Florian Pfaff

Multitarget Tracking Using Orientation Estimation for Optical Belt Sorting

Karlsruhe Series on Intelligent Sensor-Actuator-Systems

Volume 22

ISAS | Karlsruhe Institute of Technology
Intelligent Sensor-Actuator-Systems Laboratory

Edited by Prof. Dr.-Ing. Uwe D. Hanebeck

Multitarget Tracking Using Orientation Estimation for Optical Belt Sorting

by
Florian Pfaff

KIT Scientific Publishing

Karlsruher Institut für Technologie
Institut für Anthropomatik und Robotik

Multitarget Tracking Using Orientation Estimation
for Optical Belt Sorting

Zur Erlangung des akademischen Grades eines Doktors der Ingenieurwissenschaften von der KIT-Fakultät für Informatik des Karlsruher Instituts für Technologie (KIT) genehmigte Dissertation

von Florian Pfaff aus Karlsruhe

Tag der mündlichen Prüfung: 13. November 2018
Gutachter: Prof. Dr.-Ing. Uwe D. Hanebeck
Prof. Dr.-Ing. Thomas Längle

Impressum

KIT Scientific Publishing

Karlsruher Institut für Technologie (KIT)
KIT Scientific Publishing
Straße am Forum 2
D-76131 Karlsruhe

KIT Scientific Publishing is a registered trademark
of Karlsruhe Institute of Technology.
Reprint using the book cover is not allowed.

www.ksp.kit.edu

Print on Demand 2019 – Gedruckt auf FSC-zertifiziertem Papier

ISSN 1867-3813
ISBN 978-3-7315-0932-5
DOI 10.5445/KSP/1000094502

Multitarget Tracking Using Orientation Estimation for Optical Belt Sorting

zur Erlangung des akademischen Grades eines

Doktors der Ingenieurwissenschaften

von der Fakultät für Informatik
des Karlsruher Instituts für Technologie (KIT)

genehmigte

Dissertation

von

Florian Pfaff

aus Karlsruhe

Tag der mündlichen Prüfung: 13.11.2018

Erster Gutachter: Prof. Dr.-Ing. Uwe D. Hanebeck

Zweiter Gutachter: Prof. Dr.-Ing. Thomas Längle

Acknowledgment

This thesis emerged from my research performed at the Intelligent Sensor-Actuator-Systems (ISAS) laboratory at Karlsruhe Institute of Technology (KIT) as part of the *Programm zur Forderung der industriellen Gemeinschaftsforschung* (IGF) project 18798 N. First and foremost, I am utterly grateful to my Ph.D. advisor Uwe D. Hanebeck for his guidance and support. I admire him for his wisdom and intuition—certainly, he already knew I would submit this Ph.D. thesis one day when I was still an undergraduate student and had no fixed plans for the time after graduation yet. Second, I would like to thank my co-advisor Thomas Längle of the Fraunhofer Institute of Optronics, System Technologies, and Image Exploitation (IOSB). Without his efforts and expertise, the IGF project and thus also this thesis would have been unthinkable. Further, his warm greetings always made me feel welcome and comfortable during my visits at Fraunhofer IOSB.

I also owe a debt of gratitude to all other members of the IGF project, namely Georg Maier, Christoph Pieper, Benjamin Noack, Robin Gruna, Harald Kruggel-Emden, Jürgen Beyerer, Siegmar Wirtz, and Viktor Scherer. I really enjoyed how we jointly advanced our knowledge in our biweekly phone calls. In particular, I would like to thank Georg with whom I supervised quite a few students. Special thanks also go to Benjamin—not only for his contributions to the project but also for supervising me when I was getting started with research as an undergraduate student.

Even with the interesting research topics at ISAS, my time as a Ph.D. student would have never been such a pleasurable experience without the superb colleagues. I am eternally grateful to my friends and former colleagues Gerhard Kurz and Igor Gilitschenski, who awoke my passion for circles, tori, and spheres. I still vividly remember the joyful times attending conferences with them, Benjamin and many other colleagues–Christof Chlebek, Florian Rosenthal, Florian Faion, Jannik Steinbring, Selim Özgen, Maxim Dolgov, Antonio Zea, Marcus Baum, Marc Reinhardt, and Martin Pander. Martin, Jörg Fischer, and Christian Tesch were great office mates whose company I enjoyed at different times along my path to the Ph.D.

Most of the people just mentioned have already moved on to new challenges in industry or other academic institutions. I am happy they were succeeded by the nice new colleagues Kailai Li, Jana Mayer, Daniel Frisch, Susanne Radtke, and Ajit Basarur, who accompanied me during the end of my time as a Ph.D. student. Last but not least, I owe my gratitude to the secretary Dagmar Gambichler, as well as the technical staff—namely Sascha Faber, Achim Langendörfer, and Alexander Riffel—and the former colleagues Anita Oberle and Birgit Meindl. It was also a pleasure to supervise many skilled students—too many to list them all—doing seminars, lab projects as well as bachelor's and master's theses at ISAS.

Two highlights of my time as a Ph.D. student were the conferences FUSION 2016 in Heidelberg and MFI 2016 in Baden-Baden, for which I was local arrangements chair. I am grateful to the local staff at the conferences venues and the chairs, speakers, sponsors, reviewers, and participants from all around the globe for making these conferences the great successes they were.

My time as a Ph.D. student was not only exciting by itself, it was also an eventful time for me. The birth of my son Jonas truly changed my life. Together with my girlfriend Melanie, it gives me the greatest joy to watch him grow up. I am very glad and grateful I was always able to count on the wisdom of my brother Daniel, the invaluable support of my parents Heiner and Hedwig, and the encouragement of my grandmother Helga.

Karlsruhe, December 2018 Florian Pfaff

Contents

Notation

General Conventions

x	scalar
$\underline{x}$	vector
x_k	kth entry of the vector $\underline{x}$
$\underline{x}_t$	vector $\underline{x}$ at time step t
$\underline{x}^\top$	transpose of the vector $\underline{x}$
$(\underline{u} \cdot \underline{v})$	dot product of the vectors $\underline{u}$ and $\underline{v}$
$\mathbf{A}$	matrix
$\mathbf{0}_{n\times m}$	$n \times m$ zero matrix
$\mathbf{I}_{n\times n}$	$n \times n$ identity matrix
$\boldsymbol{x}$	random variable
$\Omega_{\underline{\boldsymbol{x}}}$	sample space of the random vector $\underline{\boldsymbol{x}}$
$\mathrm{E}(\underline{\boldsymbol{x}})$	expected value of the random vector $\underline{\boldsymbol{x}}$
$\mathbf{C}^{\underline{\boldsymbol{v}}}$	covariance matrix of the random vector $\underline{\boldsymbol{v}}$
$a(\cdot)$	function
$\underline{a}(\cdot)$	function with vector-valued output
e	Euler's number
$\exp(\cdot)$	exponential function (used if writing powers of e reduces readability)
$\overline{c}$	complex conjugate of c
$\dot{x}$ and $\ddot{x}$	first and second temporal derivative of x
x and y	coordinate along x- or y-axis
[KS13]	regular citation
[O1]	citation of own work
[S1]	citation of supervised student thesis

Conventions for Target Tracking

T	time between two consecutive time steps, e.g., between t and $t+1$
n	number of tracks that are currently considered by the tracker
m	number of measurements at the current time step
d	dimension of the manifold
$\mathcal{N}$	density of a normal distribution
$f_t^{\boldsymbol{w}}$	density of the random variable $\boldsymbol{w}_t$
f_t^{e}	estimated density of the state at time step t respecting all measurements up to time step t
f_{t+1}^{p}	predicted density of the state at time step $t+1$ respecting all measurements up to time step t

Conventions for Directional Estimation and Fourier Series

π	circular constant
i	imaginary unit
$\mathbb{S}^d$	d-dimensional sphere (subset of $\mathbb{R}^{d+1}$)
$\mathbb{T}^d$	d-dimensional torus
I_v	Bessel function of the first kind and order v
f_{WN}	density function of a wrapped normal distribution
$\breve{f}$	unnormalized density
N	total number of Fourier or spherical harmonic coefficients used
$\underline{c}^{\mathrm{id}}$	Fourier coefficient vector when approximating the function directly
$\underline{c}^{\mathrm{sqrt}}$	Fourier coefficient vector when approximating the square root of the function
c_k^{id}	Fourier coefficient with index k when approximating the function directly (analogous for c_k^{sqrt})
$\underline{c}_t^{\mathrm{e,id}}$	Fourier coefficient vector describing the posterior density f_t^{e} (analogous for $\underline{c}_t^{\mathrm{p,id}}$, $\underline{c}_t^{\boldsymbol{w}\mathrm{,id}}$, and $\underline{c}_t^{\mathrm{L,id}}$)
$\underline{c}_t^{\mathrm{e,sqrt}}$	Fourier coefficient vector describing the square root of the posterior density $\sqrt{f_t^{\mathrm{e}}}$ (analogous for $\underline{c}_t^{\mathrm{p,sqrt}}$, $\underline{c}_t^{\boldsymbol{w}\mathrm{,sqrt}}$, and $\underline{c}_t^{\mathrm{L,sqrt}}$)

$c_{t,k}^{\mathrm{e,id}}$	Fourier coefficient with index k of $\underline{c}_t^{\mathrm{e,id}}$ (analogous for $\underline{c}_{t,k}^{\mathrm{e,sqrt}}$)
Y_l^m	spherical harmonic function of degree l and order m
$\mathbf{C}^{\mathrm{id}}$	Fourier coefficient tensor or matrix of spherical harmonic coefficients describing a multivariate function (analogous for $\mathbf{C}^{\mathrm{sqrt}}$ describing the square root)
$c_{\underline{k}}^{\mathrm{id}}$	entry of the Fourier coefficient tensor $\mathbf{C}^{\mathrm{id}}$ with the vector-valued index $\underline{k}$
$c_{[k_1,k_2]}^{\mathrm{id}}$	entry of the Fourier coefficient matrix $\mathbf{C}^{\mathrm{id}}$ with the vector-valued index $[k_1, k_2]$
$c_l^{\mathrm{id},m}$	entry of the spherical harmonic coefficient matrix $\mathbf{C}^{\mathrm{id}}$ with degree l and order m
$\mathbf{C}_t^{\mathrm{e,id}}$	Fourier coefficient tensor or matrix of spherical harmonic coefficients at time step t describing the multivariate density f_t^{e} directly (analogous for $\mathbf{C}_t^{\mathrm{p,id}}$, $\mathbf{C}_t^{\boldsymbol{w},\mathrm{id}}$, $\mathbf{C}_t^{\mathrm{L,id}}$, and $\mathbf{C}_t^{\mathrm{T,id}}$ and the square roots thereof)
$c_{t,l}^{\mathrm{e,id},m}$	spherical harmonic coefficient of degree l and order m of the spherical harmonic approximation of the posterior density f_t^{e} (analogous for other coefficient matrices)
$\underline{\tilde{c}}$	Fourier coefficient vector representing an unnormalized density
$\underline{\check{c}}$	Fourier coefficient vector representing a normalized density that has more entries than the initial vectors of the prediction or update step
$\underline{\mathring{c}}$	Fourier coefficient vector representing an unnormalized density that has more entries than the initial vectors of the prediction or update step

General Abbreviations

BMSE	Bayesian mean squared error
CAD	computer-aided design
CFD	computational fluid dynamics
DEM	discrete element method
DFT	discrete Fourier transform
GNN	global nearest neighbor
IDFT	inverse discrete Fourier transform
IFF	Fourier identity filter
i.i.d.	independent and identically distributed
ISHF	spherical harmonics identity filter
JPDAF	joint probabilistic data association filter
LAP	linear assignment problem
LNN	local nearest neighbor
MHT	multiple hypothesis tracking
MMSE	minimum mean squared error
PDAF	probabilistic data association filter
PGF	progressive Gaussian filter
SqFF	Fourier square root filter
SqSHF	spherical harmonics square root filter
UKF	unscented Kalman filter

Abbreviated Names of the Motion Models

IV	identical velocity
CV	constant velocity
CVBC	constant velocity with bias correction
IA	identical acceleration
CA	constant acceleration
CALV	constant acceleration with limited velocity
CADSC	constant acceleration disallowing sign changes

Kurzfassung

Schüttgüter sind wichtige Industrieprodukte, die üblicherweise lose in Massen transportiert werden. Unter Schüttgüter fallen unter anderem Bergbau- und Agrarerzeugnisse sowie recyclingfähige Materialien. Schätzungen gehen davon aus, dass bis zu zehn Prozent aller weltweit produzierten Energie für die Verarbeitung von Schüttgütern aufgewandt wird. Optische Bandsortieranlagen sind vielseitig einsetzbare Anlagen, mithilfe derer Schüttgutströme aufgetrennt werden können, bei denen klassische Verfahren wie das Sieben nicht angewandt werden können.

In optischen Bandsortieranlagen wird der Schüttgutstrom durch Druckluftstöße, die getroffene Partikel ablenken, aufgetrennt. Die Druckluftstöße werden mithilfe digital gesteuerter Ventile erzeugt. In aktuell in der Industrie eingesetzten Bandsortieranlagen basieren die Steuerbefehle für die Ventile auf einer einzelnen Beobachtung eines jeden Teilchens, die durch eine Zeilenkamera gewonnen wird. Aufgrund von Verarbeitungszeiten muss die Beobachtung des Teilchens erfolgt sein, bevor es den Einflussbereich der Druckluftstöße erreicht. Daher sind Vorhersagen der Teilchenbewegung unerlässlich. In dieser Arbeit werden die Vorteile und Herausforderungen des Austauschs der Zeilenkamera durch eine Flächenkamera, die mehrere Beobachtungen eines jeden Teilchens ermöglicht, betrachtet.

Um alle Beobachtungen der einzelnen Teilchen gewinnbringend zu nutzen, wird ein Multitarget-Tracking-Verfahren hergeleitet, das auf den Anwendungsfall der Schüttgutsortierung zugeschnitten ist. Das Tracking-Verfahren basiert auf den Zentroiden der Teilchen, die mittels gegebener Bildverarbeitungsalgorithmen extrahiert werden. Für den neu vorgestellten Ansatz wird ein bestehendes Multitarget-Tracking-Verfahren abgeändert und erweitert. Des Weiteren werden potenzielle Herausforderungen des Anwendungsfalls erörtert und Lösungen für diese dargelegt. Das eingesetzte Bewegungsmodell stellt einen äußerst wichtigen Bestandteil des Tracking-Verfahrens dar. In dieser Arbeit werden neue Bewegungsmodelle vorgestellt, die Informationen über zuvor beobachtete Teilchen miteinbeziehen. Hierdurch ist es möglich, bessere Vorhersagen abzuleiten als durch Verwendung etablierter Bewegungsmodelle aus der Tracking-Literatur.

Essenziell für die erfolgreiche Anwendung des Tracking-Algorithmus ist es, zuverlässig zu urteilen, welche Beobachtungen in aufeinanderfolgenden Bildern von demselben Teilchen stammen. Hierfür wird nicht ausschließlich die vorhergesagte Position des Teilchens benutzt, sondern auch die Orientierung als zusätzliches Merkmal einbezogen. Die Bestimmung der Orientierung eines Teilchens um die Hochachse ist ein Schätzproblem, dem die Topologie des Kreises zugrunde liegt. Schätzer für diese und weitere periodische Mannigfaltigkeiten sind ein aktives Forschungsgebiet, zu dem diese Arbeit ebenfalls beiträgt. Für die Topologie des Kreises werden zwei Filter vorgestellt, die auch asymmetrische und multimodale Dichten berücksichtigen können. Bei dem ersten Filter werden priore und posteriore Dichten direkt mithilfe von Fourierkoeffizienten approximiert. Bei dem zweiten Filter werden die Quadratwurzeln der Dichten approximiert. Die zwei essenziellen Schritte für die rekursive Bayes'sche Zustandsschätzung, der Prädiktions- und der Updateschritt, werden für beide Filter erläutert. Da die Umsetzung der Bayes-Formel für den Updateschritt und der Chapman-Kolmogorov-Gleichung für den Prädiktionsschritt beschrieben wird, können die Filter für fast beliebige Schätzprobleme mit der Topologie des Kreises angewandt werden.

Des Weiteren werden die beschriebenen Filter auf komplexere Schätzprobleme in höheren Dimensionen übertragen. Während die Verallgemeinerung der Filter für die Topologie des Hypertorus nur den Einsatz multidimensionaler Fourierreihen und geringe Anpassungen erfordert, sind weitreichende Änderungen für den Übertrag auf die Topologie der Einheitskugel notwendig. Für diese werden Filter basierend auf Kugelflächenfunktionen vorgestellt.

Die beschriebenen Filter für beliebig dimensionale Hypertori sind die ersten, die Approximationen der kontinuierlichen Wahrscheinlichkeitsdichten liefern. Für die Topologie der Einheitskugel sind die Filter die bislang ersten, die eine Verbesserung der Approximationen der Dichten durch zusätzliche Parameter erlauben. Die Filter werden anhand vielfältiger Evaluationsszenarien mit unterschiedlichen Herausforderungen untersucht. In allen Szenarien erreichen die neu vorgestellten Filter hochqualitative Schätzergebnisse bei geringeren Laufzeiten als eine angepasste Version des Partikelfilters, die für periodische Mannigfaltigkeiten geeignet ist.

Darüber hinaus wird betrachtet, wie durch Schätzung der Orientierungen der Schüttgutteilchen zuverlässiger entschieden werden kann, welche Messungen von demselben Partikel stammen. Dies wird durch Einbeziehung eines zusätzlichen Terms im Multitarget-Tracking-Verfahren erreicht. Geschlossene Formeln werden für von Mises Dichten und durch Fourierreihen approximierte Dichten hergeleitet.

Die Arbeit zeigt, dass die für die Separation notwendigen Vorhersagen in optischen Bandsortieranlagen durch Verwendung von Multitarget-Tracking-Verfahren signifikant verbessert werden können, und legt die Grundlage für die Nutzung von Flächenkameras in industriellen Anlagen. Das vorgestellte Multitarget-Tracking-Verfahren arbeitet zuverlässig und wird durch Einbeziehung der Orientierung robuster gegenüber hohem Messrauschen. Durch Anwendung der verbesserten Bewegungsmodelle können die Trajektorien der Partikel bei hinreichend präzisen Messungen akkurat vorhergesagt werden.

Abstract

Bulk material is a frequently encountered type of product in industrial applications. Characteristic of bulk materials, which include mining products, grains, and recyclable materials, is that they are loosely transported in large quantities. The processing of bulk materials is estimated to consume up to 10% of all energy produced worldwide. Optical belt sorters are a versatile technology for reliably separating streams of bulk material even when classical separators such as sieves cannot be applied.

In optical belt sorters, a stream of bulk material is separated into two streams using bursts of compressed air that alter the motion of the particles that are hit. The bursts are emitted using digitally controlled valves. In sorters currently used in industry, the valves are controlled based on a single observation of each particle obtained using a line scan camera. Due to processing delays, the particles must be observed before they are in the reach of the bursts of compressed air. Therefore, a prediction of each particle's motion is required. We consider the advantages and challenges of replacing the usual line scan camera with an area scan camera, which allows us to obtain multiple observations of each particle.

To make use of all observations of a particle, a multitarget tracking algorithm tailored to the bulk material sorting task is derived. The tracking is based on the particles' centroids extracted using image processing algorithms, which are employed without modifications in this thesis. For our novel approach, we adjust and extend a classical multitarget tracking algorithm. Further, we discuss potential challenges specific to the application and suggest solutions. A particularly important component of the tracking algorithm is the motion model. In this thesis, we propose novel motion models that take knowledge about previously observed particles into account. Thus, we are able to outperform classical motion models given in the target tracking literature.

Reliably determining which observations in consecutive frames stem from the same particle is key to the success of a multitarget tracking algorithm. To achieve a high reliability, we not only rely on the predicted position of each particle but also estimate and integrate the orientation as an additional feature. Estimating the orientation of a particle around the vertical axis is an estimation problem on a circular manifold. Estimation on circular or, more generally, periodic manifolds is an active field of research to which this thesis also contributes. For circular manifolds, two filters based on Fourier series are introduced that allow representing asymmetric and multimodal densities. The first filter is based on approximating prior and posterior densities directly using Fourier coefficients. In contrast, the square roots of the densities are approximated in the second filter. The two essential steps for recursive Bayesian estimators, the update and the prediction step, are explicated for both filters. As we explain how to implement Bayes' formula for the update step and the Chapman–Kolmogorov equation for the prediction step, the filters are applicable to almost arbitrary estimation problems on the unit circle.

The presented filters are generalized for more challenging estimation problems on higher-dimensional manifolds. While the generalization to hypertoroidal manifolds only requires the use of multidimensional Fourier series and minor modifications, more extensive changes are required for adapting the concepts to estimation problems on the unit sphere. For the unit sphere, two filters based on spherical harmonics are presented.

The explained filters for arbitrary-dimensional hypertori are the first that provide continuous approximations of the probability densities. For the unit sphere, the filters are the first that allow for improvements to the approximations of the densities by increasing the number of parameters used. The filters are evaluated on a variety of scenarios with different challenges. In all scenarios, our filters achieve high-quality estimation results at lower run times than a particle filter adapted to periodic domains.

Further, we describe how the process of determining which measurements stem from the same particle can be improved by estimating the orientations of the particles. This is achieved by integrating an additional term into the multitarget tracking algorithm. Closed-form solutions are derived for von Mises densities and densities approximated using Fourier series.

Our work shows that the predictions for the separation in optical belt sorters can be significantly enhanced using multitarget tracking and paves the way for future industrial applications of area scan cameras in optical belt sorters. The multitarget tracking algorithm presented is highly reliable and, when incorporating the orientation, robust against significant measurement noise. Using the improved motion models and sufficiently precise measurements, the trajectories of the particles can be predicted accurately.

CHAPTER 1

Introduction

In the modern globalized economy, processing large quantities of products in an automated manner is an efficient means to increase cost-effectiveness and thus be competitive in the global market. One important type of product is bulk material, which are products that are commonly transported loosely in large quantities. Bulk materials include mining products, granular materials, grains, and recyclable materials. Due to technical advances in transport and processing technologies, an increasing variety of products can be treated like classical bulk materials.

It is estimated that the processing of bulk materials consumes up to 10% of all energy produced worldwide [Dur00, Section 1.2]. A significant amount of energy can be saved by ensuring early in the supply chain that only the truly important main product is shipped and processed further. For many bulk materials, the main product can be isolated using sorters based on physical properties, such as the density or shape. Sorters using physical properties include sieves, trommel screens [CHL$^+$10], magnetic separators [Obe74], and froth flotation cells [FJY07]. However, there is a variety of bulk materials for which such processes are either inapplicable or only approaches with undesirable properties exist. For example, separators based on physical properties may harm the product or result in a wet end product [Wot08].

In this thesis, we consider optical belt sorters that sort bulk materials based on image data. This type of sorter provides a means to sort a large variety of bulk materials in a dry and non-destructive manner. In the separation process of optical belt sorters, it is commonly assumed that all particles have identical motion behavior. In this thesis, we explicate a way to estimate the particles' motion behavior using appropriate tracking algorithms to improve the separation process. The algorithms are tailored to the specific problem and its real-time constraints.

In particular, we focus on estimating the orientations of the particles, which can help to improve the tracking. To estimate the orientation, a real-time capable approach is introduced that allows a flexible trade-off between processing time and estimation quality. The estimator derived is able to deal with a wide variety of estimation problems on the unit circle that are particularly hard to deal with using many state-of-the-art techniques. The novel estimator is then extended for the estimation of multiple possibly correlated angles. For multiple angles, both the topologies of the arbitrary-dimensional hypertorus and of the unit sphere are considered.

In the first section of this chapter, we introduce optical belt sorters. Insights into the machinery facilitate the understanding of the challenges and contributions of this thesis, which we lay out in the second section. Related work is presented in the third section.

1.1 Optical Belt Sorters

Optical belt sorters belong to the class of sensor-based sorters [Wot08], which can be used to sort a large variety of bulk materials. Characteristic of sensor-based sorters is the use of digital processing based on an imaging sensor's data. Optical sorters that are the focus of this thesis constitute a common type of sensor-based sorter. Such sorters are based on a grayscale or color camera. While sensor-based sorters have been in existence for over 80 years, their widespread use was deemed infeasible until about 30 years ago [Wot08].

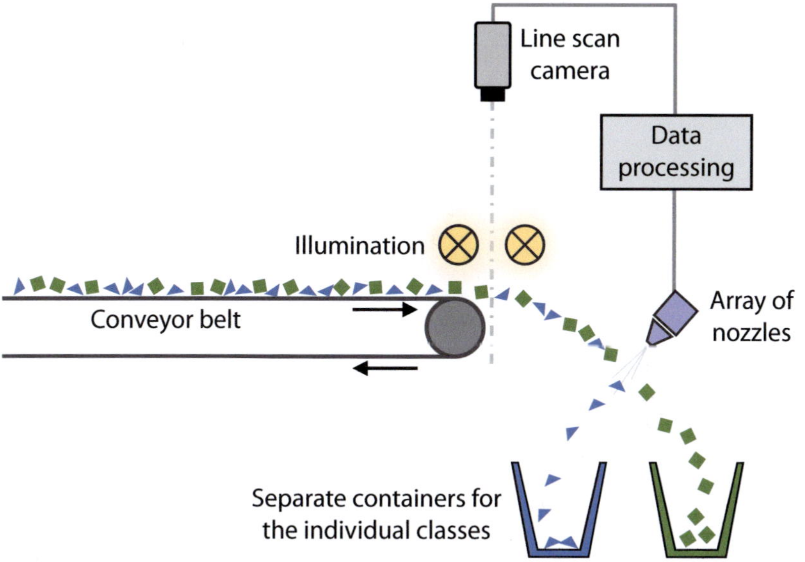

Figure 1.1.: Schematic illustration of an optical belt sorter using a line scan camera (adapted version of an illustration from [O10]).

The precise design of an optical sorter depends on the transport medium used. In this thesis, we limit ourselves to optical belt sorters. In other optical sorters, the bulk material may be transported on a large slide instead of a conveyor belt or directly go into free fall. As the separation process is similar for these sorters, many insights of this thesis can be applied to sorters employing other transport mediums.

The main components of an optical belt sorter are illustrated in Figure 1.1. How the bulk material is applied to the belt depends on previous processing steps as optical belt sorters may be integrated into large industrial processes. If an optical belt sorter is used as a stand-alone device or when the supply is highly time varying, a vibratory feeder can be used to gradually feed the bulk material to the sorter. The bulk material is usually not applied directly to the belt but rather via a small slide. On this slide, the particles accelerate along the transport direction, which reduces the difference between the belt velocity and the particles' velocities.

The belt on which the bulk material is transported is both used to accelerate the particles along the transport direction and to reduce movement orthogonal to the transport direction. In an optimal setting, which can only be achieved in theory, all particles have no relative movement to the belt and attain precisely the same velocity. Even in an optimal setting, the motion behavior of the particles on sorters using a slide instead of a belt is highly dependent on the shapes and orientations of the particles, and thus, there is significantly more variation in the particles' motions.

After the particles leave the belt, they launch in an approximately parabolic flight path. During the flight, the bulk material is inspected, and the separation is performed. Observing the particles after the end of the belt is preferred as no accumulated dirt, which could easily be confused for a particle, is visible. Further, a controlled background with a high contrast to the inspected particles can be employed.

Image processing is performed on the image data to detect the bulk material particles and determine to which class a particle belongs. Depending on the classification result, a decision is made as to which particles should fly unobstructed and which should be separated from the stream of bulk material. For the actual separation, the particles are targeted using bursts of compressed air emitted from one or multiple nozzles of an array of compressed air nozzles that are aligned orthogonally to the transport direction. The bursts are triggered using digitally controlled valves and alter the flight path of the particles that are hit, which are then collected in a different container than the rest of the bulk material.

Unlike in sorters using physical properties, the separation step is distinctly separate from the discrimination step in optical belt sorters. While this allows for high flexibility in the discrimination step, ensuring a successful separation requires particular care. The key challenge in the separation task is that due to processing times and delays, the observation and separation cannot occur simultaneously. As the particles usually have velocities considerably higher than 1 m/s, the particles move significantly during the processing times.

In industrial optical belt sorters equipped with line scan cameras, the decision of which valve to activate and when to activate it is based on the assumption of a straight flight path in the transport direction without any motion orthogonal to the transport direction. Commonly, the valves are activated at a fixed delay after the perception. As illustrated in Figure 1.2, the delay needs to be long enough to account for processing times during times of high load (i.e., when many particles are observed concurrently). However, it is also important to choose the delay as short as possible. Because the particles' trajectories become increasingly dissimilar the longer the particles are in flight, reliably hitting the particles becomes more difficult for longer delays. After a reasonable delay has been determined, the distance to the separation mechanism is usually adapted to match the delay. Since the delay is identical for all particles, the underlying assumption is that all particles take the same amount of time to reach the separation mechanism.

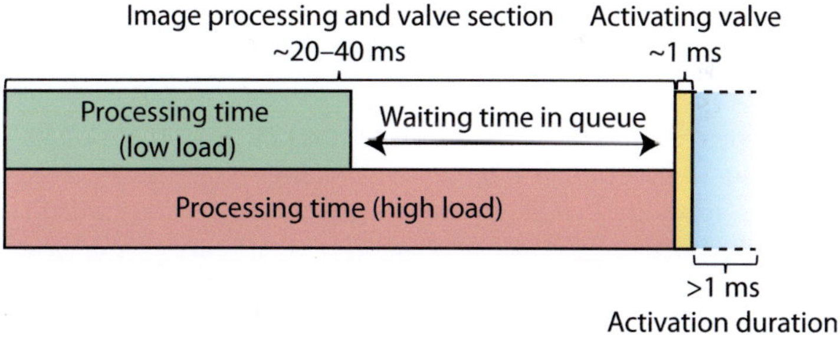

Figure 1.2.: Delays in optical belt sorters using line scan cameras. The activation duration of the valve depends on various parameters of the particle, such as its shape (adapted version of an illustration from [O9]).

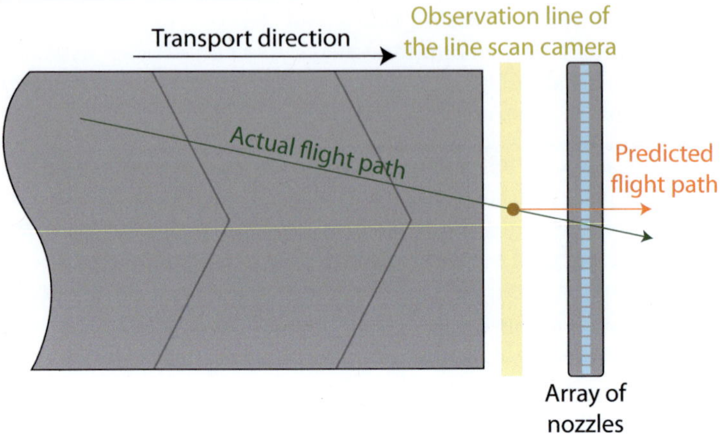

Figure 1.3.: Illustration that incorrect valves can be triggered when assuming a motion straight along the transport direction (redrawn from [S7]). We assume all nozzles are controlled by different valves.

The assumption of an identical delay and a straight flight path lead to the inherent limitations of sorters based on line scan cameras. As illustrated in Figure 1.3, the assumption of a straight flight path can cause an incorrect valve to be triggered if the particle also moves orthogonally to the transport direction. Further, if the delay between the observation and the arrival at the separation mechanism is shorter or longer than assumed, the timing of the valve activation can be incorrect. Thus, the approach is limited to bulk materials for which the assumption of a straight movement and an identical velocity of all particles is reasonably accurate.

The key idea in the novel approach that we refer to as predictive tracking is to use individualized predictions for each particle based on observations of the particles' trajectories. For this, we replace the line scan camera with an area scan camera, as illustrated in Figure 1.4. Using the area scan camera, we can observe each particle at multiple points in time[1]. Deriving high-quality predictions based on the image data in real time while enabling an accumulation of discriminatory features of the particles is a central challenge in this thesis.

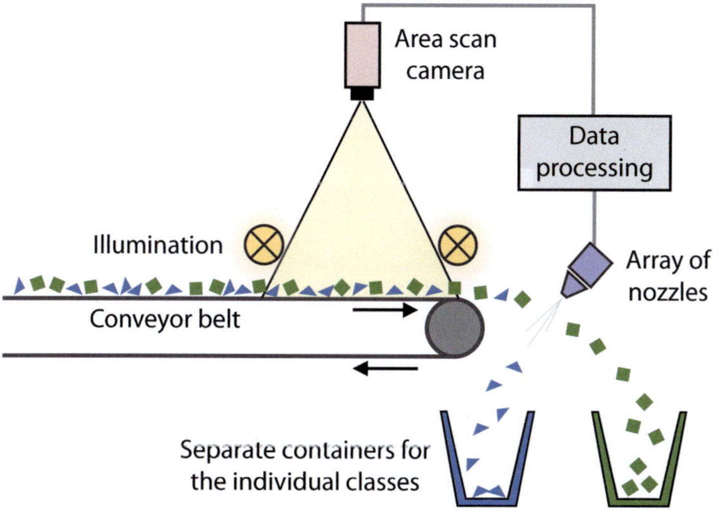

Figure 1.4.: Illustration of the novel configuration using an area scan camera (adapted version of an illustration from [O1]).

[1] As we have shown in [O5], even a color line scan camera can be used to extract some information about the motion of the particles. To achieve this, the displacement between the sensor pixels for the individual colors, which is present in many sensor layouts, is used. The quality of the estimated direction, however, depends largely on the sensor layout and the approach does not provide all the advantages obtained when using an area scan camera.

1.2 Outline and Contributions

The central research question of this thesis is how to best utilize the area scan camera's data to improve the separation results without any specialized or improved image processing routines. As illustrated in the thesis structure in Figure 1.5, we begin the thesis with some foundations in the form of an introduction and information on an experimental platform that served as the basis for many of our analyses. Then, we propose two contributions, which we summarize in the subsections of this section.

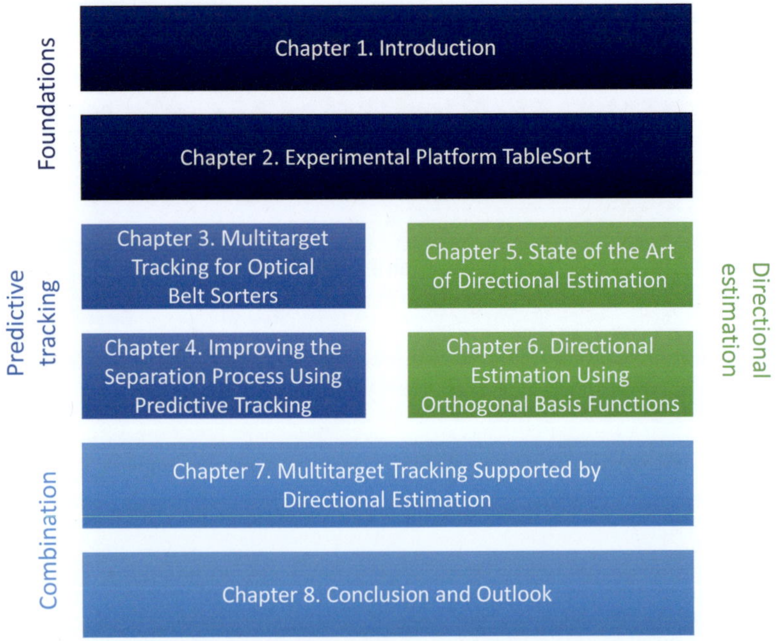

Figure 1.5.: Thesis structure. The colors in this illustration are also used as the background colors for the chapter and section numbers to indicate which part of the thesis is currently addressed.

The first contribution is an approach to generate accurate predictions for optical belt sorters based on multitarget tracking. How the tracking of the particles is realized is presented in Chapter 3. In Chapter 4, we describe how the tracking results can be used to derive accurate predictions to improve the separation quality. The tracking algorithm is further enhanced based on our second contribution, which comprises novel filters for directional estimation.

The basics and the state of the art of directional estimation are described in Chapter 5. Our novel, real-time capable algorithms for estimation of periodic quantities are presented in Chapter 6. Intermediate summaries of the presented predictive tracking and the filters for periodic manifolds are provided in Sections 4.6 and 6.6, respectively. In Chapter 7, we explicate how the orientation can be integrated into the tracking algorithm to improve its reliability. In the last chapter, we provide a conclusion and describe potential future work.

1.2.1 Predictive Tracking for Particles on a Conveyor Belt

Challenge An algorithm to track the particles and produce predictions must be developed. The algorithm needs to respect the specifics and properties of the scenario. In particular, the algorithm must be suitable for high frame rates and large numbers of particles. To be independent of the classification process, the algorithm should allow for direct accumulation of the particles' visual features.

Contribution An algorithm that allows tracking many objects simultaneously is adjusted to the bulk material sorting task. Knowledge about where particles are expected to appear and disappear is integrated. Further, the specifics of the possible challenges expected in the scenario and their implications on the tracking are discussed. Challenges include errors in the image processing component, for which strategies are explained to mitigate negative consequences. The strategies are solely based on the tracking and do not require improvements in the image acquisition and processing components. A particular adjustment was to integrate the orientation to improve the reliability of the tracking algorithm. As explained in the next subsection, accurately estimating orientations is a research problem by itself.

To generate the predictions based on the tracking results, accurate motion models are essential. While using classical motion models leads to an improvement in the selection of the valves, classical motion models can perform poorly regarding the nozzle activation timing. To alleviate this and to further improve the valve selection, novel motion models are proposed. The key idea of these models is to not merely consider each particle in isolation. By also making use of the knowledge about particles observed previously, the predictions can be further improved.

1.2.2 Adaptive Algorithms for Directional Estimation

Problem A key challenge in tracking the particles is determining which measurements stem from the same particle. Using additional visual features can help to improve the reliability of the so-called association decisions. One such additional property is the orientation. To be suitable for real-time applications such as bulk material sorting, a trade-off between estimation quality and run time is crucial. Further, the estimators derived should be as general as possible to allow for estimation of correlated angles, such as the orientations of neighboring bulk material particles.

Contribution In this thesis, we provide filters that represent densities on periodic manifolds using orthogonal basis functions. For the unit circle, we represent the periodic function on $[0, 2\pi)$ using trigonometric polynomials. Based on this representation, we lay out two filters that perform the prediction and update steps in different manners. Both filters can be flexibly configured for different trade-offs between estimation quality and processing time and the configuration can be adapted during run time.

The first filter, called the Fourier identity filter (IFF), is faster than the second filter when comparing configurations with equal numbers of parameters. The downside of this filter is that the approximation of the density may have negative function values, which is undesirable in theory and for some applications.

In the second filter, the Fourier square root filter (SqFF), we solve this problem by approximating the square root of the density instead. By calculating the square of the function values of the approximation, we can obtain an approximation of the actual density that only attains nonnegative values. A downside of this approach is that the prediction and update steps are more complicated.

Neither of the filters is inherently superior to the other. The SqFF tends to yield a better approximation of the true density and has the theoretical advantage that the approximation is nonnegative everywhere. However, the IFF is faster, and thus, more parameters can be used, which can lead to better outcomes when a point estimate is desired.

We also present extensions of the two filters to the estimation of multiple, possibly correlated angles. Such estimation problems can arise when jointly estimating the orientations of neighboring particles. The IFF and SqFF are generalized to the estimation of correlated angles using multidimensional Fourier series. Further, we provide analogues to the two filters for estimation problems on the unit sphere $\mathbb{S}^2$, which we call spherical harmonics identity filter (ISHF) and spherical harmonics square root filter (SqSHF). For these filters, we use spherical harmonics as the basis functions to represent the densities and derive suitable prediction and update steps.

1.3 Related Work

There are three fields of research related to this thesis. The first is optical belt sorting in general. The second is multitarget tracking, in particular with the use of additional features. The last field is estimation on periodic manifolds. In this section, we give a brief overview of relevant research in these fields. Additional references are provided in the respective chapters.

1.3.1 Optical Belt Sorting

Optical belt sorting is an applied research topic. Optical belt sorters are equipped with a variety of components that can be adjusted and improved. Many of the adjustments are performed by companies or license-givers that tailor optical belt sorters to specific tasks. Due to commercial interests, we believe considerable research is unpublished.

There are papers giving an overview of sensor-based sorters [Wot08], papers specifically addressing optical belt sorting [Län07], and papers addressing selected challenges in optical belt sorting [RLB15, RLB16]. In [KDJD03], multiple observations of different line scan cameras are combined. The multiple observations, however, are only used to obtain more information about the particles and are not used to improve the separation process. The most closely related work we know of is [HKK+18]. This paper also addresses the use of area scan cameras in optical belt sorting but was written well after our initial paper [O10], and tracking is not the focus of the work. The challenge addressed in [HKK+18] is easier than that of our research because the bulk material is not distributed randomly but rather forced into three separate lines.

1.3.2 Multitarget Tracking

The multitarget tracking approach presented in this thesis builds upon established multitarget tracking algorithms. In particular, classical approaches, as explained in [BP99, LIHL09], serve as the basis for the novel algorithms due to their superior run time performance and their inherent suitability to the accumulation of visual features over time. The key feature of such approaches is that (when disregarding appearing and disappearing targets), a one-to-one correspondence between the measurements and the known supposed targets is assumed and used.

Our use of the orientation to improve the association decisions, without the orientation playing a role in the motion model, is related to the concepts of feature-, attribute-, and classification-aided tracking [Dru00, Dru01, Dru03]. In these works, however, the densities are assumed to be Gaussian, which is unsuitable for periodic quantities. Alternatives not based on Gaussian distributions include feature-aided tracking without conditional probabilities of the features [SC04] or classification-aided tracking using confusion matrices [BSKG05]. We model the orientation as an additional stochastically distributed quantity, and thus, a derivation of the best association decision for Gaussian distributions [Mah07, Section 10.3] is also of interest as it can be used as a reference for the derivation for distributions on periodic manifolds.

1.3.3 Estimation on Periodic Manifolds

For circular domains, there is a variety of filters preceding our proposed IFF and SqFF. Promising alternatives are assumed density filters for circular manifolds [ARCB09, TS13] that yield fast results for simple system and measurement models. There are also widely applicable assumed density filters [KGH16a] for more complicated models. However, these filters do not allow a variable trade-off between estimation quality and run time. Further, approximating all densities using densities of a certain class can be too limiting, especially when the true density is multimodal and asymmetric.

The possibility to use Fourier series has previously been identified [WL75, Wil74a, Wil74b]. These approaches differ from ours and are not suitable for arbitrary system models. Further, the parameter reduction is performed differently and no variant is provided that ensures the nonnegativity of the approximation of the density. An approach that ensures the nonnegativity but only works in special cases was proposed in [BSH06a]. Since the invention of the IFF and SqFF, additional filters that allow a variable trade-off between estimation quality and run time have been proposed [O24, O16].

Unlike the assumed density filters, the IFF and SqFF are applicable to arbitrary-dimensional hypertori. For estimation problems on these manifolds, there are currently no alternatives except particle filters [AMGC02] that can easily be adjusted to this task. For estimation problems on the unit sphere, assumed density filters exist [CP98, TS14]. They, however, have the same limitations as assumed density filters on the circle and are thus less versatile than the ISHF and SqSHF. A more thorough overview of the related work on directional estimation is given as a historical overview in Section 5.3.

CHAPTER 2

Experimental Platform TableSort

In this chapter, we provide information on the experimental platform, called TableSort [S8], that served as the basis for several evaluations of the approaches presented in this thesis. The platform's name is derived from its small scale. Unlike most industrial optical belt sorters, TableSort fits on a standard-sized table. While algorithms presented in this thesis have also been used on data obtained from large-scale industrial optical belt sorters (e.g., in [O10]), more thorough and in-depth analyses were possible based on the TableSort system. In particular, simulations of the particle movement on TableSort based on the discrete element method (DEM) [CS79] provide reference data that help us evaluate individual components of our algorithm. In this chapter, we first explain the motivation for constructing TableSort. Then, the platform's design and key components are described. Last, we give a brief explanation of the DEM model used to generate the simulation data.

2.1 Motivation for the Experimental Optical Belt Sorter

Changing the configuration of a large industry-scale optical belt sorter is a tedious and time-consuming task. For our purpose, a suitable sorter should allow a comparison of the sorting quality of the old line scan camera-based approach with the new area scan camera-based approach. Therefore, a sorter design that takes the components of both approaches into account is desirable.

The most significant differences between a line scan camera-based layout and an area scan camera-based layout are the choice and the placement of the camera and the illumination. An example of an area scan camera-based layout is given in Figure 2.1. When using predictive tracking, it may make sense to install the area scan camera so that it can also observe particles on the belt. Therefore, an experimental platform should allow placing cameras and illuminations at different locations without a change in the overall setup.

The different cameras require different illuminations. For a line scan camera, two line lights can be employed to illuminate the observable region. For an area scan camera, a suitable light source, which does not obstruct the view of the camera but ensures a uniform illumination, is required. A ring light is sketched in Figure 2.1. Other important parameters of the belt sorter should also be easy to change. For example, being able to change the point at which the bulk material is applied to the belt allows for emulation of shorter belt lengths. Thus, experiments that provide insights on the calming effect of the belt can easily be performed.

An additional goal of the experimental platform was to allow an unobstructed view of the particles traveling through the system. This facilitates analyses of the systems using additional sensors such cameras with even higher frame rates than the one used for the tracking. TableSort was also aimed to be portable and easy to set up. Due to the sorter's portability, it was possible to set the sorter up at other research institutions to, e.g., determine relevant parameters for the DEM simulation and validate the simulation results.

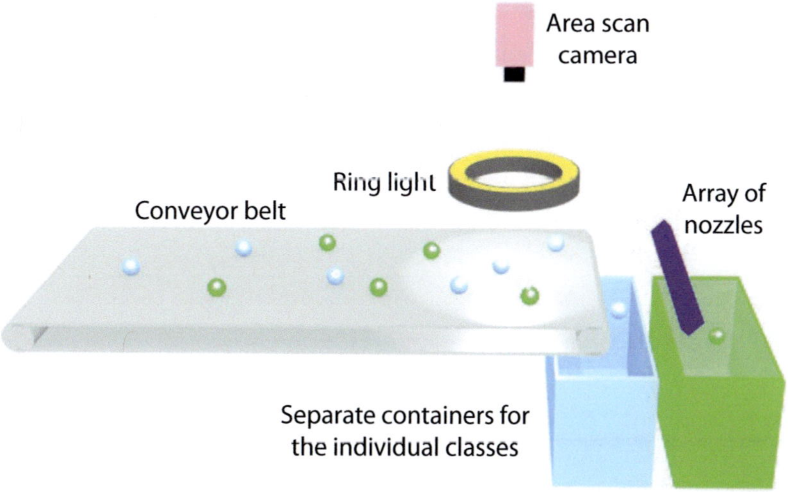

Figure 2.1.: Three-dimensional sketch of an optical belt sorter equipped with an area scan camera and a ring light.

2.2 Design of TableSort

Different designs for TableSort were analyzed in [S8]. They included designs based on multiple blocks, layouts based on mounting profiles, and designs based on panels with holes similar to optical breadboards. A panel-based design was realized as it provides high flexibility in attaching the individual components. A single panel was used because it was deemed sufficiently sturdy in theoretical analyses and practical experiments.

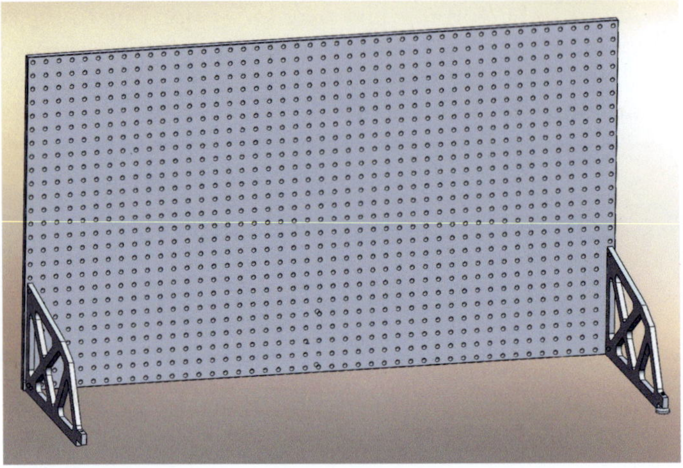

Figure 2.2.: CAD drawing of the panel to which the components are attached (from [S8]).

The construction of TableSort was based on computer-aided design (CAD) models. The panel presented in Figure 2.2 is based on an aluminum plate with a thickness of 15 mm. It is colored black to minimize the reflections of the illumination. The holes in the panel have a diameter of 8 mm and are placed on a grid at a 25 mm distance to the neighboring holes. Components of the belt sorter are attached to the panel using individualized connectors and standardized screws. As long as the components do not overlap, their locations can be chosen freely within this grid. As shown in Figure 2.3, both a line scan camera and an area scan camera can be mounted simultaneously along with suitable illuminations.

Special requirements for the individual components are considered in the design of the connectors. For example, cameras may need to be mounted significantly higher than the rest of the components. Thus, the camera mounts allow mounting the cameras at heights above the panel itself. Rotations of components can only be reproducibly realized for components attached using more than one screw. The number of possible orientations realized using multiple screws is inherently limited due to the grid. Special mounts can be used for components for which more flexibility in the choice of angles is required, such as the line lights used for illumination in line scan camera-based setups.

In addition to the camera and the illumination, a multitude of components is required for a fully functional optical belt sorter. These components include a vibratory feeder, a small slide for applying bulk material, a conveyor belt, an array of nozzles, and separate containers for the resulting streams of bulk material. Additional components for supplying the array of nozzles with compressed air may also be mounted to the front or the back. By rotating the panel by 90 degrees, a purely slide-based sorter can also be realized.

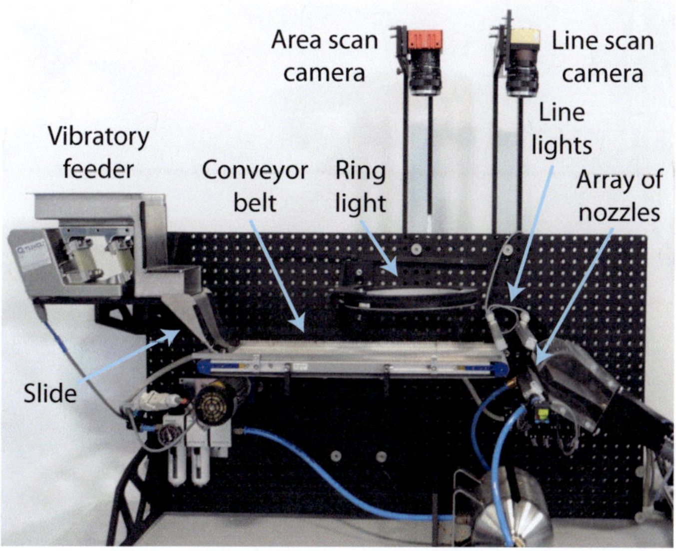

Figure 2.3.: TableSort equipped with a line scan camera, an area scan camera, and appropriate light sources.

2.3 DEM Model of TableSort

The CAD model of TableSort served as the basis for a highly accurate numerical simulation of TableSort based on the DEM [O28, O27]. Figure 2.4 illustrates the model of the sorter used in the DEM. The DEM simulation is based on approximating the effects of Newton's and Euler's equations of motion on the particles at high temporal resolutions. All interactions of the particles with each other and the solid components of the sorter, e.g., the feeder, slide, walls, and belt, are respected. Relevant parameters of the particles and of the sorter's components were determined experimentally [HWS13].

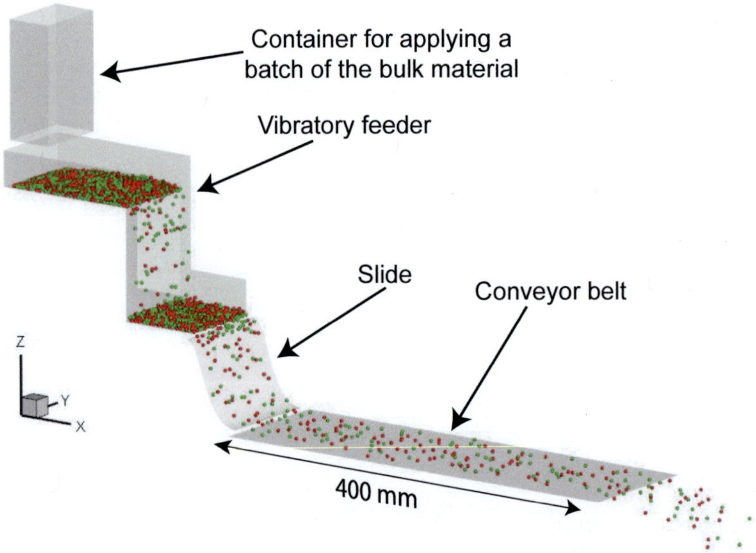

Figure 2.4.: Visualization of the DEM simulation.

In recent research, the separation process was included in the simulation [O21]. The effects of the bursts of compressed air on the particles were simulated using computational fluid dynamics (CFD), which had previously been used to analyze the ejection phase in an optical belt sorter [FGP15]. The basis for the CFD is the Navier–Stokes equation based on the finite volume method. For the CFD, a detailed and locally refined mesh was used. A one-way coupling between the CFD and the DEM was employed. The particles' positions simulated by the DEM were influenced by the CFD, but the fluid field of the CFD was assumed to be unaffected by the positions of the particles. A model to calculate the particle–fluid force that is also suitable for particles with complex shapes was employed [DF94].

The predictive tracking, as explained in the next chapters, was also integrated into this framework. The integration was realized in the form of a one-way coupling of the tracking algorithm with the DEM and a one-way-coupling with the CFD. The DEM provided the particles' positions within the (simulated) observable area to the tracking algorithm. In every time step, the tracking algorithm generated predictions as to when and where each particle recognized by the tracking algorithm was predicted to pass the separation mechanism. This information was then used to trigger the valves. The effects of the bursts of compressed air were then simulated using the CFD. Thus, a complete simulation of the sorting process based on predictive tracking was realized. This simulation was compared with an adjusted simulation in which the valve activations of line scan camera-based sorters were emulated. The comparison indicated a significant advantage of the predictive tracking approach in terms of the quality of the sorting result. In-depth information on the results are provided in [O14].

CHAPTER 3

Multitarget Tracking for Optical Belt Sorters

In this chapter, we explain how multitarget tracking is realized for the application of sorting bulk materials. In the first section, we discuss how measurements for tracking are derived from image data. An introduction to single-target tracking is given in the second section. Classical motion models for the tracking algorithms are introduced in the third section. The fourth section provides an overview of approaches to multitarget tracking. The multitarget tracking approach implemented for our application is laid out in the fifth section. How the results of the tracking are used to generate the predictions required to control the valves is explained in Chapter 4.

To be precise in our explanations without using long expressions, we define four terms. First, when we use the word *particle* (as in particle of the bulk material, not as in particle of a particle filter), we refer to a truly existing particle of the bulk material. The existence of the particle is not dependent on whether it is correctly localized or tracked. Second, when discussing multitarget tracking in general without the application in mind, we use the term *target* instead. Third, the term *measurement* is used to refer to information about a supposed particle that was obtained, e.g., using image processing in our application. As we explain in the first section of this chapter, not every particle always causes a measurement and not every measurement actually stems from a particle. Fourth, we use the term *track* to refer to information about a supposed particle derived using tracking, in particular the estimate of the particle's current state and the corresponding uncertainty. Optimally, only information about a single particle is used in each track. Further, only one track should exist per particle. This optimal result may not be achieved in real-world scenarios, especially when measurements are lacking or faulty measurements are produced by the image processing algorithm.

3.1 Deriving Measurements from Image Data

In our basic multitarget tracking approach, we estimate the particles' positions, velocities, and, depending on the model, also accelerations. As explained in Chapter 7, it can also be useful to integrate further properties, such as the orientation. Since the only sensor in our scenario is a camera, all information is derived from image data. As the first step, a background subtraction is performed. For this, an average over a series of frames is calculated, which is then subtracted from the grayscale or RGB values of the individual images. Connected-component labeling [HRG^{+}17] is then applied to find the individual particles. The centroids of the resulting connected components can then be calculated, e.g., using the first (image) moment [Bov05, Section 10.9.7.2.2]. The set of pixel coordinates of the centroids can then be directly used as measurements for tracking. However, it can be beneficial to convert the pixel coordinates to world coordinates by employing appropriate camera calibration techniques [Zha00] before passing them on to the tracking algorithm.

Since image processing algorithms are generally not free of flaws, a measurement does not necessarily stem from a real particle. For example, dirt on the belt may be seen as an additional particle. It is also not guaranteed that every particle that is visible in an image results in a measurement. Further, if multiple particles are closely spaced, they may look like a single particle. In this case, a single measurement with an incorrect centroid instead of multiple measurements of the individual particles may be derived from the image.

The image processing component is not the focus of this thesis and was thus not optimized. Errors in the image processing do not necessarily lead to errors in the separation. As we explain in more detail in Section 3.5.2, if multiple particles of the same class (i.e., only ones that are to be separated from the stream or ones that are not) are regarded as one particle over the whole tracking area, this may not lead to errors. A distinct problem occurs when multiple particles are temporarily seen as one particle. While this can cause problems for the tracking, Section 3.5.2 explains how such problems can be alleviated in the multitarget tracking algorithm. However, significant errors in the image processing component can generally not be fully compensated. Thus, while the focus of this thesis is to make the best use of the measurements obtained using image processing, it can be worthwhile to improve the image acquisition and image processing components if errors therein lead to an unsatisfactory performance in a real-world scenario.

3.2 Single-Target Tracking

In this chapter and the chapters on directional estimation, we focus on discrete-time models for recursive Bayesian estimation. Central to the Bayesian philosophy is that the state is distributed according to a probability distribution. This assumption has implications, such as that the actual initial state varies according to the distribution of the random vector $\underline{\boldsymbol{x}}_0$ when repeating the experiment [Kay93, Chapter 10]. The distribution of $\underline{\boldsymbol{x}}_0$, or at least some of its moments, are assumed to be known.

There are generally two ways to describe how the system evolves from one time step to the next and how the measurements are related to the actual state. In this chapter, we focus on describing the system evolution and the generation of the measurements based on random variables. It is also possible to provide descriptions based on densities and likelihoods, which we use later when we derive new filters for periodic manifolds.

For a system model based on random variables, the random vector $\underline{\boldsymbol{x}}_{t+1}$ for the state at time step $t+1$ is given as a (potentially nonlinear) function of the random variable $\underline{\boldsymbol{x}}_t$ at time step t, an (optional) known fixed input $\hat{\underline{u}}_t$, and a system noise term $\underline{\boldsymbol{w}}_t$ with a known distribution. The most general nonlinear (NL) model based on random variables can be written using a vector-valued nonlinear system function $\underline{a}_t$ according to

$$\underline{\boldsymbol{x}}_{t+1}^{\mathrm{NL}} = \underline{a}_t(\underline{\boldsymbol{x}}_t^{\mathrm{NL}}, \hat{\underline{u}}_t^{\mathrm{NL}}, \underline{\boldsymbol{w}}_t^{\mathrm{NL}}) \ .$$

In recursive Bayesian estimation, it is commonly assumed that the density of $\underline{\boldsymbol{x}}_{t+1}$ is conditionally independent of all $\underline{\boldsymbol{x}}_s$ and $\underline{\boldsymbol{w}}_s$ for $s < t$, given $\underline{\boldsymbol{x}}_t$, $\hat{\underline{u}}_t$, and $\underline{\boldsymbol{w}}_t$.

For the measurement step, the random variable $\underline{\boldsymbol{z}}_t$ describing the measurement is written as a (potentially nonlinear) function of the state $\underline{\boldsymbol{x}}_t$ and a noise term $\underline{\boldsymbol{v}}_t$. The most general form is the nonlinear measurement equation

$$\underline{\boldsymbol{z}}_t^{\mathrm{NL}} = \underline{h}_t(\underline{\boldsymbol{x}}_t^{\mathrm{NL}}, \underline{\boldsymbol{v}}_t^{\mathrm{NL}}) \ ,$$

which is based on a nonlinear measurement function $\underline{h}_t$.

Models that are particularly easy to handle are linear system and measurement models. A linear system model can be written as

$$\underline{\boldsymbol{x}}_{t+1}^{\mathrm{Lin}} = \mathbf{F}_t \underline{\boldsymbol{x}}_t^{\mathrm{Lin}} + \mathbf{G}_t \hat{\underline{u}}_t^{\mathrm{Lin}} + \underline{\boldsymbol{w}}_t^{\mathrm{Lin}} \tag{3.1}$$

and a linear measurement model as

$$\underline{\boldsymbol{z}}_t^{\mathrm{Lin}} = \mathbf{H}_t \underline{\boldsymbol{x}}_t^{\mathrm{Lin}} + \underline{\boldsymbol{v}}_t^{\mathrm{Lin}} \tag{3.2}$$

using the system matrix $\mathbf{F}_t$, input matrix $\mathbf{G}_t$, and measurement matrix $\mathbf{H}_t$. In this chapter and the next, we limit ourselves to linear system and measurement models.

The aim in recursive Bayesian estimation is usually to estimate relevant parameters of the state of a system based on noisy measurements. We shall assume that the entire state is to be estimated. An estimator is a function of a random variable, e.g., the measurements. When this function is applied to actual measurements, the resulting value is called an estimate. The estimate serves as an approximation of the true value that we aim to estimate.

An important measure of the quality of a Bayesian estimator is the Bayesian mean squared error (BMSE) [Kay93, Section 10.3] that is defined as the expected value of the square of the deviation between the true state and the estimate, i.e.,

$$\mathrm{BMSE}(\underline{\hat{x}}) = \mathrm{E}\big((\underline{\hat{x}}(\underline{\boldsymbol{z}}) - \underline{\boldsymbol{x}})^2\big) = \int_{\Omega_{\underline{\boldsymbol{x}}}} \int_{\Omega_{\underline{\boldsymbol{z}}}} (\underline{\hat{x}}(\underline{z}) - \underline{x})^2 f^{\underline{\boldsymbol{x}},\underline{\boldsymbol{z}}}(\underline{x}, \underline{z}) \, d\underline{x} \, d\underline{z} \ ,$$

with $\Omega_{\underline{\boldsymbol{x}}}$ and $\Omega_{\underline{\boldsymbol{z}}}$ being the sample spaces of the state and the measurement. The estimator that minimizes the BMSE is called the minimum mean squared error (MMSE) estimator. If the sample spaces are Euclidean spaces, the system and measurement models are linear, the noise terms are uncorrelated, and $\underline{\boldsymbol{x}}$ and $\underline{\boldsymbol{z}}$ are jointly Gaussian-distributed, the Kalman filter [Kay93, Chapter 13] is the MMSE estimator. If the assumption of joint Gaussianity is violated, the Kalman filter is no longer the MMSE estimator, but it is the best among the linear Bayesian estimators. The Kalman filter keeps track of an estimate $\underline{\hat{x}}$ and a corresponding covariance matrix $\mathbf{C}$. It is initialized using the mean and covariance matrix of the prior distribution. When a measurement is obtained, the updated estimate $\underline{\hat{x}}_t^{\mathrm{e}}$ and covariance matrix $\mathbf{C}_t^{\mathrm{e}}$ are calculated from the current estimate $\underline{\hat{x}}_t^{\mathrm{p}}$, the measurement $\underline{\hat{z}}_t$, the current covariance matrix $\mathbf{C}_t^{\mathrm{p}}$, and the covariance matrix of the noise term $\mathbf{C}_t^{\underline{\boldsymbol{v}}}$ according to

$$\begin{aligned}
\underline{\hat{x}}_t^{\mathrm{e}} &= \underline{\hat{x}}_t^{\mathrm{p}} + \mathbf{K}_t(\underline{\hat{z}}_t - \mathbf{H}_t \underline{\hat{x}}_t^{\mathrm{p}}) \ , \\
\mathbf{C}_t^{\mathrm{e}} &= \mathbf{C}_t^{\mathrm{p}} - \mathbf{K}_t \mathbf{H}_t \mathbf{C}_t^{\mathrm{p}} \ , \\
\mathbf{K}_t &= \mathbf{C}_t^{\mathrm{p}} \mathbf{H}_t (\mathbf{C}_t^{\underline{\boldsymbol{v}}} + \mathbf{H}_t \mathbf{C}_t^{\mathrm{p}} \mathbf{H}_t^\top)^{-1} \ .
\end{aligned}$$

$\mathbf{C}_t^{\underline{v}}$ and $\mathbf{H}_t$ are dependent on the sensor, the sensor noise and, as described in the next section, the state vector. When measurements are obtained at regular time intervals, knowledge about the state at time step $t+1$ is derived from the information about the state at time step t using the prediction step

$$\begin{aligned} \hat{\underline{x}}_{t+1}^{\mathrm{p}} &= \mathbf{F}_t \hat{\underline{x}}_t^{\mathrm{e}} + \mathbf{G}_t \hat{\underline{u}}_t \ , \\ \mathbf{C}_{t+1}^{\mathrm{p}} &= \mathbf{F}_t \mathbf{C}_t^{\mathrm{e}} \mathbf{F}_t^{\top} + \mathbf{C}_t^{\underline{w}} \ , \end{aligned}$$

which is a function of the current estimate $\hat{\underline{x}}_t^{\mathrm{e}}$, the current covariance matrix $\mathbf{C}_t^{\mathrm{e}}$, the known input vector $\hat{\underline{u}}_t$, and the covariance matrix of the system noise $\mathbf{C}_t^{\underline{w}}$. All information about the system model required by the Kalman filter is contained in the matrices $\mathbf{F}_t$, $\mathbf{G}_t$, and $\mathbf{C}_t^{\underline{w}}$. System models that are commonly used in target tracking are introduced in the next section.

3.3 Simple Discrete-Time Motion Models

The models explained in this section are linear system models (3.1) that are time-invariant, i.e., all matrices describing the model are identical for all time steps. We can thus neglect the time index t for the matrices. Further, we only present models without any input. Thus, no matrix $\mathbf{G}$ is required. Due to the different assumptions of the motion models, the quantities estimated also vary. We now consider one particle in isolation and use x_t to denote the position of the particle along the transport direction and y_t for the position orthogonal to the transport direction. The first temporal derivatives describing the velocities are denoted by $\dot{\mathsf{x}}_t$ and $\dot{\mathsf{y}}_t$ and the second temporal derivatives describing the accelerations by $\ddot{\mathsf{x}}_t$ and $\ddot{\mathsf{y}}_t$. There is more than one variant of the constant velocity and constant acceleration model [LJ03]. We always choose the discrete-time model that is derived from the respective continuous-time model. More information on the continuous-time models is given in the next chapter. Using the models based on the continuous-time models is recommended in [LJ03] as the actual movements are continuous in time. The variants directly defined in discrete time use the same system matrices and mainly differ in how the noise term affects the system.

For the constant velocity model, our state vector $\underline{x}_t$ is

$$\underline{x}_t = \begin{bmatrix} \mathsf{x}_t \\ \dot{\mathsf{x}}_t \\ \mathsf{y}_t \\ \dot{\mathsf{y}}_t \end{bmatrix} .$$

The accelerations are not part of the state vector as accelerations are assumed to be only caused by the system noise. The system matrix for the constant velocity model is

$$\mathbf{F} = \begin{bmatrix} 1 & T & 0 & 0 \\ 0 & 1 & 0 & 0 \\ 0 & 0 & 1 & T \\ 0 & 0 & 0 & 1 \end{bmatrix} ,$$

with T denoting the time between two subsequent time steps. No input is used by the system model. When disregarding the input and the noise term, using the matrix $\mathbf{F}$ in the linear model (3.1) causes the position components to change according to the current velocities, and the velocities are kept constant. Assuming the noise term has a power spectral density of $S_{\boldsymbol{w}}$ along both axes, the noise covariance is given by

$$\mathbf{C}^{\underline{w}} = S_{\boldsymbol{w}} \begin{bmatrix} T^3/3 & T^2/2 & 0 & 0 \\ T^2/2 & T & 0 & 0 \\ 0 & 0 & T^3/3 & T^2/2 \\ 0 & 0 & T^2/2 & T \end{bmatrix} .$$

If there are additional sources of acceleration not respected by the system model, a larger covariance matrix should be used. This allows for, e.g., tracking maneuvering targets using a constant velocity model. In our case, we need a larger covariance matrix because particles may accelerate or decelerate due to the influence of the belt, the air resistance, or collisions with walls or other particles.

As only the position of the particle can be observed, the measurement matrix of a linear measurement model is a 2×4 matrix. If the measurements are given in pixel coordinates, information on the camera calibration may be used to generate a suitable measurement matrix. For simulations in which the positions are directly accessible or when the measurements have already been converted to world coordinates, the measurement matrix

$$\mathbf{H} = \begin{bmatrix} 1 & 0 & 0 & 0 \\ 0 & 0 & 1 & 0 \end{bmatrix}$$

can be used. When the measurements are given in pixel coordinates, this matrix can also be used to perform the tracking in pixel coordinates. In this case, the tracking may be less accurate because image distortions are not accounted for. The measurement covariance matrix $\mathbf{C}^{\underline{v}}$ is a 2×2 matrix that has to respect both the image acquisition and image processing error. Assuming that the errors are stochastically distributed is a convenient assumption that facilitates tractability but constitutes an approximation in our application.

The constant acceleration model allows for incorporating an acceleration, such as the one induced by the belt or the deceleration caused by the air resistance during the flight. For the constant acceleration model, we define the state vector as

$$\underline{x}_t = \begin{bmatrix} \mathsf{x}_t \\ \dot{\mathsf{x}}_t \\ \ddot{\mathsf{x}}_t \\ \mathsf{y}_t \\ \dot{\mathsf{y}}_t \\ \ddot{\mathsf{y}}_t \end{bmatrix} .$$

Changes in the acceleration, e.g., due to collisions or because the effect of the belt on the particle changes, are not respected in the model and can only be accounted for in the noise term. The noise is modeled in the form of the third order temporal derivative of the position, which is called the jerk. For the variant of the constant acceleration model we use, which is called the Wiener-sequence acceleration model, the system matrix is

$$\mathbf{F} = \begin{bmatrix} \mathbf{F}_{\mathsf{x}} & \mathbf{0}_{3\times3} \\ \mathbf{0}_{3\times3} & \mathbf{F}_{\mathsf{y}} \end{bmatrix} , \quad \mathbf{F}_{\mathsf{x}} = \mathbf{F}_{\mathsf{y}} = \begin{bmatrix} 1 & T & T^2/2 \\ 0 & 1 & T \\ 0 & 0 & 1 \end{bmatrix} ,$$

with $\mathbf{0}_{3\times3}$ being a 3×3 matrix of zeros. We assume the power spectral densities of the noise terms for the x- and y-axis are both $S_{\boldsymbol{w}}$, i.e., they are identical and known. The covariance matrix of $\underline{\boldsymbol{w}}$ is then

$$\mathbf{C}^{\underline{w}} = \begin{bmatrix} S_{\boldsymbol{w}}\mathbf{Q} & \mathbf{0}_{3\times3} \\ \mathbf{0}_{3\times3} & S_{\boldsymbol{w}}\mathbf{Q} \end{bmatrix} , \quad \mathbf{Q} = \begin{bmatrix} T^5/20 & T^4/8 & T^3/6 \\ T^4/8 & T^3/3 & T^2/2 \\ T^3/6 & T^2/2 & T \end{bmatrix} .$$

Only the position components of the state vector can be measured. Under the same assumption as in the constant velocity model, we obtain

$$\mathbf{H} = \begin{bmatrix} 1 & 0 & 0 & 0 & 0 & 0 \\ 0 & 0 & 0 & 1 & 0 & 0 \end{bmatrix}$$

as the measurement matrix. For the measurement covariance matrix $\mathbf{C}^{\underline{v}}$, the same matrix as in the constant velocity model can be used.

3.4 Overview of Multitarget Tracking Algorithms

In the previous sections, we explained how single targets can be tracked and described suitable motion models. To apply the Kalman filter to a single-target tracking scenario, we only have to choose one of the models and provide a measurement noise covariance matrix and the power spectral density of the system noise.

The state of a multitarget tracking problem comprises the states of all targets involved. To solve a multitarget tracking problem directly using a Kalman filter, the number of targets would need to be known. Further, it would be necessary to know which measurement stems from which target to provide a suitable measurement matrix. This information is unavailable in our scenario. Since we do not keep track of the correlations of the positions of the particles (doing so for all particles would be infeasible in our real-time application), there is no need to have a single state vector containing the states of all particles. Instead, the states of the individual targets can be split into multiple state vectors for the individual targets.

This strategy is frequently applied in multitarget tracking and makes the multitarget tracking algorithm easier to comprehend and analyze. Further, estimating the states of all particles separately facilitates the integration of new targets and the elimination of no longer relevant tracks.

Multitarget tracking algorithms can be subdivided into three important classes. First, there are algorithms that are said to perform explicit or hard association decisions. The underlying assumption is that each target gives rise to one measurement, and if all measurements are correctly associated with the respective tracks, the multitarget tracking problem can be treated like multiple single-target tracking problems. Second, there are approaches that use soft association decisions, i.e., do not enforce one-to-one assignments and allow using a single measurement to update the information about multiple tracks. Third, there are approaches in which the data association is only performed implicitly or not at all. We give an outline of all the three classes in the following paragraphs.

Trackers Using Hard Association Decisions Two common algorithms using hard association decisions are the local nearest neighbor (LNN) and the global nearest neighbor (GNN) [BP99, Section 6.4], [Mah07, Section 10.3.1.3]. Both are based on an uncertainty-aware distance called the Mahalanobis distance. For both approaches, a matrix as depicted in Figure 3.1 containing the squared Mahalanobis distances between the current estimates of each track and the measurements is computed. The calculation is in $O(nm)$ for n tracks and m measurements and in $O(n^2)$ when m and n are approximately equal.

We now address the variant of the LNN in which each measurement is assigned to a single track and vice versa. This prevents, e.g., multiple tracks representing different targets from following only a single target. In the LNN, we consider the tracks (or measurements) consecutively and determine the most compatible measurement (or track). This pairing is then fixed, and the measurement and the track will not be associated again when considering the next tracks. This procedure can be visualized using the association matrix as follows. Consider the rows in Figure 3.1 one after another. Look for the entry with the lowest value in the current column. The indices of the row and the column in which the cell lies then describe the track–measurement pair that is fixed. The column and the row are struck out and will not be used for future associations. If the number of tracks is equal to the number of measurements, all cells are struck out at the end. As we only have to iterate over all entries of the matrix once, this approach is in $O(n^2)$.

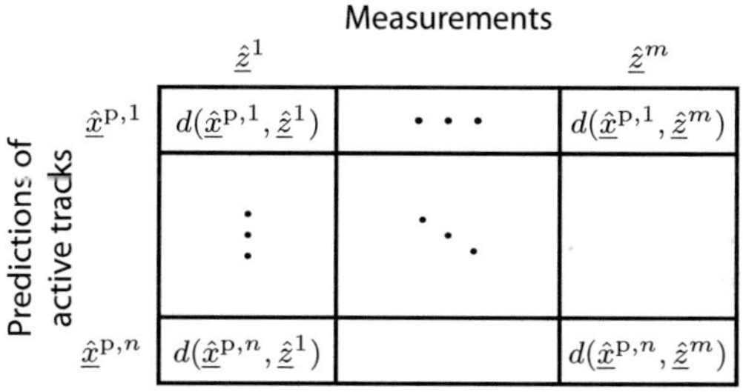

Figure 3.1.: Matrix used to determine the association decisions (adapted version of an illustration from [O7]). The upper indices are used to distinguish the individual measurements and targets. d denotes the squared Mahalanobis distance, which does not only depend on the measurement and the prior estimate but also the respective uncertainties.

The LNN can lead to incorrect association decisions even in simple scenarios. In particular, the LNN is dependent on the order in which the columns are considered. An example illustrating this problem is presented in Figure 3.2. To make the scenario easy to comprehend, we assume that the uncertainties are identical in both directions. In this case, the squared Mahalanobis distance corresponds to the squared Euclidean distance scaled by a scalar. We further assume that the uncertainties are equal for all measurements and tracks, in which case the same scalar applies to all measurement–track pairs.

If we begin with track 1 with the predicted position $\hat{\underline{x}}^{p,1}$, this track is associated with the most compatible measurement $\hat{\underline{z}}^1$. Then, however, track 2 can only be associated with the measurement $\hat{\underline{z}}^2$, which runs contrary to the intuition on how the correct association should look like. If we had started with track 2, this track would have been assigned to measurement 1 as expected. A technique that can be adopted from graph partitioning is to iterate through the entries of the matrix in ascending order [MS07]. If an entry has not yet been struck out, the measurement–track pair described by the entry is incorporated into the association decision and the column and row are struck out. The complexity increases to $O(n^2 \log n)$ because a sorting operation is required to determine the order for the iteration. By considering the measurement–track combination with the lowest distance first, the scenario illustrated in Figure 3.2 could be solved optimally. In more complicated scenarios, however, the outcome can still be suboptimal.

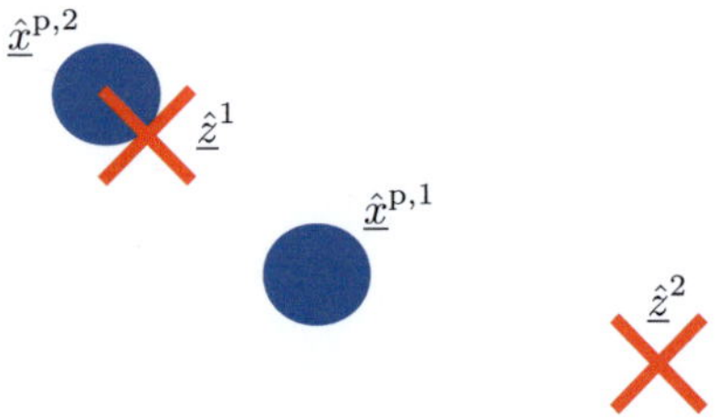

Figure 3.2.: Example in which the LNN may perform badly.

Stated informally, the weakness of the LNN is that it may be necessary to include measurement–track pairs that are not optimal when considered by themselves to maximize the overall quality of the association decision. The GNN solves this by determining the association decision that minimizes the sum of the squared Mahalanobis distances of all track–measurement pairs. As we will see in the next section, minimizing the squared Mahalanobis distances corresponds to finding the most likely association when all densities involved are Gaussian. As Chapter 7 explains, this does not apply to other densities. After the association decision has been fixed according to the LNN or GNN, a Kalman filter is used to update each track with the corresponding measurement. We choose the GNN for our application because it has proven to be real-time capable, reliable, and suitable for our application. More details on the GNN and the track management implemented for this thesis are provided in the next section.

A popular extension of the approaches using hard association decisions is the use of multiple hypotheses. In multi-hypotheses tracking (MHT) [Bla04], [BP99, Section 6.7], more than a single association decision is considered. A tree of multiple possible hypotheses is generated and maintained over multiple time steps. If an estimate is to be provided, the currently most likely hypothesis is output. However, the most likely hypothesis can change because less likely hypotheses can become more likely as new measurements are obtained. Visually speaking, if there are two almost equally likely association decisions in one time step, the GNN would decide on one option and assume it to be correct. This is a potential problem as even a single false association decision may result in the loss of a track [Bla04]. In MHT, both hypotheses are considered possible in the hope that it will become evident which hypothesis is correct as new information emerges. With time, past ambiguities may resolve while new ambiguities may arise.

Since considering all possible association decisions is generally intractable, the first step in MHT is to perform gating. When performing gating, a threshold is used beyond which a measurement–track pair is deemed unlikely to be part of the best association decision. For each hypothesis, an assessment is given that respects all aspects of the model, including not only the compatibility of the observation with the track but also knowledge about the frequency and distribution of measurements that do not stem from actual targets. It is common to not directly work with the individual association decisions but to rather provide values that indicate the total compatibility of the track–measurement pairs based on all plausible association decisions. If the ambiguities are limited to a few of the tracks, the association decision can be finalized for the others. When maintaining only the compatibility of the past measurements with the tracks, it is necessary to ensure that no measurement is doubly used when fixing measurement–track pairs. Since each hypothesis can give rise to several new hypotheses in every time step, the number of hypotheses would increase exponentially if no means to reduce the number of hypotheses were employed. The reduction of the number of hypotheses is a key part of a multi-hypothesis tracker and several strategies exist. Due to the higher computational costs of multi hypothesis trackers, we did not consider them for our real-time application.

Trackers Using Soft Association Decisions Soft association decisions are used in the joint probabilistic data association filter (JPDAF) [BSDH09], [BP99, Section 6.6], which is based on the probabilistic data association filter (PDAF) [BP99, Section 6.6.1] for single-target tracking. The gist of the PDAF is that when there is clutter (i.e., false measurements that did not originate from an actual target), it may be reasonable to partially use multiple measurements instead of deciding on one measurement that might be clutter. How much each measurement affects the state is determined by the compatibility of the measurement with the track. Measurements that are far away from the expected measurement are inherently weighted very little. In practice, using gating is essential to exclude unlikely association decisions that negatively affect the run time. The joint probabilistic data association filter transfers the concept of the PDAF to the multitarget tracking case. Each track is potentially updated using multiple measurements. While this approach can (assuming everything is modeled correctly) achieve a lower BMSE than the approaches based on the GNN or LNN, it also has its disadvantages. First, if two targets are very close, the measurements of both targets may be used to update both tracks. This may also apply to more than two targets and can lead to all tracks following a path in between the actual targets. This is a type of so-called track coalescence common to JPDAF-based trackers [Ken08]. Second, even when using gating, the JPDAF is expensive to calculate. Therefore, fast approximations [Bau15] are often employed. Experiments with a fast JPDAF were performed in this project, but the increase in the complexity of the algorithm was not rewarded with a significant improvement in the estimation quality. For this reason, and because collecting features for the classification would have to be handled differently if a JPDAF-based tracker was used, we did not consider the JPDAF further.

Trackers Using Implicit Data Association and Association-Free Approaches One approach to implicit data association is to use a single measurement equation for all targets that is invariant under any permutation of the targets [BH13]. An approach that is free of associations is the probability hypothesis density (PHD) filter [Mah03], in which the multitarget tracking problem is interpreted in a finite set statistics [Mah07] framework. Since the PHD filter was proposed, a variety of modifications and ways to implement it efficiently have been proposed [UEW07]. There are also other filters than the PHD filter that are based on finite set statistics [HB15]. As such filters are not suitable for accumulating features of the individual particles, we have not considered such approaches in this thesis.

3.5 Implemented Multitarget Tracking Algorithm

In this section, we detail how we have realized a multitarget tracking algorithm for the scenario of tracking bulk material particles on a conveyor belt based on the GNN. The entire processing chain is depicted in Figure 3.3. The image acquisition and processing components, the sorting decision, and the valve selection are not addressed in detail in this thesis. The GNN comprises several steps. In addition to the prediction and update steps of the filter, the association distances are calculated and the association is performed. Further, in the track management, new tracks are generated for new particles and existing tracks are deleted for particles that have left the observable area. All of these steps are explained in this chapter. The prediction for the separation that is specific to our predictive tracking for optical belt sorting is addressed in detail in the next chapter.

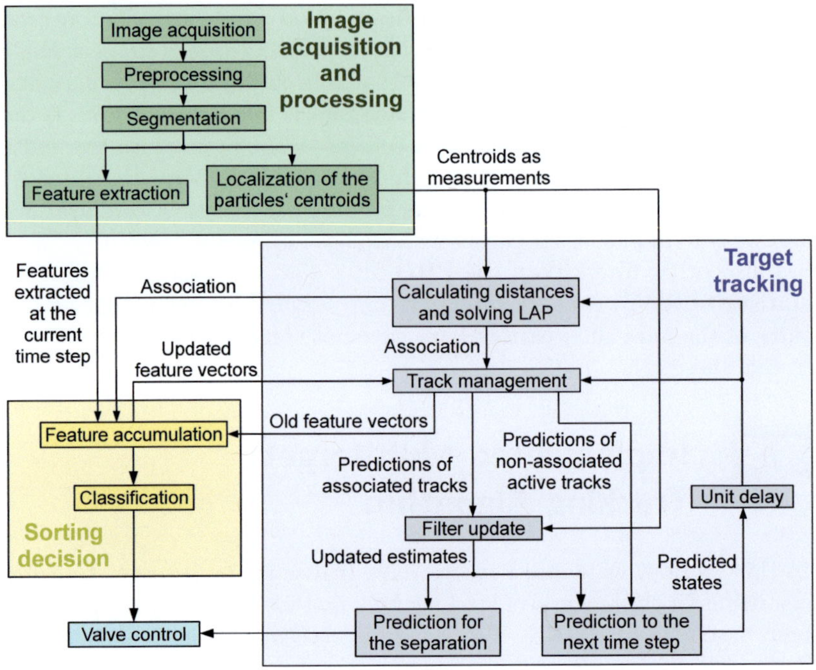

Figure 3.3.: Processing chain for the predictive tracking approach.

In the first subsection of this section, we explain the motivation for the use of squared Mahalanobis distances for the GNN and provide insights on how to efficiently solve the association problem. While we assume that a valid association decision comprising only one-to-one assignments exists in the first subsection, we describe how the approach can be extended to handle newly appearing as well as disappearing particles in the second subsection.

3.5.1 Solving the Association Problem

The motivation for the use of squared Mahalanobis distances in the association matrix as shown in Figure 3.1 is based on the association likelihoods [Mah07, Section 10.3]. When all densities involved are Gaussian densities in a Euclidean space, the association likelihood for a measurement $\hat{\underline{z}}$ with the measurement covariance $\mathbf{C}^{\underline{v}}$ stemming from the ith track with mean $\hat{\underline{x}}^{\mathrm{p},i}$ and covariance $\mathbf{C}^{\mathrm{p},i}$ is (see also [Mah07, Section 10.3, Equations (10.19)–(10.26)])

$$\begin{aligned} \ell(\hat{\underline{z}}|i) &= \int_{\mathbb{R}^n} \ell(\hat{\underline{z}}, \underline{x}^i|i)\, d\underline{x}^i = \int_{\mathbb{R}^n} \mathcal{N}(\hat{\underline{z}}; \mathbf{H}\underline{x}^i, \mathbf{C}^{\underline{v}})\, \mathcal{N}(\underline{x}^i; \hat{\underline{x}}^{\mathrm{p},i}, \mathbf{C}^{\mathrm{p},i})\, d\underline{x}^i \\ &= \frac{1}{\sqrt{\det 2\pi(\mathbf{H}\mathbf{C}^{\mathrm{p},i}\mathbf{H}^\top + \mathbf{C}^{\underline{v}})}} \\ &\quad \cdot \exp\left(-\frac{1}{2}(\hat{\underline{z}} - \mathbf{H}\hat{\underline{x}}^{\mathrm{p},i})^\top (\mathbf{H}\mathbf{C}^{\mathrm{p},i}\mathbf{H}^\top + \mathbf{C}^{\underline{v}})^{-1} (\hat{\underline{z}} - \mathbf{H}\hat{\underline{x}}^{\mathrm{p},i}) \right). \end{aligned} \tag{3.3}$$

We now say we have n measurements $\hat{\underline{z}}^1, \dots, \hat{\underline{z}}^n$ and n tracks. In this case, an association can be seen as a permutation τ of $\{1, \dots, n\}$. Then, the most probable association maximizes [LIHL09, Section 11.3]

$$\ell(\hat{\underline{z}}^{\tau(1)}, \hat{\underline{z}}^{\tau(2)}, \dots, \hat{\underline{z}}^{\tau(n)}|1, 2, \dots, n) = \prod_{i-1}^{n} \ell(\hat{\underline{z}}^{\tau(i)}|i) \ .$$

The best permutation also minimizes the negative log thereof, i.e., it minimizes

$$-\log \ell(\hat{\underline{z}}^{\tau(1)}, \hat{\underline{z}}^{\tau(2)}, \dots, \hat{\underline{z}}^{\tau(n)}|1, 2, \dots, n) = -\sum_{i=1}^{n} \log \ell(\hat{\underline{z}}^{\tau(i)}|i) \ . \tag{3.4}$$

Inserting (3.3) into the right-hand side of (3.4), we get

$$
\begin{aligned}
&\sum_{i=1}^{n}\left(\frac{1}{2}\log\left(\det 2\pi(\mathbf{H}\mathbf{C}^{\mathrm{p},i}\mathbf{H}^\top+\mathbf{C}^{\underline{v}}\right)\right.\\
&\left.+\frac{1}{2}(\hat{\underline{z}}^{\tau(i)}-\mathbf{H}\hat{\underline{x}}^{\mathrm{p},i})^\top(\mathbf{H}\mathbf{C}^{\mathrm{p},i}\mathbf{H}^\top+\mathbf{C}^{\underline{v}})^{-1}(\hat{\underline{z}}^{\tau(i)}-\mathbf{H}\hat{\underline{x}}^{\mathrm{p},i})\right)\\
&=\underbrace{\frac{1}{2}\sum_{i=1}^{n}\log\left(\det 2\pi(\mathbf{H}\mathbf{C}^{\mathrm{p},i}\mathbf{H}^\top+\mathbf{C}^{\underline{v}})\right)}_{\text{independent of }\tau}\\
&+\frac{1}{2}\sum_{i=1}^{n}\left(\underbrace{(\hat{\underline{z}}^{\tau(i)}-\mathbf{H}\hat{\underline{x}}^{\mathrm{p},i})^\top(\mathbf{H}\mathbf{C}^{\mathrm{p},i}\mathbf{H}^\top+\mathbf{C}^{\underline{v}})^{-1}(\hat{\underline{z}}^{\tau(i)}-\mathbf{H}\hat{\underline{x}}^{\mathrm{p},i})}_{\Lambda}\right),
\end{aligned}
\tag{3.5}
$$

when assuming the measurement covariance $\mathbf{C}^{\underline{v}}$ is identical for all measurements. When determining the permutation that minimizes the expression, we can omit the part independent of τ. The remaining term is proportional to the sum of the squared Mahalanobis distances.

In this form, we can show that lower system and measurement noise terms can significantly improve the reliability of the GNN. We now assume that the measurement covariance is fixed and only the system model can be improved, which leads to a smaller $\mathbf{C}^{\underline{w}}$ regarding the Löwner partial ordering. In this partial ordering, a matrix $\mathbf{P}$ is larger than (or as large as) a matrix $\mathbf{R}$ if $\mathbf{P}-\mathbf{R}$ is positive semidefinite. If $\mathbf{C}^{\underline{w}}$ is consistently smaller, $\mathbf{C}^{\mathrm{p},i}$ will also be smaller after prediction steps have been performed. Thus, $\mathbf{H}\mathbf{C}^{\mathrm{p},i}\mathbf{H}^\top+\mathbf{C}^{\underline{v}}$ decreases and $(\mathbf{H}\mathbf{C}^{\mathrm{p},i}\mathbf{H}^\top+\mathbf{C}^{\underline{v}})^{-1}$ increases [Nor89]. Due to the improvement in the prediction accuracy, $\hat{\underline{z}}^{\tau(i)}-\mathbf{H}\hat{\underline{x}}^{\mathrm{p},i}$ decreases on average if the measurement $\hat{\underline{z}}^{\tau(i)}$ stems from the track i. For the correct association, the two effects cancel out on average in Λ. However, if $\hat{\underline{z}}^{\tau(i)}$ does not stem from the measurement i, $\hat{\underline{z}}^{\tau(i)}-\mathbf{H}\hat{\underline{x}}^{\mathrm{p},i}$ does not decrease on average. Since $(\mathbf{H}\mathbf{C}^{\mathrm{p},i}\mathbf{H}^\top+\mathbf{C}^{\underline{v}})^{-1}$ increases nonetheless, Λ increases for incorrect associations. Thus, incorrect associations can be distinguished more reliable from correct ones. Therefore, the reliability of the multitarget tracker can be improved by employing superior motion models.

We can arrange the squared Mahalanobis distances in a matrix as shown in Figure 3.1. The task of finding the best association can then be reinterpreted as a linear assignment problem (LAP). Linear assignment problems can be solved in $O(n^3)$ using the Hungarian algorithm [Kuh55]. Efficient optimal LAP solvers in $O(n^3)$ that are tailored to the use in modern computers include, e.g., the LAPJV [JV87], which is named after its authors.

One way to improve the run time is to use gating. While gating is not as important for the GNN as it is for multiple hypothesis trackers and the JPDAF, a significant reduction in the run time can be achieved. Gating allows splitting the assignment problem into multiple smaller ones. Then, the employed LAP solver only needs to be applied to each of the smaller problems. Gating entails the risk of voiding the optimality. The risk, however, can be negligible depending on the size of the gating regions.

A different way to improve the run time is to use the auction algorithm [Ber09], which can be significantly faster than the Hungarian algorithm. The auction algorithm is not guaranteed to yield the optimal result. However, a bound for the deviation from the optimal result can be given. The auction algorithm is highly parallelizable. In [O18], we proposed an implementation of the auction algorithm on the GPU that makes heavy use of parallelization and atomic operations. The described implementation outperformed the GPU implementation of the auction algorithm proposed in [VR09]. If the GNN is too costly even with all optimizations, it is possible to temporarily replace the GNN with an LNN to ensure the real-time performance of the system [O18].

If the run times are unsatisfactory even when using an LNN, or when a GNN should be used even for tight real-time requirements, there is a variety of strategies to further reduce the run time. A simple approach is to discard individual frames. When skipping a frame, it is important to perform another prediction step of the individual tracks' Kalman filters to account for the missing measurements. Further, it is possible to only consider a part of the observable area. When using this strategy, adjustments to the track management, which is explained in the next subsection, are required. It is also possible to combine the two approaches and observe different regions at different frame rates. This combination allows for observing the particles over a large field of view while also facilitating high-quality estimates toward the end of the belt. The former is useful for accumulating visual features for the classification, and the latter is important for generating precise predictions.

3.5.2 Track Management

In the previous section, we have only regarded the case in which no new particles appear in the field of view and no particles disappear from the field of view. In the bulk material sorting task, particles appear and disappear on a regular basis, making procedures to handle the particle appearance and disappearance an important part of our algorithm. In the first part of this subsection, we explain how new tracks are initialized. In the second part, we describe how we determine which measurements stem from already known tracks, which measurements stem from new tracks, and which tracks were not observed at the current time step. In the third part, we explain how the reliability of the tracking can be improved in the presence of missing measurements and clutter.

Initialization of Tracks Regardless of the model used, it is necessary to provide a prior distribution for each new track. A common strategy is to initialize the prior with a large uncertainty and then rely on the measurements to eliminate the mean of the prior, which may be a random guess or some other value[1]. In our application, the state is only partially observable. If we initialized the state of a particle for a CV model with $\underline{x}_0^{\mathrm{p}} = \begin{bmatrix} 0 & 0 & 0 & 0 \end{bmatrix}^\top$ and a very high uncertainty, only the x- and y-components would be updated in the first update. The components $\dot{\mathsf{x}}_0^{\mathrm{e}}$ and $\dot{\mathsf{y}}_0^{\mathrm{e}}$ would still be zero, leading to the prediction that the particles stay stationary. While the velocity components would be corrected

[1] Strictly speaking, this goes against the Bayesian philosophy because the prior does not actually describe the distribution of the initial state when the experiment is repeated. As initializing the state with a high uncertainty is a just a trick to be able to use the easy formulae of Bayesian estimators such as the Kalman filter, one should be aware that certain properties and implications of recursive Bayesian estimation may not actually apply.

eventually in a single-target tracking scenario, significant problems can arise in the multitarget tracking case. If we assume that the particles stay stationary, the prediction of a particle's position may be closer to a measurement of a new particle than to the actual next measurement of the respective particle. This may lead to incorrect association decisions and could even lead to a complete breakdown of the multitarget tracking algorithm. Therefore, we use a reasonable value for the velocity $\dot{\mathsf{x}}_0^{\mathrm{p}}$ along the transport direction. For the first particles, an initial guess provided by the user is employed. In our experience, a rough guess is sufficient to start the tracking reliably. Once a sufficient number of particles has been observed, the initial value for the velocity is refined based on the average velocity of the observed particles and the corresponding uncertainty is reduced. Using values for the prior distribution that are based on previous observations is in line with the empirical Bayes [LC98, Section 4.1] approach. The initial guess for the velocity $\dot{\mathsf{y}}_0^{\mathrm{p}}$ is zero because we commonly have no reason to believe the particles are more likely to move more in one direction orthogonal to the transport direction than in the other. For the CA model, we initialize $\dot{\mathsf{x}}_0^{\mathrm{p}}$ and $\dot{\mathsf{y}}_0^{\mathrm{p}}$ as in the CV model. We initialize the accelerations components $\ddot{\mathsf{x}}_0$ and $\ddot{\mathsf{y}}_0$ for the CA model with zero. However, it would also be possible to refine the initial accelerations with time.

Recognizing Disappeared Tracks and Measurements of New Particles

To account for appearing and disappearing particles, we extend the original association matrix shown in Figure 3.1 that only allows for one-to-one assignments. As illustrated in Figure 3.4, additional columns are added for tracks of particles that are not observed again and rows are added for measurements that stem from particles that have not been observed yet.

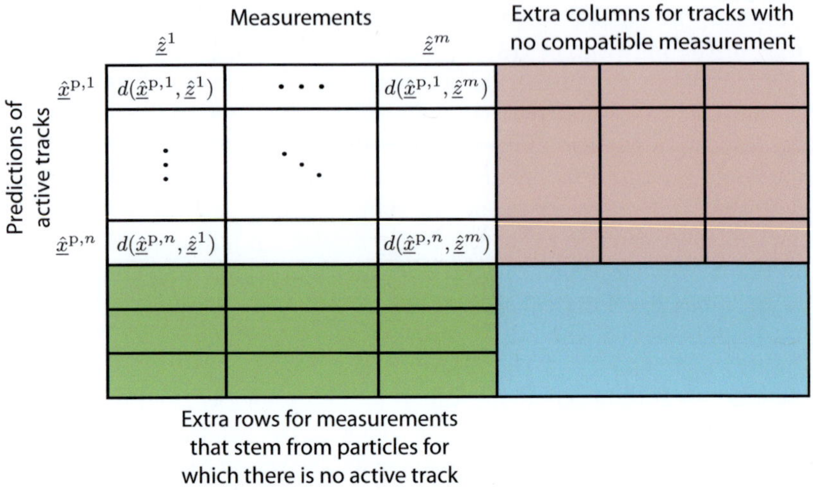

Figure 3.4.: Matrix used to determine the association decision that includes extra columns and rows for the track management (adapted version of an illustration from [O7]).

In the new columns and rows, we insert distance-like penalty terms. The precise values used depend on the location of the measurement or the predicted position of the particle. The penalty terms are based on probability densities, as illustrated in Figure 3.5. If a measurement is at the beginning of the field of view and within the area reachable within one time step given our current value for the initial velocity $\dot{\mathrm{x}}_0^{\mathrm{P}}$, the probability that the measurement belongs to a new track is higher than thereafter. We do not know the precise distribution of the initial velocities and instead assume they are distributed according to the assumed distribution of the initial velocities that we use for the track initialization. This leads to a smooth transition to a lower value in the likelihood function in Figure 3.5. Since the transition depends on the prior distribution of the initial velocity, it is dependent on whether the initial guess provided by the user or the refined value is used.

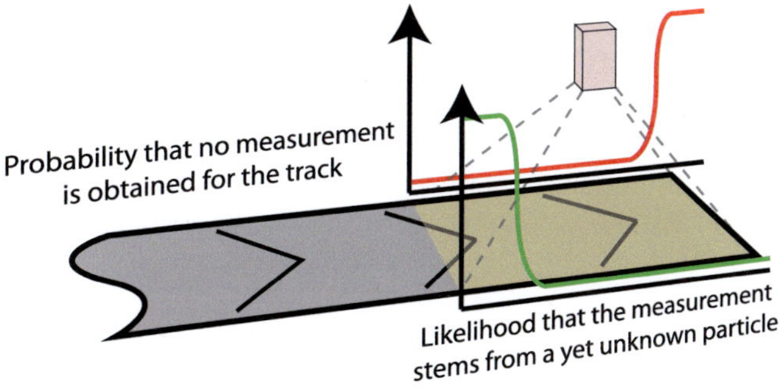

Figure 3.5.: Likelihood that a measurement stems from a new particle or that a particle being tracked is not observed again.

In our implementation, we do not allow the likelihood to reach zero to permit an initialization of new tracks everywhere on the belt. This may be necessary, for example, if a particle was erroneously missed in previous frames, if two particles were seen as a single particle in previous steps, or if a particle of the bulk material breaks apart. Because we assume that we have no further knowledge about where particles separate or previously missed particles appear, we preserve the low value over the whole remaining area, as depicted in Figure 3.5.

The probability that no further measurements of a particle that is being tracked are obtained depends on the predicted position of the tack. The probability is low at the beginning of the belt and then smoothly transitions to higher values for predictions outside the observable area. It is possible to incorporate the uncertainty of the prediction of the position in the probability. A nonzero value in the beginning and the middle of the field of view ensures that particles that actually vanish in an unintended way (e.g., because they jump over the boundaries of the belt), can be accounted for. Further, the nonzero probability also allows us to discontinue tracks that were caused by erroneous observations, e.g., dirt on the belt.

For an easier implementation, the smooth transitions can be replaced by step functions. When using a step function, the likelihood for the appearance should at least stay high in the area that can be reached in one time step given the current estimate of the initial velocity. An additional safety margin should be added to account for the uncertainties that would otherwise not be respected by the step function.

Thus far, we have discussed how the values for the white, green, and red cells in Figure 3.4 are derived. The cells in blue are set to an appropriate penalty term to ensure no problems occur when the number of extra columns or rows is higher than necessary. However, using significantly more columns or rows than necessary causes higher run times due to the higher problem size of the LAP. For the auction algorithm, it may make sense to include some additional variation in the penalty terms to further reduce the computation time spent on the extra column and rows.

Having too few additional columns and rows to account for all appearing and disappearing particles may cause significant problems. If there are too few additional columns, not all tracks of the particles that have disappeared can be labeled as disappeared. In this case, tracks have to be associated with measurements of new tracks or of other existing tracks. If there are too few additional rows, new measurements must be associated with existing tracks or tracks of particles that have disappeared. These effects significantly reduce the tracking accuracy and can even lead to a breakdown of the tracker.

Dealing with False Measurements and Clutter In our multitarget tracking scenario, it is possible that measurements are missed or that dirt on the belt is falsely recognized as a particle. To reduce the impact of these errors on the tracking, we use track scores [BP99, Chapter 6]. When a measurement is determined to stem from a yet unknown particle, a new track is initiated and initialized with a low track score. In each time step in which a measurement is associated with the track, its track score increases. A cap is used to prevent the track score from rising indefinitely. If no measurement is associated with the track, the track score decreases. If the track score falls below a certain threshold, the track is no longer seen as a valid track in the observable area and is removed from the multitarget tracking problem. If the track score is still above the threshold, the track is further preserved. Since no measurement is associated with the track, the update step is skipped. However, the same prediction step is used as for tracks associated with a measurement. If the supposed particle is to be separated from the stream of bulk material, the track score can be used to judge whether to activate suitable valves. A low track score may indicate that the image processing does not always see the supposed particle as an actual particle. A potential cause is that dirt on the belt is causing the irregular measurements. Therefore, if the track score is low, it may make sense to not trigger the valves at all or to only activate them if there is no risk of hitting particles that should not be hit in the vicinity.

There are additional ways to reduce the effect of dirt on the belt on the separation decision even if the image processing component always classifies the dirt as a particle. As dirt on the belt consistently travels at the speed of the belt, its motion behavior differs significantly from that of actual particles whose motion behavior progressively adapts to the belt. At the time the separation decision is made, the trajectory of the particle can be used to assess whether the particle may be, in fact, dirt on the belt.

A particular challenge in our application occurs if multiple particles are detected as a single particle by the image processing component. This can occur, for example, if the particles collide or touch over multiple time steps. We first address the latter case. As briefly mentioned previously, the erroneous detection of multiple particles as a single particle in the whole observable area may not necessarily lead to errors in the separation. This particularly holds if all or none of the particles are to be separated from the stream. If none of the particles should be separated from the stream, the separation mechanism will not be triggered if the classification is accurate. Thus, no error will occur. If all of the particles should be separated from the stream, they can be hit reliably if the classification is correct, the activation duration is long enough, and the activated valves cover the entire area of the supposed single particle. If two particles of different classes are seen as a single particle at all time steps, errors may be inevitable. For example, if damages are detected on one particle, the neighboring particle that is considered to be a part of the particle will also be separated from the stream. If such errors have a significant impact on the sorting quality, improving the image acquisition or image processing component should be attempted.

If multiple particles that were previously detected as separate particles collide at some point, we may obtain too few measurements at the time of the collision. Further, the measurement will not be close to the centroid of one of the particles but rather somewhere in between. By adding an additional processing step, we can alleviate negative effects on the tracking in many cases. If our predictions indicate that two particles are supposed to be neighboring in the next time step and only one larger particle is observed instead, it is reasonable to assume that the image processing has determined the two particles to be a single particle. In this case, we can split the particle before passing the measurements on to the multitarget tracking algorithm.

CHAPTER 4

Improving the Separation Process Using Predictive Tracking

In the previous chapter, we described how we perform the tracking of the particles in the observable area. In this chapter, we first explain how the process to generate the predictions for the separation is changed for systems based on area scan cameras. In Section 4.2 on page 52, we go into detail on how the CA and CV models can be formulated to generate predictions for the separation. In Section 4.3 on page 55, we assess the suitability of the CA and CV models. New models tailored for use in bulk material sorting are provided in Section 4.4. An evaluation of the performance of the novel models is provided in the last section.

4.1 Phases of Predictive Tracking

For the prediction for the separation, we subdivide the transport of the bulk material into multiple phases. Before we explicate the phases of our novel approach, we describe the phases in the line scan camera-based approach, as illustrated in Figure 4.1. Transporting the particles on the belt serves to bring the particles to an identical velocity along the transport direction and decrease the motion orthogonal to the transport direction. As the relative movement between the particles and the belt is to be reduced, we refer to the phase on the belt as the *calming phase.* When the particles leave the belt, they transition into the *flight phase.* During the flight phase, the particles are observed by the line scan camera. As there may be dirt on the belt, it is advantageous to observe the particles after they have left the belt. Further, the background can be adapted to suit the sorting task. For each particle, we only obtain a single observation, which is used to predict the position and point in time at which the particle reaches the separation mechanism. We refer to the phase between the observation and the separation as the *prediction phase.* As a single observation does not allow deriving information about the motion orthogonal to the transport direction, a straight movement is assumed. If the particle should be separated from the stream, one or multiple valves are activated. Since we have no knowledge about the speed of the particles, the valves are triggered after a fixed delay. As the prediction phase is of identical length for all particles, the underlying implicit assumption is that all particles have the same velocity.

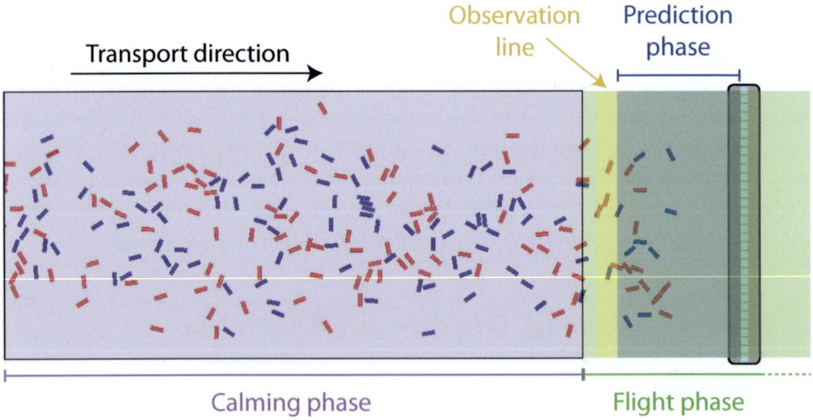

Figure 4.1.: Phases of the particle transport when using a line scan camera.

Now, we consider the phases of the predictive tracking approach as illustrated in Figure 4.2 for comparison. Until a particle enters the observable area of the camera, it is only calmed by the belt. Once a particle comes into the field of view of the area scan camera, it enters the *tracking phase* that is new in the predictive tracking approach. In this phase, the tracking as described in Chapter 3 is performed. As long as the particles are on the belt, the calming function of the belt also applies in the tracking phase. During the tracking phase, the remaining time until the particle reaches the separation mechanism can be calculated as explained in the next section. At some time step, there is too little time remaining to postpone the valve activation decision for the particle until the next time step. In this time step, a decision whether the particle should be separated from the stream is made based on the classification result. If the particle should be hit, one or multiple valves are chosen and a point in time for the activation is specified.

Since the estimated velocities of the particles are not necessarily identical, the position along the transport direction at which a particle may be at the last usable observation is particle-dependent. Thus, unlike in line scan camera-based sorters, the position at which the particles transition into the prediction phase is different for the individual particles. In Figure 4.2, we emphasize this by drawing the tracking phase so that it includes particles that are very likely to be observed again in time, while not including particles for which the sorting decision has already been made. Under the assumption that one particle cannot jump ahead of another particle even if it is faster, it is possible to visualize the tracking phase as a continuous region. The regions are only used for visualization purposes, and the border between the tracking phase and the prediction phase changes depending on the estimated velocities of the particles.

Unlike in line scan camera-based sorters, the particles are usually observed while they are still on the belt. As explained in Section 3.5.2, problems caused by dirt on the belt can be alleviated using the tracking approach. Therefore, there is less need to observe the particles in flight. While the prediction phase can start during the flight phase, we assume that it starts while the particles are still on the belt. This way, the flight phase can be kept short. As the deviation between the assumed and the actual flight path grows for longer flight paths, a separation close to the edge of the belt is desirable. However, since the separation can only occur in flight, there is always some overlap between the prediction phase and the flight phase.

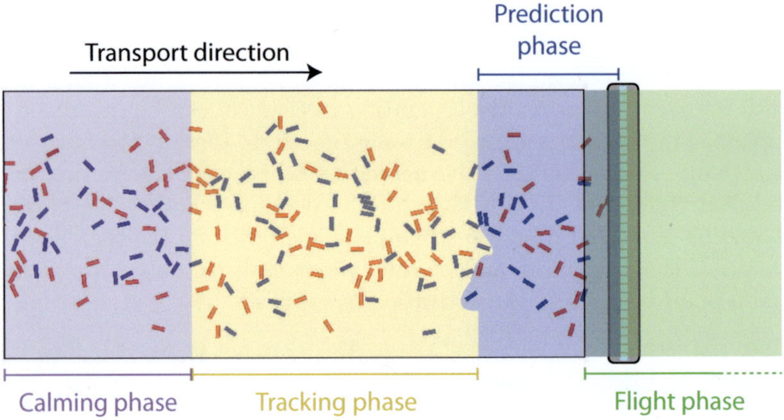

Figure 4.2.: Phases of the particle transport when using predictive tracking.

4.2 Determining Predictions Based on Motion Models

To perform the prediction for the separation, we first have to define a coordinate $\mathsf{x}^{\text{PredTo}}$ along the x-axis to predict to, such as the coordinate along the x-axis of the center or the beginning of the separation mechanism. By defining a line parallel to the y-axis at the chosen coordinate along the x-axis, we obtain a predefined line to which we predict each particle's motion. The predicted time t^{Pred} describing when the particle arrives at the predefined line is used to determine when the valve should be triggered. The selection of the valve to activate is based on the predicted point y^{Pred} at which the particle crosses the predefined line. If the particle passes the array of nozzles in between two nozzles that are controlled by different valves, it can make sense to trigger both valves. The precise number of valves to trigger may also be determined based on the size of the particle and the sizes of the nozzles.

To obtain the best prediction, it is generally not advisable to simply perform multiple prediction steps in discrete time and then take the prediction closest to the predefined line. First, the coordinate along the x-axis will not be perfectly matched, which causes an additional imprecision in the prediction of the position along the y-axis if the estimated velocity along this axis is nonzero. Second, if the controller for the valves features higher clocking rates than the sensor, a higher precision of the temporal prediction may lead to improved separation results.

For the CV model, it is possible to derive an accurate prediction based on the discrete-time model. For this, we perform prediction steps until we obtain a point after the predefined line. Then, we linearly interpolate the position between the last prediction before passing the predefined line and the point thereafter and calculate the intersection with the predefined line. The coordinate along the y-axis of the intersection corresponds to the spatial prediction. To obtain the temporal prediction, we divide the distance between the point of intersection and the last prediction before the intersection by the distance between the last prediction before the predefined line and the point thereafter. The result is then the fraction of a time step that needs to be added to the time step of the last prediction before the intersection to obtain the precise temporal prediction.

A linear interpolation between two predictions only yields an approximation if the velocity does not stay constant. Thus, this approach should not be applied to other models such as the CA model. A generally applicable strategy is to use models in continuous time. If we have a continuous-time model for the evolution of $\mathsf{x}(t)$ and $\mathsf{y}(t)$, we can determine when the particle reaches the predefined line by solving

$$\mathsf{x}(t) = \mathsf{x}^{\text{PredTo}}$$

for t. The resulting time t^{Pred} can then be inserted into the model for the motion along the y-axis to obtain the predicted position y^{Pred} according to

$$\mathsf{y}^{\text{Pred}} = \mathsf{y}(t^{\text{Pred}}) \ .$$

In the following paragraphs, we provide continuous-time versions of the CV model and the CA model. We only consider the generation of predictions and do not go into detail on the evolution of the uncertainties. As we will see in the evaluation of the models, there are effects not respected by the models that cause, e.g., biases. Due to such effects, we would not obtain an accurate assessment of the uncertainties.

Constant Velocity Model When disregarding the noise term, the continuous-time constant velocity model [LJ03] for the two-dimensional tracking scenario on the belt can be given as a differential equation according to

$$\dot{\underline{x}}(t) = \mathbf{A}\underline{x}(t) \ , \qquad \mathbf{A} = \begin{bmatrix} 0 & 1 & 0 & 0 \\ 0 & 0 & 0 & 0 \\ 0 & 0 & 0 & 1 \\ 0 & 0 & 0 & 0 \end{bmatrix} \ .$$

To perform a prediction based on an estimate of our discrete-time Kalman filter, we convert the time index of the Kalman filter into a point in time. The time at which the last observation before the prediction is obtained is called t^{Last}. We call the estimates for the position and velocity along the x-axis at this point in time x^{Last} and $\dot{\mathsf{x}}^{\text{Last}}$ and obtain

$$\mathsf{x}(t) = \mathsf{x}^{\text{Last}} + (t - t^{\text{Last}})\dot{\mathsf{x}}^{\text{Last}}$$

as the formula for the evolution of the position along the x-axis in continuous time. We can then determine the point in time $t^{\text{Pred,CV}}$ at which the particle passes the predefined line at $\mathsf{x}^{\text{PredTo}}$ by solving

$$\mathsf{x}^{\text{PredTo}} = \mathsf{x}^{\text{Last}} + (t - t^{\text{Last}})\dot{\mathsf{x}}^{\text{Last}}$$

for t.

The position along the y-axis similarly follows the equation

$$\mathsf{y}(t) = \mathsf{y}^{\text{Last}} + (t - t^{\text{Last}})\dot{\mathsf{y}}^{\text{Last}} \ . \tag{4.1}$$

The position $\mathsf{y}^{\text{Pred,CV}}$ along the y-axis at which the particle passes the predefined line is obtained by inserting the predicted time $t^{\text{Pred,CV}}$ into (4.1).

Constant Acceleration Model For the continuous-time constant acceleration model, the differential equation for the six-dimensional state vector including the accelerations is

$$\underline{\dot{x}}(t) = \mathbf{A}\underline{x}(t) \ , \qquad \mathbf{A} = \begin{bmatrix} \mathbf{A}_{\mathsf{x}} & \mathbf{0} \\ \mathbf{0} & \mathbf{A}_{\mathsf{y}} \end{bmatrix} , \qquad \mathbf{A}_{\mathsf{x}} = \mathbf{A}_{\mathsf{y}} = \begin{bmatrix} 0 & 1 & 0 \\ 0 & 0 & 1 \\ 0 & 0 & 0 \end{bmatrix} .$$

From this formula, we can derive

$$\begin{aligned} \mathsf{x}(t) &= \mathsf{x}(t^{\text{Last}}) + \int_{t^{\text{Last}}}^{t} \dot{\mathsf{x}}(t) dt = \mathsf{x}^{\text{Last}} + \int_{t^{\text{Last}}}^{t} \dot{\mathsf{x}}^{\text{Last}} + (t - t^{\text{Last}}) \ddot{\mathsf{x}}^{\text{Last}} \, dt \\ &= \mathsf{x}^{\text{Last}} + (t - t^{\text{Last}}) \dot{\mathsf{x}}^{\text{Last}} + \frac{1}{2}(t - t^{\text{Last}})^2 \, \ddot{\mathsf{x}}^{\text{Last}} \ , \\ \mathsf{y}(t) &= \mathsf{y}^{\text{Last}} + (t - t^{\text{Last}}) \dot{\mathsf{y}}^{\text{Last}} + \frac{1}{2}(t - t^{\text{Last}})^2 \, \ddot{\mathsf{y}}^{\text{Last}} \ . \end{aligned} \tag{4.2}$$

Analogous to the continuous-time CV model, we can solve $\mathsf{x}(t) = \mathsf{x}^{\text{PredTo}}$ for t and then insert the result $t^{\text{Pred,CA}}$ into (4.2).

4.3 Evaluating Predictions in Simulation Scenarios

In this section, we describe evaluation scenarios that we use to assess the suitability of the motion models for the predictive tracking approach. As no ground truth for the motion of the particles is available in real-world scenarios, we use the noise-free simulation data obtained using the DEM. The DEM simulation also allows for generating image data (sample frames are used as the basis for the Figures 4.1 and 4.2). However, in [O7], we have observed that including the image processing in the evaluation makes the quality differences between the models harder to assess. Therefore, our evaluation of the models is directly based on the DEM data in world coordinates.

The simulated scenarios are based on the TableSort system. The length of the belt employed is 40 cm, and the belt is configured to run at 1.5 m/s. We assume the separation is performed directly after the end of the belt and set the predefined line to the edge of the belt. The edge of the belt is chosen for two reasons. First, a separation directly after the end of the belt can make sense because short flight paths are desirable as explained in Section 4.1. Second, the simulation does not respect the air resistance, and thus, becomes less realistic the longer the particles are in flight. To evaluate the precision of the prediction without any additional effects, the CFD component of the simulation that induces the separation is disabled. The prediction for each particle is generated before it reaches $\frac{5}{8}$ of the belt length, which means the prediction phase spans at least 15 cm. The models are evaluated based on the position data sampled at 200 Hz. Our evaluation criterion is the temporal and spatial deviation from the actual time and place at which the particles reach the predefined line. It is generally reasonable to assume that an improvement of the prediction accuracy results in a higher hit rate for particles that should be hit and a potential decrease in the number of falsely ejected particles.

Three different bulk materials that are expected to differ in regard to their motion behavior are considered. The particles of the bulk materials are modeled after actual wooden particles that were also used for tests on the real TableSort system. The necessary parameters of the bulk materials were derived using a process explained in [HWS13]. The first bulk material comprises spheres with a radius of 2.5 mm. As the second bulk material, cylinders with a height of 9 mm and a radius of 1.5 mm are considered. Wooden cuboids with edge lengths of 2 mm, 5 mm, and 6 mm are used as the third bulk material. The data sets contain 3713 spheres, 4427 cylinders, and 4357 cuboids. Each batch weighs approximately 0.2 kg.

To determine the ground truth for the evaluation, the DEM data are used with a sampling rate of 1000 Hz. To determine the time and place of the intersection used as ground truth, all centroid positions of each particle are utilized. In particular, positions beyond the tracking phase are included. For each particle, the last position before the edge of the belt and the first position thereafter is determined. Then, a linear interpolation, as illustrated in Figure 4.3, is performed between the two positions. Using a linear interpolation, we implicitly assume that the velocity during each interval of length 1×10^{-4} s is constant. This assumption is an approximation. However, the precision of the determined values is generally much higher than the precision of the predictions generated at least 15 cm before the end of the belt based on data sampled at 200 Hz. Thus, the interpolated values can be reasonably used as ground truth.

Based on the ground truth time and position t^{GT} and y^{GT} for each particle, the temporal and spatial deviations are calculated according to

$$
\begin{aligned}
t^{\mathrm{Err}} &= t^{\mathrm{Pred}} - t^{\mathrm{GT}} \,, \\
\mathsf{y}^{\mathrm{Err}} &= \mathsf{y}^{\mathrm{Pred}} - \mathsf{y}^{\mathrm{GT}} \,.
\end{aligned}
$$

As we only calculate the difference and do not take the absolute value, we can differentiate between predicted values that are larger and ones that are smaller than the respective ground truth values. The sign of the temporal error is of particular interest. For $t^{\mathrm{Err}} > 0$, the particle arrived earlier than predicted, whereas the particle arrived later than predicted for $t^{\mathrm{Err}} < 0$.

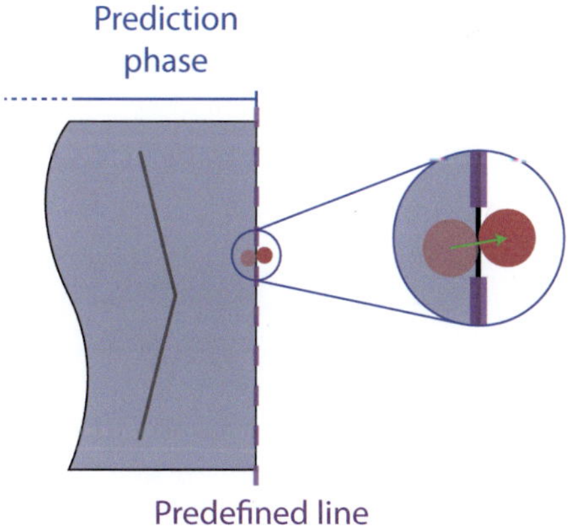

Figure 4.3.: Illustration of the calculation of the ground truth intersection. The edge of the belt is used as the predefined line to which the motion of the particles is predicted.

Using the noise-free measurements of the DEM at a sampling rate of 200 Hz, the association decisions can be determined reliably using the approach described in Section 3.5. Further, as there is no measurement uncertainty, only few observations before the start of the prediction phase are required to perform the predictions according to the CA or CV model as explained in Section 4.2. The temporal and spatial deviations are visualized as boxplots. Each box ranges from the 25% to the 75% percentile. The red line in the middle of each box marks the median. The upper and lower whiskers extend to the highest and lowest value that deviates no more than 2.7 standard deviations from the median. For normally distributed deviations, the range of ± 2.7 standard deviations translates to a coverage of about 99.3%.

The evaluation results for the accuracy of the temporal predictions are displayed in Figure 4.4. It is evident that the CA model is clearly the better model in this scenario. Applying the CV model results in a significant bias. That most particles arrive later than expected implies that the velocity does not stay constant and that the particles still accelerate further in the prediction phase. We confirm this in an analysis of the particles' velocities in the next section. The variance of the deviations, however, is higher for the CA model in the spheres and cylinders data sets. While the velocity affects the position linearly in time, the effect of the acceleration is quadratic. Therefore, small deviations between the estimated and the true acceleration can result in significant deviations in the temporal prediction. In the next section, we address how we can mitigate the bias without using the estimated acceleration.

For the spatial deviation, we examined three models. In addition to the CA and CV models, we consider a model that assumes that the particles move straight in the transport direction. This model is supposed to emulate the model used by line scan camera-based sorters that assume an absence of motion orthogonal to the transport direction. The evaluation results are presented in Figure 4.5. The tracking-based predictions using the CV or CA model are clearly superior to the predictions straight in the transport direction. This indicates that an improvement in the valve selection can be achieved using the predictive tracking approach. For the spheres data set, the constant velocity model performs best. For the cuboids and cylinders data sets, the CA model performs significantly better than the CV model.

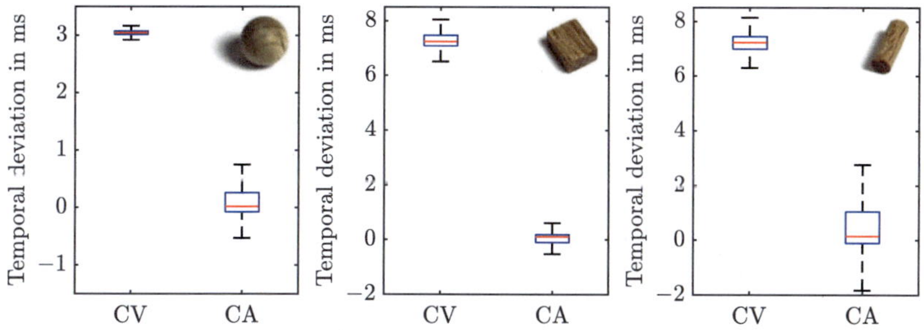

(a) Results for the spheres data set. **(b)** Results for the cuboids data set. **(c)** Results for the cylinders data set.

Figure 4.4.: Temporal deviations for all three scenarios for the CV and CA models.

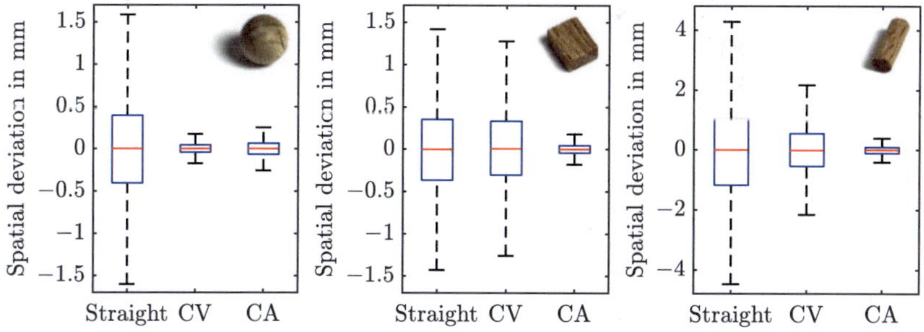

(a) Results for the spheres data set. **(b)** Results for the cuboids data set. **(c)** Results for the cylinders data set.

Figure 4.5.: Spatial deviations for all three scenarios for the prediction straight in the transport direction and the CV and CA models.

4.4 Scenario-Specific Motion Models

In this section, we derive motion models tailored to the scenario at hand. For this, we integrate our knowledge about the motion of the conveyor belt into our model. As the conveyor belt only moves in the transport direction, it can make sense to consider different motion models for the x-axis and the y-axis. In Section 4.2, we explained that the temporal component of the prediction can be calculated first and the spatial displacement can then be calculated based on the temporal prediction. Thus, we can easily combine different models for the individual axes. As the temporal prediction must be calculated first, we begin by analyzing the motion behavior of the particles along the transport direction. Afterward, we consider the motion orthogonal to the transport direction.

4.4.1 Models for the Temporal Prediction

To derive new motion models for our application, we regard the velocities of the particles over the course of the belt. In Figure 4.6, we depict interpolations of the particles' average velocities and the corresponding standard deviations depending on the position of the particles on the belt. The particles clearly tend to accelerate further while they are on the belt. This also applies to the prediction phase that ranges from 0.25 m to 0.40 m, which explains the bias of the CV model. The rate at which the particles accelerate depends on the shape of the particles. While care has to be taken when assessing the acceleration based on this plot with the position on the belt on the abscissa, the plot implies that the velocities approximately follow a constant acceleration. The plot also suggests that the CA model was only able to obtain nearly bias-free results because most particles do not reach their maximum velocity. If, however, the belt was longer, a significant bias could also arise for the CA model as the particles would stop accelerating during the prediction phase. Further, if the belt was so long that the particles reached their maximum velocity before entering the prediction phase, the results of the CV model would show less bias. If the scenario was changed so that the predefined line was, e.g., 0.1 m after the end of the belt, the deceleration during the prediction phase would lead to a bias for the CA model.

The aim of our new models is to achieve little bias without any requirements for the belt length, i.e., the belt should neither need to be long enough to be suitable for the CV model nor so short that the particles accelerate during the whole prediction phase as assumed by the CA model. The key idea behind the novel models is that if the particles' motion behavior is sufficiently similar, some particles can be observed at the end of the prediction phase to improve the prediction results for future particles. Data about the motion behavior can, e.g., be obtained in experiments with a deactivated separation mechanism and a field of view that includes the entire prediction phase. With a suitable field of view, data about the particles' motion behavior can also be accumulated while the system is in regular use as long as the effects of the bursts of compressed air are taken into account.

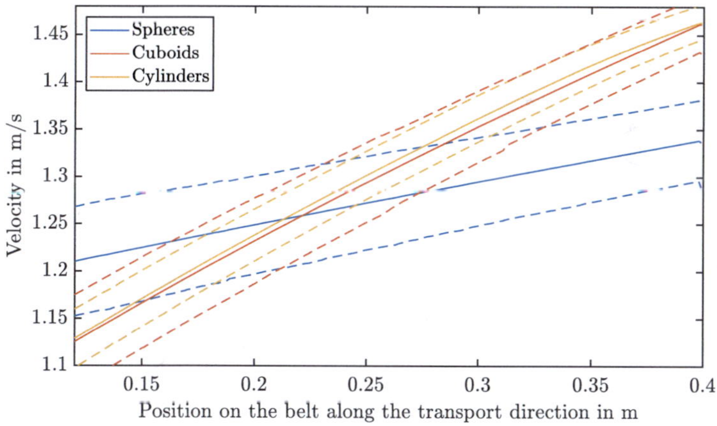

Figure 4.6.: Mean velocities and standard deviations plotted for a part of the belt for all data sets. The dotted lines indicate $\pm 1\sigma$ added to the mean.

In the following paragraphs, we give the temporal predictions as point estimates. If the uncertainty in a prediction is asymmetric around the estimate (e.g., if it is much more likely that the particle arrives later than earlier), then basing the valve activation only on this point estimate may not be optimal. However, approaches to fine-tune the valve activations should be based on real-world experiments for the bulk material sorting task to also take deviations from the assumed motion model into account.

We start with an explanation of the model implicitly used by sorters equipped with line scan cameras. Because only a single observation of each particle is used, information about previously observed particles is indispensable to activate the valves at the correct point in time.

Identical Delay Model We start by regarding how predictions as to when the centroid of a particle arrives at the predefined line can be generated using line scan cameras. Line scan cameras yield one-dimensional images that are concatenated into a two-dimensional image. When two-dimensional image processing routines are applied to extract the centroid, one coordinate describes the centroid's position orthogonal to the transport direction. The other coordinate describes the time t^{Obs} at which the centroid passed the observable line.

Assuming the line scan camera is aligned perfectly parallel to the y-axis, the position at which the camera observes the particle along the x-axis is fixed. Since the image processing component cannot determine the centroid with perfect accuracy, there is an error in the point in time at which the centroid passes the observable line. However, this error can be kept small as line scan cameras may feature sampling rates of 10 kHz and higher, yielding a high resolution along the time axis.

The valve is triggered after a fixed delay after the time of the observation t^{Obs}. The predicted time at which the valve should be triggered can thus be calculated using the time of the observation and a fixed offset t^{Offset}. The formula for this model, which we refer to as the identical delay (ID) model, is thus

$$t^{\text{Pred,ID}} = t^{\text{Obs}} + t^{\text{Offset}}$$

for line scan camera-based sorters. The optimal offset depends on the hardware setup and the bulk material sorting task. Usually, the temporal offset is fixed based on the processing times in cases of high load, as explained in Section 1.1, and the sorter is adjusted to the offset. The placement of the separation mechanism is refined based on experiments to ensure that the timing of the valve activation is suitable to hit the particles.

We now adapt this model to sorters using area scan cameras, which allow for multiple observations of each particle but cannot ensure that the particle is observed at the same coordinate along the x-axis. To derive the parameters for the model, we assume that some particles have previously been observed and tracked. For the previously observed particles, we determine an approximation of the best point in time at which the valve should have been triggered, i.e., when the particle reached the predefined line. Then, we calculate the average delay t^{Avg} between the time of the last observation before the prediction phase and the time at which the predefined line was reached. To generate a prediction for a newly observed particle, the offset t^{Avg} is then added to the time of the last observation before the prediction phase t^{Last}. Thus, the formula for the ID model for the use in area scan camera-based sorters is

$$t^{\mathrm{Pred,ID}} = t^{\mathrm{Last}} + t^{\mathrm{Avg}} \ .$$

Identical Velocity Model When using an area scan camera, the last observation before the prediction phase may occur at different coordinates along the x-axis. By respecting the coordinate along the x-axis at t^{Last}, the ID model can be enhanced for sorters equipped with area scan cameras.

In a model that we refer to as the identical velocity (IV) model, the delay between the last observation before the prediction phase and the moment the predefined line is reached is not considered identical for all particles. Instead, we assume that all particles have an identical velocity. For all previously observed particles, we determine the velocity for which the prediction result would have been identical to the approximation of the actual point in time at which the predefined line was reached.

We then calculate $\dot{\mathsf{x}}^{\text{Avg}}$ as the median or mean of all these velocities. For each newly observed particle, the predicted time $t^{\text{Pred,IV}}$ can then be calculated based on $\dot{\mathsf{x}}^{\text{Avg}}$, the position of the last observation of the particle along the x-axis x^{Last}, and the x-coordinate of the predefined line $\mathsf{x}^{\text{predTo}}$ according to

$$t^{\text{Pred,IV}} = t^{\text{Last}} + \frac{\mathsf{x}^{\text{PredTo}} - \mathsf{x}^{\text{Last}}}{\dot{\mathsf{x}}^{\text{Avg}}} .$$

Bias-Corrected Constant Velocity Model We now address how the CV model, as presented in Section 4.2, can be improved. As Section 4.3 explains, using a CA model can result in a larger variance than using a CV model. By eliminating the bias detrimental to the performance of the CV model, we can achieve an improved model that performs better than the CA model in two of the three scenarios. For this, we determine the bias t^{Bias} for the previously observed particles and then subtract it from the predictions for future particles. Under the assumption that the bias is similar for future particles, we obtain a bias-corrected variant of the CV model by calculating the temporal prediction according to

$$t^{\text{Pred,CVBC}} = t^{\text{Pred,CV}} - t^{\text{Bias}} .$$

Identical Acceleration Model In the biased-corrected version of the CV model, the correction term is independent of the last position at which the particle was observed. In the identical acceleration (IA) model, we strive to also incorporate the last position of the particle by assuming that the temporal deviation is caused by an additional acceleration, which is similar for all particles. For previously observed particles, we have an approximation of the point in time t^{GT} at which each particle reached the predefined line. We now add an acceleration term to the CV model to obtain a formula similar to that of the CA model. For each previously observed particle with index i, we solve the equation

$$\mathsf{x}^{\text{PredTo}} = \mathsf{x}^{\text{Last},i} + (t^{\text{GT},i} - t^{\text{Last},i})\dot{\mathsf{x}}^{\text{Last},i} + \frac{1}{2}(t^{\text{GT},i} - t^{\text{Last},i})^2\,\ddot{\mathsf{x}}^{\text{Optimal},i}$$

for $\ddot{x}^{\text{Optimal},i}$ to obtain the acceleration that would have resulted in the optimal temporal prediction for the particle. Using this equation, we assume that the particle accelerates uniformly in the prediction phase.

We now define $\ddot{x}^{\text{Avg}}$ to be the median or mean of all $\ddot{x}^{\text{Optimal},i}$ that are available for the previously observed particles. For each new particle, we predict the particle's position based on the average acceleration $\ddot{x}^{\text{Avg}}$ and the individually estimated velocity $\dot{x}^{\text{Last}}$. The prediction $t^{\text{Pred,IA}}$ is then determined by solving

$$x^{\text{PredTo}} = x^{\text{Last}} + (t - t^{\text{Last}})\dot{x}^{\text{Last}} + \frac{1}{2}(t - t^{\text{Last}})^2\,\ddot{x}^{\text{Avg}}$$

for t.

Constant Acceleration Model with Limited Velocity While the particles still clearly accelerate in the prediction phase in the considered scenarios, we know that they should never accelerate beyond the belt velocity during the prediction phase. As the average velocities in Figure 4.6 indicate, had the belt been 10 cm longer (or significantly slower), the particles' accelerations would have changed while the particles are on the belt as their velocities would not exceed the belt velocity. To make the CA model more suitable for scenarios in which the particles reach their maximum velocity during the prediction phase, we define a constant acceleration model with limited velocity (CALV).

Depending on the feeding process and the speed of the belt, it is possible that particles arrive at the belt at a velocity higher than the belt velocity. However, as this does not occur in our scenarios, we limit ourselves to the case in which the particles are slower than the belt velocity. As the first step, we determine when the belt velocity $\dot{x}^{\text{Belt}}$ will be reached according to the prediction of a CA model by solving

$$\dot{x}^{\text{Last}} + \ddot{x}^{\text{Last}}t = \dot{x}^{\text{Belt}}$$

for t. The result shall be called t^{MaxVel}. We only need to consider particles that are accelerating, i.e., for which $\ddot{x}^{\text{Last}} > 0\,\text{m/s}^2$ holds in our coordinate system. If the belt velocity is expected to be surpassed after the predefined line to which we predict, then limiting a particle's velocity does not affect the prediction result. Thus, we first calculate $t^{\text{Pred,CA}}$ according to the CA model. If t^{MaxVel} is larger than $t^{\text{Pred,CA}}$, then the belt velocity is not reached and $t^{\text{Pred,CA}}$ can be used as the prediction. If the maximum velocity is reached before $t^{\text{Pred,CA}}$, we use a CA model until t^{MaxVel} and a CV model with $\dot{\mathsf{x}}^{\text{Belt}}$ as the velocity thereafter. We accomplish this by calculating the remaining distance at t^{MaxVel}, dividing it by the belt velocity, and adding t^{MaxVel}. This results in the formula

$$t^{\text{Pred,CALV}} = t^{\text{MaxVel}} + \big(\mathsf{x}^{\text{PredTo}} - \mathsf{x}^{\text{Last}} - \dot{\mathsf{x}}^{\text{Last}}(t^{\text{MaxVel}} - t^{\text{Last}}) \\ - \frac{1}{2}\ddot{\mathsf{x}}^{\text{Last}}(t^{\text{MaxVel}} - t^{\text{Last}})^2\big)/\dot{\mathsf{x}}^{\text{Belt}}$$

for the predicted time $t^{\text{Pred,CALV}}$.

4.4.2 Models for the Motion Orthogonal to the Transport Direction

The evaluation results in Section 4.3 indicate that respecting the motion orthogonal to the transport direction can significantly reduce prediction errors. Due to the symmetry of the sorter design, spatial deviations in one direction are as likely as deviations in the opposite direction. Therefore, treating both directions equally does not result in a bias. The absence of a bias for the simple motion models can be seen in Figure 4.5.

As the distribution of the velocities is also approximately symmetric, the average velocities are close to zero. Therefore, we visualize the velocities of individual particles over the course of the belt in Figure 4.7. For all types of particles, abrupt changes in the velocities occur due to collisions. We do not attempt to model collisions as this would be computationally expensive and may necessitate knowledge about certain physical properties of the particles that is usually unavailable in practice.

As depicted in Figure 4.7a, the spherical particles tend to arrive at the belt at lower velocities orthogonal to the transport direction than the cuboids and cylinders presented in Figures 4.7b and 4.7c. For the spheres, comparably little deceleration occurs, which suggests that a CV model is

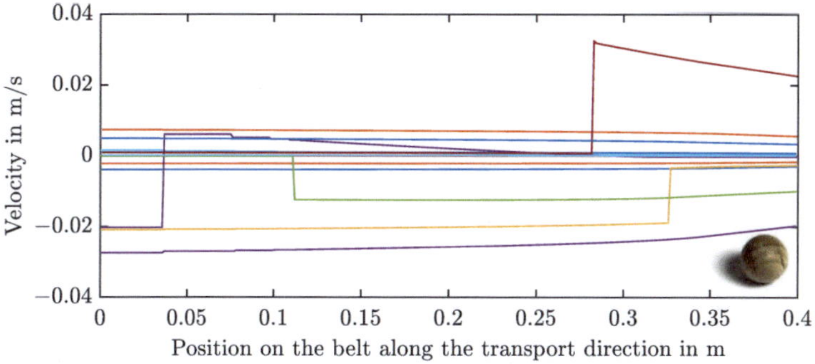

(a) Velocities for the spheres data set.

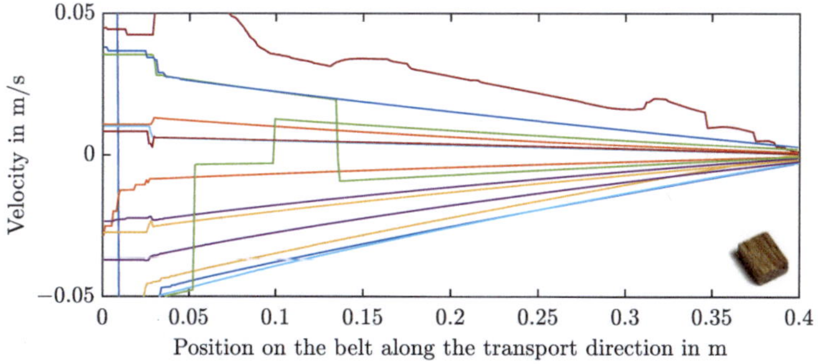

(b) Velocities for the cuboids data set.

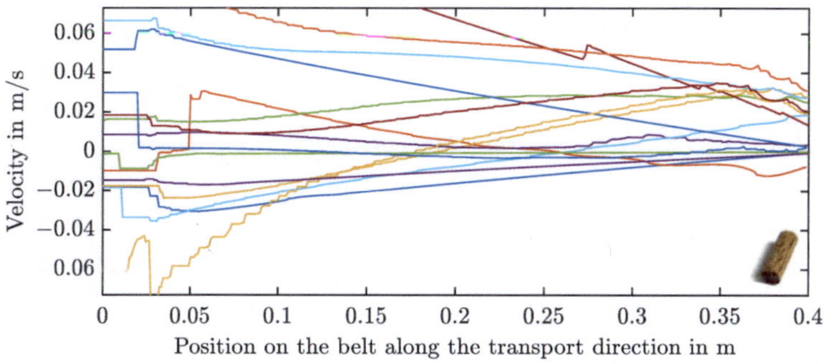

(c) Velocities for the cylinders data set.

Figure 4.7.: Velocities orthogonal to the transport direction of 15 particles of each bulk material plotted over the position on the belt.

suitable for predicting the motion orthogonal to the transport direction. A significantly higher deceleration can be observed for the cuboids in Figure 4.7b. The velocities do not stay constant but rather change at a constant rate, which makes a CA model appear more suitable than a CV model.

The velocities of the cylinders illustrated in Figure 4.7c indicate a much more diverse behavior, and there are effects that cannot be observed in the other data sets. In the cuboids data set, the velocities show a clear trend to a velocity of $0\,\mathrm{m/s}$. While the particles also decelerate on average in the cylinders data set, the velocities of some particles clearly cross the zero line. These particles show an increase in the absolute value of the velocity orthogonal to the transport direction. Such an increase can also be observed for particles that do not cross the zero line. The cylinders speed up due to the form of the particles and the difference between the velocities of the particles and the velocity of the belt. Unless the particles are aligned with their long sides pointing in the transport direction, the difference to the belt velocity induces a rolling motion. Depending on the orientations of the cylinders, this rolling motion may cause an acceleration orthogonal to the transport direction.

In the following paragraphs, two non-standard motion models for predicting the motion of bulk material particles orthogonal to the transport direction are presented. Both models use an acceleration in addition to the currently estimated velocity. However, the acceleration used is not the currently estimated acceleration as used by the CA model.

Constant Acceleration Model Disallowing Sign Changes In this model, we use our knowledge that the spheres and cuboids tend to experience a reduction in their absolute velocities. Thus, when the velocity orthogonal to the transport direction reaches approximately $0\,\mathrm{m/s}$, it should stay close to $0\,\mathrm{m/s}$ in the absence of collisions. Since one of the purposes of the belt is to reduce the motion orthogonal to the transport direction, this property is expected to hold for a variety of bulk materials. In contrast, the use of a classical CA model would result in a predicted increase in the velocity in the opposite direction once the velocity of $0\,\mathrm{m/s}$ is reached.

In the constant acceleration model disallowing sign changes (CADSC) of the velocity, we first determine the point in time $t^{\text{SignChange}}$ at which a velocity of $0\,\text{m/s}$ is reached under the assumption of a CA model. Based on the last estimates of the velocity $\dot{\mathsf{y}}^{\text{Last}}$ and acceleration $\ddot{\mathsf{y}}^{\text{Last}}$ before the start of the prediction phase, we can calculate $t^{\text{SignChange}}$ as

$$t^{\text{SignChange}} = t^{\text{Last}} + \frac{-\dot{\mathsf{y}}^{\text{Last}}}{\ddot{\mathsf{y}}^{\text{Last}}} .$$

If the sign change is predicted to occur after the predicted time t^{Pred} at which the predefined line is supposedly reached, i.e., $t^{\text{SignChange}} \geq t^{\text{Pred}}$, the CA model can be used without any modification. We can also use the prediction of the CA model if $t^{\text{SignChange}} < t^{\text{Last}}$, which occurs when the signs of $\dot{\mathsf{y}}^{\text{Last}}$ and $\ddot{\mathsf{y}}^{\text{Last}}$ are identical. If none of these two conditions holds, we assume that the velocity orthogonal to the transport stays $0\,\text{m/s}$ after $t^{\text{SignChange}}$. Hence, the particles are assumed to move only along the transport direction after $t^{\text{signChange}}$. Thus, we can obtain $\mathsf{y}^{\text{Pred,CADSC}}$ by using a CA model until $t^{\text{SignChange}}$, which can be achieved by inserting $t^{\text{SignChange}}$ into (4.2).

Ratio-Based Deceleration Model In this model, we also use observations of previously observed particles as in the IA model for the temporal prediction. In the cuboids and the spheres data sets, we observed a tendency toward deceleration. We now say that all particles decelerate similarly and evenly during the prediction phase. For the particles observed previously, we calculate the ratio of the velocity at the end of the prediction phase to the last estimated velocity before the start of the prediction phase. We then calculate the median r of these ratios and assume that the ratio is similar for future particles. It is particularly important to use the median and not the mean to be robust against potentially large ratios that can occur when $\left|\dot{\mathsf{y}}^{\text{Last}}\right|$ is very small. Further, the median prevents an influence of particles with massive changes due to collisions.

We now say that the change in the velocity occurs evenly over time and model it as an acceleration. For each particle that enters the prediction phase in the next time step, we calculate the acceleration that results in a velocity of $r\dot{\mathsf{y}}^{\text{Last}}$ at the end of the prediction phase. This acceleration can be calculated according to

$$\ddot{\mathsf{y}}^{\text{Ratio}} = \frac{-(1-r)\cdot\dot{\mathsf{y}}^{\text{Last}}}{t^{\text{Pred}} - t^{\text{Last}}} .$$

The acceleration $\ddot{\mathsf{y}}^{\text{Ratio}}$ can then be used instead of the estimated acceleration $\ddot{\mathsf{y}}^{\text{Last}}$ in the CA model. When inserting t^{Pred} in (4.2), we obtain

$$\mathsf{y}^{\text{Pred,Ratio}} = \mathsf{y}^{\text{Last}} + (t^{\text{Pred}} - t^{\text{Last}})\dot{\mathsf{y}}^{\text{Last}} + \frac{1}{2}(t^{\text{Pred}} - t^{\text{Last}})^2\,\ddot{\mathsf{y}}^{\text{Ratio}}$$

as our prediction.

4.5 Performance Comparison of the Motion Models

In this section, we extend the evaluation given in Section 4.3. We no longer limit ourselves to the classical CV and CA models and also consider combinations of one model for the temporal prediction with a different model for the spatial prediction. In particular, we combine the most promising model for the temporal prediction with different models for the spatial prediction. If the assumptions of the model for the motion orthogonal to the transport direction are accurate, using a more precise point in time should result in better spatial predictions. For our novel models that depend on previously observed particles, we use the first 10% of the particles to determine the relevant parameters. To compare our approaches with the optimal performance of a line scan camera-based sorter, we make an exception for the identical velocity model. For the IV model, we use 100% of the available data to calculate the median to allow this model to achieve its optimal performance.

In Figure 4.8, we provide the temporal deviations between the ground truth and the predictions generated by the new models for the scenarios described in Section 4.3. To facilitate a comparison with the simple motion models, we also provide the results of the CA model, which are also presented in Figure 4.4. The CV model is omitted due to its large bias. Figure 4.8 shows that the CA model with limited velocity only provides a significant improvement over the regular CA model in the cylinders data set. For the spheres and the cuboids data sets, the CV model with the simple bias correction outperforms the CA model. The IA model performs best in all scenarios. The IV model performs the worst out of the models shown in Figure 4.8.

In Figure 4.9, we depict multiple combinations of models for the prediction along the transport direction with models for the prediction orthogonal to the transport direction. For comparison with the simple motion models, we provide the results for the CA model along both directions (CA–CA). For all data sets, combining the CALV model with the CADSC model does not yield an improvement compared with the regular CA model. Combining the IA model with the CV model only yields good results for the spheres data set, for which the regular CV model also performed favorably. Combining the IA model with the CA model does not yield a significantly different performance than the regular CA model. This suggests that the improvement in the temporal prediction only has a minor impact on the spatial prediction. For the spheres and the cuboids data sets, the ratio-based model performs best. This does not hold for the cylinders data set. Since the cylinders may accelerate or decelerate orthogonal to the transport direction, assuming that the accelerations for all particles are similar is not warranted. Thus, it is better to use a simple CA model for the predictions orthogonal to the transport direction in this scenario. For the cylinders, deriving motion models that take the orientations of the individual particles into account may yield further improvements.

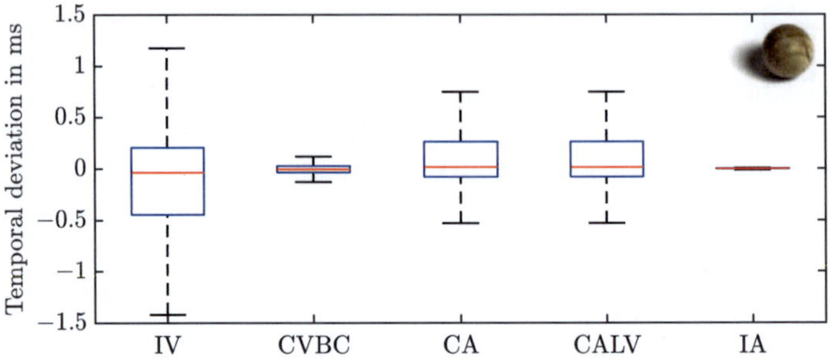

(a) Results for the spheres data set.

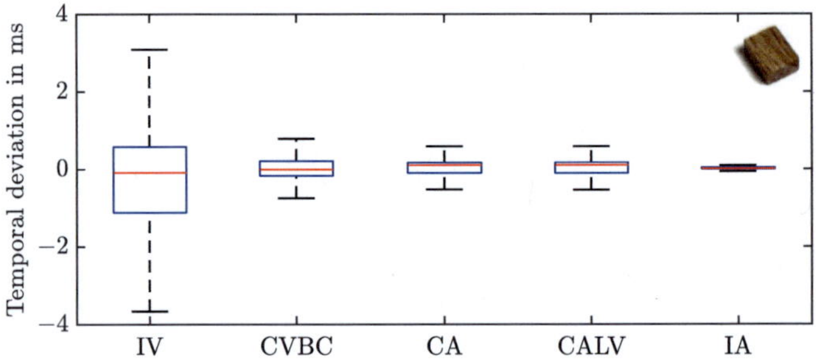

(b) Results for the cuboids data set.

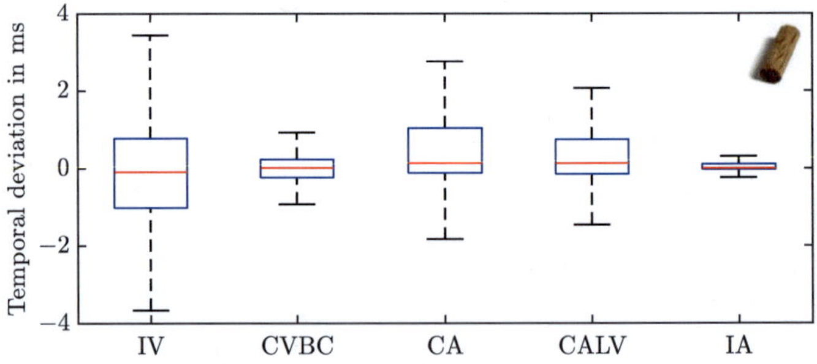

(c) Results for the cylinders data set.

Figure 4.8.: Evaluation results for the temporal deviation in all three scenarios. A list of the abbreviations used is given on page x.

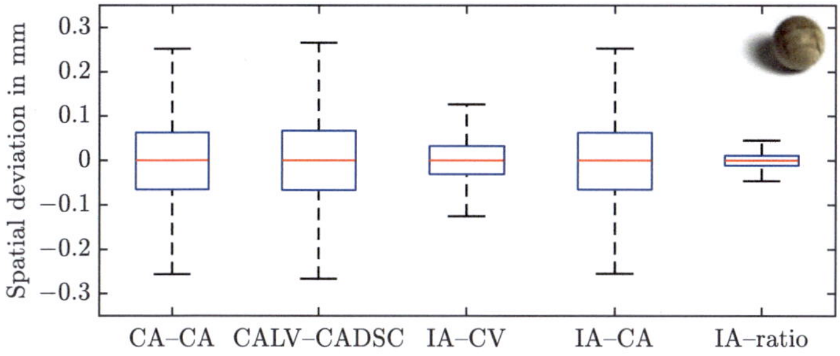

(a) Results for the spheres data set.

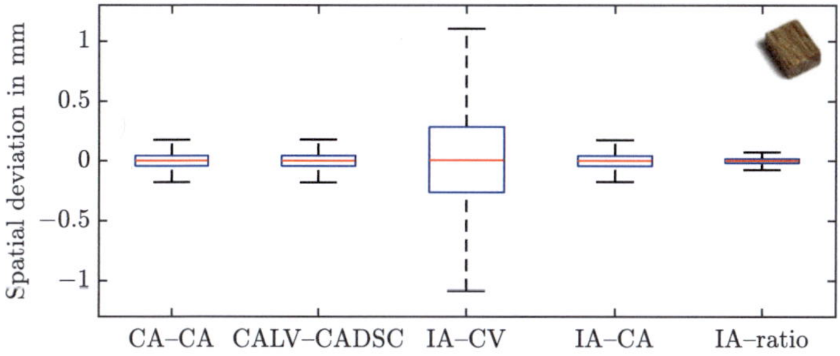

(b) Results for the cuboids data set.

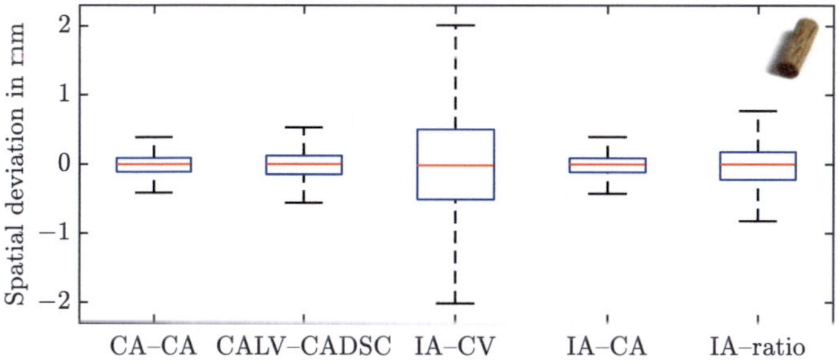

(c) Results for the cylinders data set.

Figure 4.9.: Evaluation results for the spatial deviation in all three scenarios. A list of the abbreviations used is given on page x.

All in all, the evaluation results show that by using motion models tailored to the scenario, we can achieve almost bias-free results with only a fraction of the deviations of the models based on the assumptions of line scan camera-based sorters. Using the novel models is particularly important for improving the accuracy of the temporal prediction. For the spatial prediction, the new ratio-based model can lead to significant improvements over the CV and CA models if the particles are similar in their acceleration behavior.

4.6 Summary and Discussion

In the current and previous chapter, we have explained a basic approach to predictive tracking that will be further extended in Chapter 7. In Chapter 3, we gave an introduction to single-target and multitarget tracking. Further, we described our implemented approach for the application of tracking bulk material particles on a conveyor belt. The approach is based on finding the most likely association between the tracks and the measurements. Moreover, we addressed particular challenges to realizing a reliable tracking in the bulk material sorting scenario.

In the current chapter, we described how predictions for the separation can be realized based on information obtained using multitarget tracking. For this, we first highlighted the differences between predictions of line scan camera-based sorters and predictions based on tracking. Initially, classical motion models were used for predictive tracking. While these motion models already allowed for an improvement in the spatial predictions, the precision of the temporal predictions was evidently suboptimal. To improve both the accuracy of the temporal and spatial predictions, novel models were developed that integrate information on previously observed particles' trajectories. Using these models, a clear improvement in the accuracy of the temporal predictions was attained. A significant improvement in the spatial predictions was also achieved for two of the three bulk materials considered.

The evaluation of the motion models was based on data from the DEM simulation that are not influenced by measurement noise. As observed in [O7], the differences in the prediction accuracy of different motion models are less pronounced when there are measurement errors stemming from the image processing. When using the novel motion models, the accuracy of the image processing may become the new limiting factor for the accuracy of the predictions. Another challenge arising in the presence of measurement noise is that the association decisions may no longer be reliable. To facilitate reliable association decisions even in the presence of significant measurement noise, we integrate orientation estimates into the association decisions in Chapter 7. In the following two chapters, we address the challenge of estimating periodic quantities and propose filters for periodic manifolds that are suitable for real-time applications, such as bulk material sorting.

CHAPTER 5

State of the Art of Directional Estimation

Estimating the orientation of a bulk material particle is an estimation problem with the topology of the unit circle. A multitude of benefits can be gained by estimating the orientations of bulk material particles. First, the separation can be improved if the orientations of elongated particles are known. Second, new motion models incorporating the orientation could be derived for, e.g., cylinders. Third, the reliability of the association process in the multitarget tracking algorithm can be improved by incorporating the orientation, which is addressed in detail in Chapter 7.

Future improvements to the tracking may involve jointly tracking clusters of particles. If the particles are in contact, jointly estimating their positions and orientations in one state vector may result in a higher estimation quality because the states of the particles are correlated. Further, we can use different measurement models based on whether the cluster was detected to be a single or multiple particles by the image processing component. The estimation problem can be significantly simplified by assuming that the orientation of each particle is independent of its position. Even with this simplification, we arrive at multivariate estimation problems. For the multivariate estimation problem for the position component, which is on a linear manifold, efficient filters for simple system and measurement models exist. The multivariate estimation problem for the orientation component poses a greater challenge. As we will see in this chapter, there are only few filters for multivariate estimation problems with the appropriate topology. In Chapter 6, we describe our novel filters that allow jointly estimating multiple correlated angles.

In the context of statistics, it has been known for over a century [Sch17] that periodic manifolds need to be treated differently than linear manifolds. In the field of recursive Bayesian estimation, which has received significant attention since the advent of the Kalman filter [Kal60], researchers have been tackling estimation on periodic manifolds as a special problem in nonlinear estimation [BM75]. Before we explain the different topologies, we first provide an example that illustrates that the straightforward use of a Kalman filter, which does not respect the periodicity of the underlying domain, is not advisable for periodic manifolds. In the example, we regard a circular manifold, which is the simplest periodic manifold.

Example 1. In this example, we perform a single update step and compare the result of a Kalman filter with the true posterior density. First, we approximate the periodic prior density and likelihood on the circle using Gaussian densities with corresponding means, as depicted in Figures 5.1a and 5.1b. The result obtained using a Kalman filter is plotted as a dark red dashed line in Figure 5.1c. In green, we show the true posterior density. The mean of the posterior Gaussian given by the Kalman filter may be a reasonable estimate when $[0, 2\pi)$ is regarded as an interval. However, when interpreting $[0, 2\pi)$ as a circle, the result is unsatisfactory. Instead of parameterizing a periodic function using a scalar $x \in [0, 2\pi)$, unit vectors in the circular subset $\{\underline{x} \in \mathbb{R}^2 : \|\underline{x}\| = 1\}$ of the real plane $\mathbb{R}^2$ can be used. This allows us to plot the functions in a way that makes the periodicity more evident. In Figure 5.1d, we illustrate the prior density, the likelihood, and the true posterior density in a three-dimensional plot. The peak of the true posterior density is

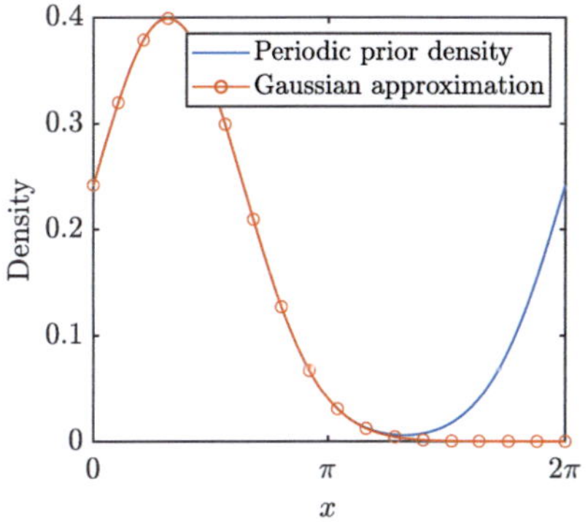

(a) True prior density and approximation thereof.

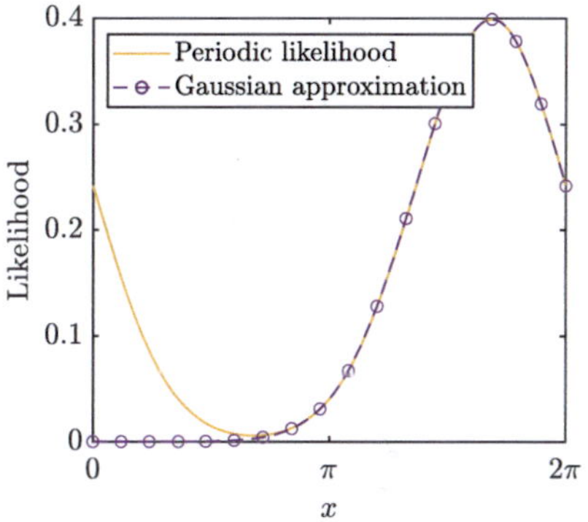

(b) True likelihood and approximation thereof.

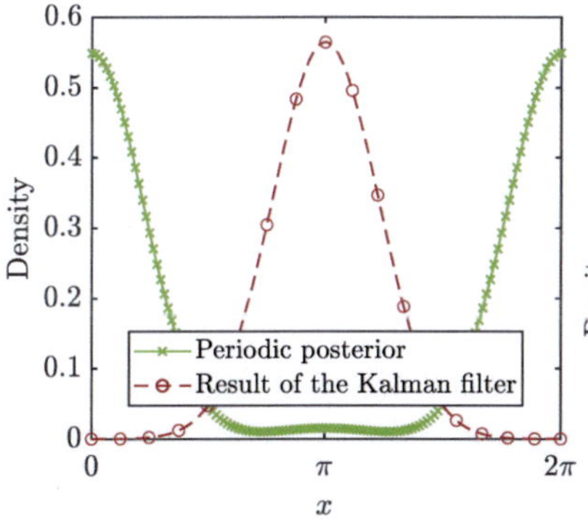

(c) True posterior density and result of the Kalman filter.

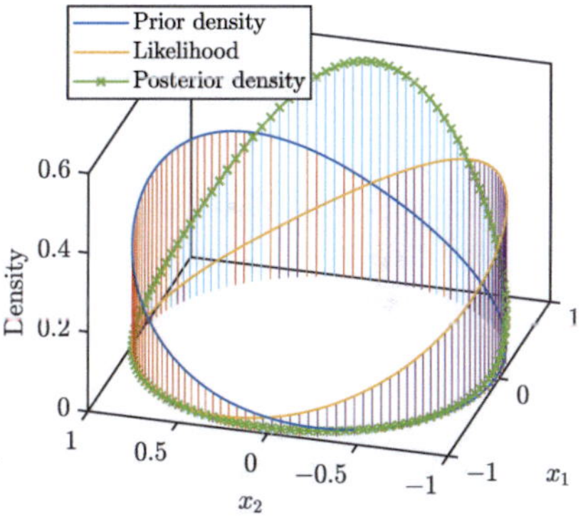

(d) Prior density, likelihood, and true posterior density. The circle is embedded in $\mathbb{R}^2$ in this plot.

Figure 5.1.: Example of the application of a Kalman filter to estimate a periodic quantity. The Gaussian densities have probability mass outside the $[0, 2\pi)$ interval shown in the plot.

located where the function values of both the prior density and the likelihood are high. As apparent in Figure 5.1c, the peak of the density given by the Kalman filter is on the opposite side of the circle. The estimate provided by the Kalman filter is thus of very low quality.

The example above only demonstrates a single weakness of treating periodic domains like linear ones. In the example, the correct mean could be obtained by shifting the border of periodicity. However, even with such an adjustment, the uncertainties of the Kalman filter can be misleading, particularly if the prior density and the likelihood are (nearly) contradictory. Using directional statistics, no such problems arise as the periodicity is properly accounted for.

For univariate periodic estimation problems, the circle $\mathbb{S}^1$ that can be parameterized by $x \in [0, 2\pi)$ is considered. If the densities are, e.g., π-periodic or repeat at every integer, they can be scaled appropriately and treated like 2π-periodic densities. More detail on this is given in the context of extracting orientations from ambiguous image data in Chapter 7 and Appendix E.2. The domains do not have to start at 0 as merely additions and subtractions are required to be able to use the standard parameterization internally.

Estimation problems on periodic manifolds are particularly challenging for random vectors with high numbers of variates. As in the case of nonlinear estimation on linear domains, the higher the dimensionality, the more challenging the estimation problem becomes. When considering a multivariate estimation problem with a toroidal or hypertoroidal manifold, the user should thus first check whether the estimation problem can be separated into multiple independent estimation problems with lower numbers of variates. This is trivial when the individual random variables are independent. Independence, however, is not always required to be able to reformulate the estimation problem as one involving only independent random variables.

When facing an estimation problem with multiple angles, it is necessary to be aware of the underlying topology. There are two classes of topologies of particular interest, both of which are generalizations of the unit circle. One generalization is the hypertorus. The hypertorus

$\mathbb{T}^d$ is a d-dimensional manifold that is the Cartesian product of d unit circles. If we generate a random vector comprising two independent random variables on $\mathbb{S}^1$, the underlying topology of the random vector is that of a torus. In our context, the hypertorus is thus a quite natural generalization of the circular topology. A different generalization is the d-dimensional hypersphere $\mathbb{S}^d$. When embedding the hypersphere $\mathbb{S}^d$ in $\mathbb{R}^{d+1}$, the sphere can be described as

$$\mathbb{S}^d = \{\underline{x} \in \mathbb{R}^{d+1} : \|\underline{x}\| = 1\} .$$

Special cases are the unit circle $\mathbb{S}^1$ and the unit sphere $\mathbb{S}^2$. An embedding of the unit circle in $\mathbb{R}^2$ can be seen in Figure 5.1d.

Fields in which circular statistics find application include biology [Bat81], modeling of wind directions [CBR08], and geology [Sch17, KS04]. Algorithms for recursive Bayesian estimation on circular manifolds have been applied to, e.g., speaker tracking [TS13] and phase estimation [LW75, WL75, BCM70, BM75]. Directional statistics on the sphere are used, e.g., in geosciences [Mar81, Wat56] and for analyzing crystal structures [CWN$^+$15a, CWN$^+$15b]. Estimation problems on spheres include multiple speaker tracking [TS14], tracking on a sphere [CP98], and estimating the spin on a ball based on quaternions [GK14]. Important applications of statistics on toroidal and hypertoroidal manifolds can be found in the field of bioinformatics [MTS07, BMT$^+$08, MHTS08, Hug07]. Estimation problems on hypertoroidal manifolds include the estimation of correlated angles, such as angles on a robotic arm [O6]. Further, jointly estimating multiple orientations of separate objects in a two-dimensional space is an estimation problem on a hypertoroidal manifold. In the context of bulk material sorting, the orientations of neighboring particles may be estimated jointly to improve the estimation accuracy.

The remainder of this section is structured as follows. We provide the basics of recursive Bayesian estimation in the first subsection. Afterward, we lay out the basics of directional statistics in the second subsection and provide a brief overview of recursive Bayesian estimation on periodic manifolds in the third subsection.

5.1 Nonlinear Recursive Bayesian Estimation

In Section 3.2, we limited ourselves to describing the system evolution and the generation of measurements using linear models. Further, we only addressed how to describe the system and measurement models using random vectors. While the description using random vectors may often be more intuitive, there is a second approach to describe the system evolution and the generation of the measurements that is based on probability densities. This approach helps to understand the theory behind many recursive Bayesian estimators.

To describe the system evolution using probability densities, a transition density $f_t^{\mathrm{T}}(\underline{x}_{t+1}|\underline{x}_t)$ describing the density at $\underline{x}_{t+1}$ for a given $\underline{x}_t$ is used. To describe the generation of the measurements, a likelihood function $f_t^{\mathrm{L}}(\underline{z}_t|\underline{x}_t)$ describing the density of $\underline{z}_t$ for a given $\underline{x}_t$ is used. It is important to note that once the actual measurement $\hat{\underline{z}}_t$ is obtained, the measurement is fixed and the function thus only depends on $\underline{x}_t$. The function obtained when varying the variable $\underline{x}_t$ that the likelihood is conditioned on is not a probability density function in general.

As we describe in detail in Section 5.3, other measures of error than the Euclidean distance make more sense for periodic manifolds. Thus, the best estimate for a given posterior density should also be calculated differently. Common to all recursive Bayesian estimators, however, is that approximating the posterior density as accurately as possible is generally helpful in deriving the best estimate. In $\mathbb{R}^d$, the mean of the posterior density f^{e} is often of interest as it constitutes the estimate that minimizes the BMSE [Kay93, Section 10.3]. We later discuss a similar property for posterior densities on $\mathbb{S}^1$ for a different measure of the error. Not all filters focus on approximating f^{e}. Some approaches, such as the particle filter [AMGC02], do not provide a proper approximation of the continuous probability density but do allow approximating properties of the density, such as the mean of f^{e}, over multiple time steps.

In the following paragraphs, we describe the theoretically optimal predicted and posterior densities. Beginning with the initial prior $f_0^{\mathrm{p}}(\underline{x}_0)$, update and prediction steps are usually performed alternatingly. Practical implementation of these steps often only yield approximations of the true densities. We start by describing the update step that allows for incorporating the measurement information. Then, we describe the prediction step used to obtain the prior density for the next time step. For both the update and prediction step, we introduce models for periodic domains.

Update Step Given the prior density $f_t^{\mathrm{p}}(\underline{x}_t|\hat{\underline{z}}_1, \dots, \hat{\underline{z}}_{t-1})$ depending on all measurements until $t-1$ (or none at time step 0), the posterior density $f_t^{\mathrm{e}}(\underline{x}_t|\hat{\underline{z}}_1, \dots, \hat{\underline{z}}_t)$ can be given according to Bayes' rule [Kay93, Section 10.3] as

$$f_t^{\mathrm{e}}(\underline{x}_t|\hat{\underline{z}}_1, \dots, \hat{\underline{z}}_t) = \frac{f_t^{\mathrm{L}}(\hat{\underline{z}}_t|\underline{x}_t) f_t^{\mathrm{p}}(\underline{x}_t|\hat{\underline{z}}_1, \dots, \hat{\underline{z}}_{t-1})}{\int_{\Omega_{\underline{x}}} f_t^{\mathrm{L}}(\hat{\underline{z}}_t|\underline{x}_t) f_t^{\mathrm{p}}(\underline{x}_t|\hat{\underline{z}}_1, \dots, \hat{\underline{z}}_{t-1})\, d\underline{x}_t} ,$$

with the sample space $\Omega_{\underline{x}}$, state $\underline{x}_t$, and the measurements $\hat{\underline{z}}_1, \dots, \hat{\underline{z}}_t$ of all time steps so far. As the denominator is independent of $\underline{x}_t$, we can describe the posterior density via

$$f_t^{\mathrm{e}}(\underline{x}_t|\hat{\underline{z}}_1, \dots, \hat{\underline{z}}_t) \propto f_t^{\mathrm{L}}(\hat{\underline{z}}_t|\underline{x}_t) f_t^{\mathrm{p}}(\underline{x}_t|\hat{\underline{z}}_1, \dots, \hat{\underline{z}}_{t-1}) ,$$

in which $\propto$ indicates that the left-hand side is equivalent to the right-hand side except for a scaling factor that is independent of $\underline{x}_t$.

For linear domains, a simple measurement model is the identity model (IM) with additive noise

$$\underline{\boldsymbol{z}}_t^{\mathrm{IM}} = \underline{\boldsymbol{x}}_t^{\mathrm{IM}} + \underline{\boldsymbol{v}}_t^{\mathrm{IM}} ,$$

which is a special case of the linear measurement model (3.2). Adapted to circular or, more generally, hypertoroidal domains, we define the measurement model

$$\underline{\boldsymbol{z}}_t^{\mathrm{TAIM}} = \underline{\boldsymbol{x}}_t^{\mathrm{TAIM}} + \underline{\boldsymbol{v}}_t^{\mathrm{TAIM}} \mod 2\pi , \tag{5.1}$$

which we refer to as the topology-aware identity model (TAIM) with additive noise. If the random vector $\underline{\boldsymbol{v}}_t^{\text{TAIM}}$ is defined on $[0, 2\pi)^d$, the likelihood can be given as

$$f_t^{\text{L,TAIM}}(\hat{\underline{z}}_t|\underline{x}_t) = f_t^{\underline{\boldsymbol{v}},\text{TAIM}}(\hat{\underline{z}}_t - \underline{x}_t \mod 2\pi) \ .$$

In the more general case of a topology-aware nonlinear (TANL) measurement model with additive noise for hypertoroidal manifolds, we can use the model

$$\underline{\boldsymbol{z}}_t^{\text{TANL}} = \underline{a}_t(\underline{\boldsymbol{x}}_t^{\text{TANL}}) + \underline{\boldsymbol{v}}_t^{\text{TANL}} \mod 2\pi \ , \tag{5.2}$$

for which the corresponding likelihood is

$$f_t^{\text{L,TANL}}(\hat{\underline{z}}_t|\underline{x}_t) = f_t^{\underline{\boldsymbol{v}},\text{TANL}}(\hat{\underline{z}}_t - \underline{a}_t(\underline{x}_t) \mod 2\pi) \ . \tag{5.3}$$

Prediction Step To make statements about future time steps and to make use of the information obtained from measurements of previous time steps in the current time step, prediction steps can be utilized. Based on probability densities, the prediction step can be described by the Chapman–Kolmogorov equation according to

$$f_{t+1}^{\text{p}}(\underline{x}_{t+1}|\hat{\underline{z}}_1, \ldots, \hat{\underline{z}}_t) = \int_{\Omega_{\underline{\boldsymbol{x}}}} f_t^{\text{T}}(\underline{x}_{t+1}|\underline{x}_t) f_t^{\text{e}}(\underline{x}_t|\hat{\underline{z}}_1, \ldots, \hat{\underline{z}}_t)\, d\underline{x}_t \ . \tag{5.4}$$

Similar as for the measurement model, the identity model with additive noise can be used as a system model on linear domains. This model is given by

$$\underline{\boldsymbol{x}}_{t+1}^{\text{IM}} = \underline{\boldsymbol{x}}_t^{\text{IM}} + \underline{\boldsymbol{w}}_t^{\text{IM}} \ . \tag{5.5}$$

Based thereon, we define a topology-aware variant for hypertoroidal manifolds according to

$$\underline{\boldsymbol{x}}_{t+1}^{\text{TAIM}} = \underline{\boldsymbol{x}}_t^{\text{TAIM}} + \underline{\boldsymbol{w}}_t^{\text{TAIM}} \mod 2\pi \ . \tag{5.6}$$

Similar to (5.2), we also formulate a topology-aware nonlinear model with additive noise

$$\underline{\boldsymbol{x}}_{t+1}^{\text{TANL}} = \underline{a}_t(\underline{\boldsymbol{x}}_t^{\text{TANL}}) + \underline{\boldsymbol{w}}_t^{\text{TANL}} \mod 2\pi \ . \tag{5.7}$$

If we have a system model based on random variables, the transition densities must be derived to use the Chapman–Kolmogorov equation. The transition densities corresponding to the models (5.5), (5.6), and (5.7) are

$$
\begin{aligned}
f_t^{\mathrm{T,IM}}(\underline{x}_{t+1}|\underline{x}_t) &= f_t^{\underline{\boldsymbol{w}},\mathrm{IM}}(\underline{x}_{t+1} - \underline{x}_t) \;, \\
f_t^{\mathrm{T,TAIM}}(\underline{x}_{t+1}|\underline{x}_t) &= f_t^{\underline{\boldsymbol{w}},\mathrm{TAIM}}(\underline{x}_{t+1} - \underline{x}_t \mod 2\pi) \;, \\
f_t^{\mathrm{T,TANL}}(\underline{x}_{t+1}|\underline{x}_t) &= f_t^{\underline{\boldsymbol{w}},\mathrm{TANL}}(x_{t+1} - \underline{a}_t(x_{t+1}) \mod 2\pi) \;.
\end{aligned}
$$

There is also a variety of other models, such as models involving multiplicative noise, for which the transition densities can be easily derived.

For $\Omega_{\underline{\boldsymbol{x}}} = \mathbb{R}^d$, the prediction step for the identity model with additive noise (5.5) can be reformulated to use the convolution operator $*$ as

$$
\begin{aligned}
f_{t+1}^{\mathrm{p}}(\underline{x}_{t+1}|\hat{\underline{z}}_1, \dots, \hat{\underline{z}}_t) &= (f_t^{\underline{\boldsymbol{w}}} * f_t^{\mathrm{e}})(\underline{x}_{t+1}) \\
&= \int_{\mathbb{R}^d} f_t^{\underline{\boldsymbol{w}}}(\underline{x}_{t+1} - \underline{x}_t) f_t^{\mathrm{e}}(\underline{x}_t|\hat{\underline{z}}_1, \dots, \hat{\underline{z}}_t) \, d\underline{x}_t \;.
\end{aligned}
$$

For the topology-aware identity model with additive noise on $\mathbb{T}^d$, the topology-aware convolution defined as

$$
(f_t^{\underline{\boldsymbol{w}}} * f_t^{\mathrm{e}})(\underline{x}_{t+1}) = \int_{\mathbb{T}^d} f_t^{\underline{\boldsymbol{w}}}(\underline{x}_{t+1} - \underline{x}_t \mod 2\pi) f_t^{\mathrm{e}}(\underline{x}_t|\hat{\underline{z}}_1, \dots, \hat{\underline{z}}_t) \, d\underline{x}_t \quad (5.8)
$$

needs to be used if $f_t^{\underline{\boldsymbol{w}}}$ is only defined on $[0, 2\pi)$. However, the integral in the Chapman–Kolmogorov equation cannot always be simplified to a simple operation based on the posterior density and the noise density. As we later discuss, there is no direct analogue to the identity model with additive noise on the unit sphere $\mathbb{S}^2$.

5.2 Fundamentals of Directional Statistics

Directional statistics [MJ99, JS01] is a subfield of statistics concerned with statistical models for periodic quantities. To facilitate the understanding of directional estimation, we introduce some densities on the periodic manifold and analogues to properties on linear manifolds, such as moments and the mean. Furthermore, measures of distance on periodic manifolds are introduced.

5.2.1 Densities on Periodic Manifolds

We first introduce the popular von Mises and wrapped normal distributions. Both are derived, albeit in different ways, from the normal distribution and constitute the foundation for popular filters. Afterward, we explain a multitude of other densities. While there are no filters for periodic manifolds that directly work with, e.g., the wrapped exponential distribution, such densities can be approximated in the Fourier filters described in the next chapter.

Wrapped Normal Distribution Visually speaking, the wrapped normal distribution [JS01, Section 2.2.6] can be obtained by taking the density of a regular normal distribution on $\mathbb{R}$ and wrapping it around the unit circle. This is equivalent to summing up the density of all points mapped to the same value when taking the input value modulo 2π. The density can be written in a series representation as

$$f_{\text{WN}}(x;\mu,\sigma) = \sum_{j\in\mathbb{Z}} \mathcal{N}\big(x + 2\pi j;\mu,\sigma\big)$$

based on the mean μ (taken modulo 2π) and standard deviation σ of the normal distribution that is wrapped. Integrating this density over $[0, 2\pi)$ yields the same result as integrating the normal distribution over $\mathbb{R}$, which is why the density is inherently normalized.

Von Mises distribution The von Mises distribution [MJ99, Section 3.5.4] (also called circular normal in [JS01, Section 2.2.4]) is not derived using wrapping. Instead, this distribution can be derived by considering only the probability density along the unit circle of a bivariate normal distribution on $\mathbb{R}^2$ with a mean $\|\underline{\mu}\| = 1$ and a scaled identity matrix $\kappa \mathbf{I}_{2\times 2}$ as the covariance matrix. To ensure the normalization of the density, a normalization constant is required. The density of the normalized von Mises distribution can be expressed in analytic form as

$$f_{\mathrm{VM}}(x; \mu, \kappa) = \frac{\mathrm{e}^{\kappa \cos(x-\mu)}}{2\pi I_0(\kappa)} \, .$$

The normalization involves the Bessel function of the first kind and order zero $I_0(\cdot)$.

Circular Uniform Distribution The circular uniform distribution is a uniform distribution on the unit circle. Unlike on $\mathbb{R}^d$, it is possible to have a density that uniformly covers the entire space. The density is $\frac{1}{2\pi}$ at all points on the circle so it normalized to 1 when integrated over $[0, 2\pi)$. It is easy to generalize the circular uniform distribution for the hypertorus and the hypersphere. The value of the density function just has to be adapted to ensure the normalization when the density is integrated over the entire domain.

Other Wrapped Distributions Several other distributions can be obtained similarly to the wrapped normal distribution. By wrapping the density of a Cauchy distribution, the density of the wrapped Cauchy distribution [JS01, Section 2.2.7], [MJ99, Section 3.5.7]

$$\begin{aligned} f_{\mathrm{WC}}(x; \mu, \sigma) &= \frac{1}{2\pi}\left(1 + 2\sum_{k=1}^{\infty} \mathrm{e}^{-k\sigma} \cos\left(k(x-\mu)\right)\right) \\ &= \frac{1}{2\pi} \frac{1 - \mathrm{e}^{-2\sigma}}{1 + \mathrm{e}^{-2\sigma} - 2\mathrm{e}^{-\sigma}\cos(x-\mu)} \end{aligned}$$

is obtained. The wrapping performed for the wrapped exponential distribution [JK04] is slightly different as the exponential distribution is only defined on $\mathbb{R}^+$. Therefore, the density on $\mathbb{R}^+$ is wrapped onto the unit circle, resulting in the density

$$f_{\mathrm{WE}}(x;\lambda) = \sum_{k=0}^{\infty} \lambda \mathrm{e}^{-\lambda(x+2\pi k)} = \frac{\lambda \mathrm{e}^{-\lambda x}}{1-\mathrm{e}^{-2\pi\lambda}} \ .$$

Multivariate Wrapped Normal Distribution Based on the idea of the bivariate wrapped normal (also called wrapped bivariate normal [JS01, Section 2.3.2]) distribution, we define the density of the arbitrary-dimensional wrapped normal distribution as

$$f_{\mathrm{WN}}(\underline{x};\underline{\mu},\mathbf{C}) = \sum_{\underline{j}\in\mathbb{Z}^d} \mathcal{N}(\underline{x}+2\pi\underline{j};\underline{\mu},\mathbf{C}) \ . \tag{5.9}$$

The parameters $\underline{\mu}$ and $\mathbf{C}$ are the mean and covariance matrix of the underlying normal distribution. To approximate the values of the density, a partial sum can be calculated. However, if we, e.g., ensure that all terms for $\underline{j} \in \{-3,\dots,3\}^d$ are used in the approximation, the evaluation becomes exponentially more costly with increasing dimension. As an alternative, there are also multivariate generalizations of the von Mises distribution [MHTS08], which we do not go into detail on.

Von Mises–Fisher Distribution The von Mises–Fisher distribution [MJ99, Section 9.3.2] is a generalization of the von Mises distribution to arbitrary-dimensional hyperspheres. We limit ourselves to the case of the unit sphere $\mathbb{S}^2$. For all vectors $\underline{x} \in \mathbb{R}^3$ of unit norm, the density is defined as

$$f_{\mathrm{VMF}}(\underline{x};\underline{\mu},\kappa) = c(\kappa)\mathrm{e}^{\kappa\underline{\mu}^\top\underline{x}} \tag{5.10}$$

with the normalization constant

$$c(\kappa) = \frac{\kappa}{4\pi\sinh(\kappa)}$$

for $\underline{\mu} \in \mathbb{S}^2$, and $\kappa > 0$. The function $\sinh(\cdot)$ denotes the hyperbolic sine function. The von Mises–Fisher distribution is radially symmetric around $\underline{\mu}$.

5.2.2 Moments and Measures of Location and Correlation

On linear domains, the most common measures of location, dispersion, and correlation are the mean, variance, and covariance, respectively. The mean is the first moment and the variance is the second central moment. These moments are also referred to as power moments to distinguish them from other types of moments. A different type of moment that is particularly useful for periodic domains is the trigonometric moment. After introducing trigonometric moments, we explicate the mean direction and give an outline of angular correlation coefficients. These two concepts constitute measures of location and correlation of random variables on periodic manifolds.

Trigonometric Moments Trigonometric moments for scalar random variables are defined as [JS01, Section 2.1]

$$m_k = \mathrm{E}(\mathrm{e}^{ik\boldsymbol{x}}) = \int_0^{2\pi} f(x)\mathrm{e}^{ikx}dx \tag{5.11}$$

for $k \in \mathbb{Z}$. Due to the complex exponential function, m_k is commonly a complex number with a real and an imaginary part. In the context of the trigonometric moment problem [Ger46], the trigonometric moments are often defined with an additional minus sign in the argument of the exponential function. The trigonometric moments can also be split into two components that reflect the real and imaginary parts of m_k [MJ99, Section 3.4.1], [JS01, Section 2.1]. We use the definition involving complex numbers in this thesis as the relationship to Fourier series is more apparent in this formulation.

As the trigonometric moment consists of two components (in our case, the real and imaginary parts), the first trigonometric moment can contain information about both the location and the dispersion of the density. In particular, if the first trigonometric moment m_1 of a von Mises distribution or wrapped normal distribution is known, it is possible to determine both parameters of the distribution.

While the reference works on directional statistics [MJ99, JS01] do not provide a definition for the trigonometric moments of multivariate densities, these moments have been defined in the context of the multivariate trigonometric moment problem [ILL10, KPRvdO16] for vectors of integers $\underline{k}$. After adapting the sign in the exponential function to be consistent with (5.11), we obtain the formula

$$m_{\underline{k}} = \mathrm{E}(\mathrm{e}^{i\underline{k}\cdot\underline{\boldsymbol{x}}}) = \int_{[0,2\pi)^d} f(\underline{x})\mathrm{e}^{i(\underline{k}\cdot\underline{x})}\, d\underline{x} \tag{5.12}$$

for the trigonometric moment with vector-valued index $\underline{k}$, in which $\cdot$ denotes the dot product. For convenience, we define the trigonometric moment vector $\underline{m}_k$ of scalar index k for multivariate densities as the vector of all moments of vector-valued index $m_{\underline{k}}$ that have k as one index and 0 as all others, i.e.,

$$\underline{m}_k = \begin{bmatrix} m_{[k,0,\ldots,0]} \\ m_{[0,k,\ldots,0]} \\ \vdots \\ m_{[0,0,\ldots,k]} \end{bmatrix} = \begin{bmatrix} \mathrm{E}(\mathrm{e}^{ik\boldsymbol{x}_1}) \\ \mathrm{E}(\mathrm{e}^{ik\boldsymbol{x}_2}) \\ \vdots \\ \mathrm{E}(\mathrm{e}^{ik\boldsymbol{x}_d}) \end{bmatrix} = \begin{bmatrix} \int_{[0,2\pi)^d} f(\underline{x})\mathrm{e}^{ikx_1} d\underline{x} \\ \int_{[0,2\pi)^d} f(\underline{x})\mathrm{e}^{ikx_2} d\underline{x} \\ \vdots \\ \int_{[0,2\pi)^d} f(\underline{x})\mathrm{e}^{ikx_d} d\underline{x} \end{bmatrix}. \tag{5.13}$$

Although the individual entries only describe the trigonometric moment of a single variate of the random vector, a d-dimensional integral is required to simultaneously marginalize out the other $d-1$ dimensions. The definition (5.13) was first used for the torus in [KGDH14] and for the hypertorus in [O6]. The entries of the vector $\underline{m}_k$ will be referred to as $m_{k,1}$ to $m_{k,d}$ in the following paragraphs. While there are also concepts for trigonometric moments on the sphere [KGH16b, KMvdO16], we will not use these in this thesis.

Mean Direction In linear spaces, the first power moment is the mean of the distribution, which is a frequently used measure of the location of the density. In contrast, the first trigonometric moment also contains information about the dispersion. It is, however, possible to derive a quantity that only describes the location of the density from the first trigonometric moment. For random variables on the circle, the so-called mean direction can be calculated from the first trigonometric moment according to [JS01, Section 2.1]

$$\mu = \text{atan2}(\mathcal{I}(m_1), \mathcal{R}(m_1)) \tag{5.14}$$

using the four-quadrant arctangent [Hab11] that is commonly referred to as atan2. If $m_1 = 0$, then the mean direction is undefined. For example, this is the case for the circular uniform distribution. As is implied in the naming of the parameter, the mean direction of the densities parameterized by a location parameter μ is commonly μ.

As in [KH17, O6], we define the mean direction in the multivariate case to be the stacked mean directions of the individual variates, which results in the formula

$$\underline{\mu} = \begin{bmatrix} \text{atan2}(\mathcal{I}(m_{1,1}), \mathcal{R}(m_{1,1})) \\ \vdots \\ \text{atan2}(\mathcal{I}(m_{1,d}), \mathcal{R}(m_{1,d})) \end{bmatrix}$$

based on the entries of the trigonometric moment vector of scalar index $\underline{m}_1$.

For quantities on the sphere, the mean direction is the normalized expected value of the random variable on the sphere [MJ99, Section 9.2.1], i.e.,

$$\underline{\mu} = \text{E}(\underline{\boldsymbol{x}}) \left(\sum_{i=1}^{d} \text{E}(\boldsymbol{x}_i)^2 \right)^{-\frac{1}{2}} .$$

For the von Mises distribution, the mean direction corresponds to the parameter $\underline{\mu}$ of the density. There are also densities on the sphere, such as the spherical uniform distribution, for which the mean direction is undefined.

Angular Correlation Coefficient Defining a measure of correlation for directional quantities is less straightforward than for linear quantities. In the literature, several correlation coefficients have been proposed, such as the ones by Johnson and Wehrley [JW77] and Jupp and Mardia [JM80].

For two random variables $\boldsymbol{x}_1$ and $\boldsymbol{x}_2$ defined on $\mathbb{S}^1$, we can formulate a covariance matrix

$$\begin{aligned}\boldsymbol{\Sigma}^{\text{Torus}} = \mathrm{E}\Bigg(&\left(\begin{bmatrix}\cos(\boldsymbol{x}_1)\\ \sin(\boldsymbol{x}_1)\\ \cos(\boldsymbol{x}_2)\\ \sin(\boldsymbol{x}_2)\end{bmatrix} - \mathrm{E}\left(\begin{bmatrix}\cos(\boldsymbol{x}_1)\\ \sin(\boldsymbol{x}_1)\\ \cos(\boldsymbol{x}_2)\\ \sin(\boldsymbol{x}_2)\end{bmatrix}\right)\right)\\ &\left(\begin{bmatrix}\cos(\boldsymbol{x}_1)\\ \sin(\boldsymbol{x}_1)\\ \cos(\boldsymbol{x}_2)\\ \sin(\boldsymbol{x}_2)\end{bmatrix} - \mathrm{E}\left(\begin{bmatrix}\cos(\boldsymbol{x}_1)\\ \sin(\boldsymbol{x}_1)\\ \cos(\boldsymbol{x}_2)\\ \sin(\boldsymbol{x}_2)\end{bmatrix}\right)\right)^\top\Bigg)\end{aligned} \tag{5.15}$$

that contains information about the correlation of the two random variables. Using entries of this covariance matrix, all the aforementioned correlation coefficients can be determined. Therefore, the matrix described by (5.15) is used to determine these correlation coefficients in our library for directional estimation [O13]. Using the first trigonometric moment $\underline{m}_1$, we can obtain the inner expected value in (5.15) according to

$$\begin{aligned}&\mathrm{E}\left(\begin{bmatrix}\cos(\boldsymbol{x}_1) & \sin(\boldsymbol{x}_1) & \cos(\boldsymbol{x}_2) & \sin(\boldsymbol{x}_2)\end{bmatrix}\right)^\top\\ &\qquad = \begin{bmatrix}\mathcal{R}(m_{1,1}) & \mathcal{I}(m_{1,1}) & \mathcal{R}(m_{1,2}) & \mathcal{I}(m_{1,2})\end{bmatrix}^\top .\end{aligned}$$

For d-dimensional random vectors, this matrix can be generalized to

$$\begin{aligned}\boldsymbol{\Sigma}^{\text{Hypertorus}} = \mathrm{E}\Bigg(&\left(\begin{bmatrix}\cos(\boldsymbol{x}_1)\\ \sin(\boldsymbol{x}_1)\\ \vdots\\ \cos(\boldsymbol{x}_d)\\ \sin(\boldsymbol{x}_d)\end{bmatrix} - \mathrm{E}\left(\begin{bmatrix}\cos(\boldsymbol{x}_1)\\ \sin(\boldsymbol{x}_1)\\ \vdots\\ \cos(\boldsymbol{x}_d)\\ \sin(\boldsymbol{x}_d)\end{bmatrix}\right)\right)\\ &\left(\begin{bmatrix}\cos(\boldsymbol{x}_1)\\ \sin(\boldsymbol{x}_1)\\ \vdots\\ \cos(\boldsymbol{x}_d)\\ \sin(\boldsymbol{x}_d)\end{bmatrix} - \mathrm{E}\left(\begin{bmatrix}\cos(\boldsymbol{x}_1)\\ \sin(\boldsymbol{x}_1)\\ \vdots\\ \cos(\boldsymbol{x}_d)\\ \sin(\boldsymbol{x}_d)\end{bmatrix}\right)\right)^\top\Bigg) ,\end{aligned}$$

which is a $2d \times 2d$ matrix that describes the correlations of the individual variates of the random vector. This matrix is a special case of a matrix used to describe correlations in [Kur15, Section 2.2.3]. Obtaining the entries of $\mathbf{\Sigma}^{\text{Hypertorus}}$ is nontrivial for arbitrary densities. However, as explained in [O6, Appendix. C], the values are easy to derive based on the Fourier coefficients of the density.

5.2.3 Distance Measures on Periodic Manifolds

On periodic domains, we should not simply use distance measures defined on linear domains as they do not properly respect the periodicity of the domain. As an easy example, on a circle, 0 and $2\pi - 0.1$ are closer to each other than 0 and π. Using the Euclidean distance, we would obtain distances of $2\pi - 0.1$ and π, respectively. Since $(2\pi - 0.1) > \pi$, the points of the latter pair would appear closer to each other, which violates our intuition about distances on the circle.

The absolute value, however, can be easily modified to take the periodicity of the domain into account. Using [JS01, Section 1.3.2]

$$d_0(\alpha, \beta) = \min(\alpha - \beta, 2\pi - (\alpha - \beta)) \ ,$$

we always obtain the smaller of the two arc lengths as the distance between the angles α and β. A completely different distance is given by [JS01, Section 1.3.2]

$$d_{\cos}(\alpha, \beta) = 1 - \cos(\alpha - \beta) \ , \tag{5.16}$$

which we refer to as the cosine distance. The cosine itself increases as the topology-aware distance d_0 between the two angles increases. The minus ensures that the distance increases the further the two angles are apart. The additional 1 in (5.16) ensures that the distance is always nonnegative and

$$d_{\cos}(\alpha, \beta) = 0 \Leftrightarrow \alpha = \beta \ .$$

Illustrations of the two distance measures for the unit circle are given in [Kur15, Section 2.2.2].

We now generalize d_0 to higher-dimensional manifolds. Our generalization, which is a topology-aware adaptation of the Euclidean distance, is defined for the vectors of angles $\underline{\alpha}$ and $\underline{\beta}$ as

$$d_0(\underline{\alpha}, \underline{\beta}) = \sqrt{\sum_{i=1}^{d} \left(\min(\alpha_i - \beta_i, 2\pi - (\alpha_i - \beta_i)) \right)^2} \ .$$

We first used this distance measure in [O6].

To define a distance on the sphere $\mathbb{S}^2$, we need to take a different approach. One possible distance can be obtained by considering the space $\mathbb{R}^3$ in which $\mathbb{S}^2$ can be embedded and then determining the Euclidean distance between the two points on the unit sphere. However, this does not respect the curvature of the sphere. If we consider a point on the sphere $\mathbb{S}^2$ embedded in $\mathbb{R}^3$, we can define a vector going from the origin $\underline{0} = \begin{bmatrix} 0 & 0 & 0 \end{bmatrix}^\top$ to the respective point. If we have two points, we can determine the vectors for both points and consider the angle between them at $\underline{0}$. This measure of distance between the two points $\underline{u}$ and $\underline{v}$ on the sphere is called angular distance [KS13, Section 7.2.1] and can be calculated according to

$$d_{\text{ang}}(\underline{u}, \underline{v}) = \text{acos}(\underline{u} \cdot \underline{v}) \ . \tag{5.17}$$

For the unit sphere, the length of the shortest arc on the surface between the two points (also called orthodromic distance) is equal to the angle between the two vectors in radian [KS13, Section 7.2.1].

5.3 Recursive Bayesian Estimation on Periodic Manifolds

In this section, we provide a brief historical overview of approaches to Bayesian estimation on periodic manifolds in discrete time. The filters have different strengths and weaknesses and vary in terms of the system and measurement models that can be employed. Thus far, no direct analogue to the Kalman filter that can be used to efficiently deal with estimation problems with hundreds of dimensions is known. However, the limited size of the domain can be used to derive filters that take different approaches than filters on linear domains. When we state that a filter can be used for arbitrary system or measurement models in the following paragraphs, we do this without considering special cases, such as densities that can only be described using Dirac delta distributions [KGH13]. Further, the applicability of a filter to an estimation problem does not imply accurate estimation results.

Filters for Circular Manifolds Early work on estimation for circular domains was performed by the engineering community for phase-locked loop problems. Although the authors deal with an estimation problem with the topology of the unit circle, they never refer to the field of directional statistics and do not use its terminology. We believe the reason for this is that the important reference books were yet to be written and important terms of directional statistics were either not coined or not sufficiently popularized yet. In the work [BCM70], the authors use $2d_{\cos}$ as a measure of distance on the circle and provide a formula to obtain the estimate that minimizes the expected distance for a given density. The formula essentially describes the mean direction (5.14). The update step given in [BCM70] can provide the optimal result when only update steps are performed and all densities and likelihoods involved are von Mises-distributed. Fourier series are used in the prediction step. However, an important problem of Fourier series approximations is disregarded, namely that using a limited number of coefficients can cause negative function values in the approximation. Further, the formulae are tailored to von Mises distributions and have a run time complexity of $O(N^2)$ when consistently employing N Fourier coefficients.

In the papers [WL75, Wil74a, Wil74b], the authors use $d_{\cos}$ as the measure of error and provide some insights based on Fourier series. The focus is put on wrapped normal (therein called folded normal) distributions. In [Wil74a], the authors discuss the prediction formula for the topology-aware identity model with additive noise (5.6) and the update step using Bayes' formula. In [WL75, Wil74a], they point out that the operations of the update step look like discrete convolutions and discuss the need for parameter reduction. The authors propose to, e.g., only preserve the N largest coefficients [WL75]. A practical implementation and experimental results are provided in [Wil74b]. The authors only consider using seven coefficients and state that a straightforward truncation does not work because the higher order coefficients become more important as the uncertainty decreases. Therefore, they suggest approximating the results with wrapped normal distributions instead.

A filter based on Fourier series for intervals was presented in [BSH06a] and a generalization to higher dimensions was proposed in [BSH06b]. In these works, the Fourier series represents a potentially complex-valued function. The square of the complex norm of the function value at each point approximates the value of the density at the respective point. However, the formulae for the transformation and the prediction step only work in special cases.

An early filter using the terminology of directional statistics was presented in [ARCB09]. As all densities and likelihood functions are assumed to be von Mises-distributed, we refer to this filter as the von Mises filter. The prediction step is restricted to the topology-aware identity model with additive noise. The filter is exact for the update step as the class of von Mises distributions is closed under multiplication with a subsequent normalization [ARCB09]. An approximation is performed for the prediction step. The prediction step can be understood as follows. Both von Mises distributions are approximated using wrapped normal distributions, which are then convolved. As the class of wrapped normal distributions is closed under convolution [JS01, Section 2.2.6], a wrapped normal distribution is obtained. This wrapped normal distribution is then approximated using a von Mises distribution for the next update step.

A different filter for circular manifolds was proposed in [TS13]. It is based on using wrapped normal distributions and assuming that only a finite number of terms are relevant. The system is assumed to evolve according to the topology-aware identity model with additive noise and the likelihood is assumed to be wrapped normally distributed.

A filter suitable for nonlinear system models with additive noise was proposed in [KGH13]. The prediction step can be interpreted as an adaptation of the unscented Kalman filter (UKF) [JU04] to circular domains. Analogous to the UKF, the approximation of the resulting density is again of the same type, i.e., von Mises-distributed. For the update step, the likelihood is assumed to be Mises-distributed, and the step is performed as in [ARCB09]. In [KGH14], an update step allowing the use of arbitrary likelihood functions was introduced. For this, the ideas of the progressive Gaussian filter (PGF) [Han13, SH14] were adapted to the circular case. The most general variant of the filter was proposed in [KGH16a]. In this variant, the noise term in the system model does not need to be additive.

In [O11, O8], we proposed a Fourier filter that we describe in more detail in the next chapter. In this filter, a nonnegative approximation of the density is obtained by calculating the Fourier coefficients of the square root of the density. The variant described in [O11] has a complexity of $O(N \log N)$ for N Fourier coefficient and allows the use of arbitrary likelihood functions in the update step and the topology-aware identity model with additive noise in the prediction step. A more general prediction step with a complexity of $O(N^2 \log N)$ that supports arbitrary transition densities is described in [O8].

Since then, so-called discrete filters have been proposed for circular domains [O24]. These filters involve approximations of the density function in one of two ways. In the Dirac-based approach, the continuous probability density function is converted into a discrete probability mass function describing the probabilities on an equidistant grid. The probability mass function is only defined on the grid points. In the second approach, the approximation of the density is defined on $[0, 2\pi)$ and is a piecewise constant function. The interval $[0, 2\pi)$ is subdivided into equally-sized regions in which the function value stays constant. The integral over each region of the piecewise constant function is supposed to be equivalent to the integral of the actual density over the same region. The discrete filters are also widely applicable and can handle highly nonlinear system and measurement models. Depending on the estimation problem and the variant used, however, the filters may involve one-dimensional or two-dimensional integrals.

Filters for Hypertoroidal Manifolds To our knowledge, the first filter for toroidal manifolds was presented in [KGDH14]. The filter can be used when the system and measurement models are identity models with additive noise. This filter is based on bivariate wrapped normal distributions and uses the vector-valued trigonometric moment as defined in (5.13) and one of the circular correlation coefficients. In [KH15], an update step for a bivariate von Mises distribution was introduced. A filter for nonlinear models that adapts the ideas of the PGF to wrapped normal distributions on toroidal domains was proposed in [O22]. The filter can be used for arbitrary system models and likelihoods. One significant limitation of the filter is that an approximation with a bivariate wrapped normal distribution is performed in every time step.

Extending the filters [KGDH14, O22] to arbitrary-dimensional hypertoroidal manifolds is nontrivial and, to our knowledge, no assumed density filters exist yet for $d \geq 3$. However, it is easy to adapt the particle filter [AMGC02] to hypertoroidal domains. An implementation of a particle filter for hypertoroidal domains is provided in our library [O13]. In [O6], we formulated Fourier filters for multivariate estimation problems on the hypertorus. A promising future approach to filtering on the hypertorus would be to generalize the discrete filters used on the circle.

Filters for Hyperspherical Manifolds A filter that is based on the von Mises–Fisher distribution (therein called Langevin distribution) was proposed in [CP98]. The authors note that finding a transition density that causes the resulting predicted density to be von Mises-distributed is difficult and describe methods to perform prediction steps in an approximate fashion. In [TS14], the authors state they match von Mises–Fisher distributions with wrapped normal distributions to perform the prediction step and then match a von Mises–Fisher distribution to the result. A filter for hyperspherical manifolds based on the antipodally symmetric Bingham distribution [Bin74] is given in [KGJH14]. The formulae for the update step produce an exact posterior density for arbitrary dimensions. The prediction step given, however, is an approximation and is limited to $\mathbb{S}^1$ and $\mathbb{S}^3$. An adaptation of the ideas of the UKF to estimation problems on the hypersphere was presented in [GKJH16]. A filter based on spherical harmonics was proposed by us in [O2]. It adopts the ideas of the IFF and allows for the use of certain types of transition densities and arbitrary likelihood functions. The filter based on spherical harmonics is presented alongside a novel variant in the next chapter.

CHAPTER 6

Directional Estimation Using Orthogonal Basis Functions

In the previous chapter, we have shown that there are a multitude of filters for estimation problems on the circle. Except for the Bingham filter that allows for two modes due to its antipodal symmetry, none of the filters based on probability distributions are suitable for multimodal estimation problems. As we address in more detail in Chapter 7, the likelihoods for measuring orientations of bulk material particles based on image data may have multiple modes and may not be antipodally symmetric. Furthermore, only the particle filter exists for estimation problems with $d \geq 3$. For jointly estimating the state of multiple bulk material particles in clusters in future work, filters allowing for higher numbers of modes are required.

In this chapter, we first explain the concepts of Fourier series, trigonometric polynomials, and spherical harmonics. Then, we propose new filters based on orthogonal basis functions that allow for multimodal estimation problems on the circle and can also be applied to higher dimensional estimation problems with the topology of a hypertorus. After describing filters for the hypertorus, filters for the unit sphere are given. In the first filter for circular and hypertoroidal domains, which we call Fourier identity filter (IFF), we approximate the densities directly using Fourier series. In the second filter for circular and hypertoroidal domains, called Fourier square root filter (SqFF), we approximate the square root of the density. Approximating the square root allows us to maintain an approximation of the prior and posterior densities with only nonnegative function values. When approximating a density directly, expressions can be given that, if fulfilled, ensure that the approximation is nonnegative. However, ensuring that the expressions hold is nontrivial. For example, the expressions given in [FD04] can essentially be interpreted as stating that an approximation is nonnegative if there is a series describing a real-valued function that is the square root of the approximation. Instead of always enforcing this condition, we directly work with the square root to arrive at less costly filters that always yield approximations of the densities with only nonnegative function values. While the SqFF has the advantage that the approximation is nonnegative for all input values, the IFF is, as our evaluation will show, faster for configurations with equal numbers of coefficients. The Fourier series approximations of densities on hypertoroidal manifolds are based on trigonometric polynomials, and spherical harmonics are used for densities on the unit sphere. As the filters for estimation problems on the unit sphere that we present later in this chapter are not straightforward generalizations of the IFF and SqFF, we refer to them as the spherical harmonics identity filter (ISHF) and spherical harmonics square root filter (SqSHF).

The Fourier filters are versatile and do not suffer from most disadvantages of the filters for the unit circle mentioned in Section 5.3. Unlike the filters that approximate the density functions using a unimodal density in every time step [ARCB09, TS13, KGH14, KDH15, KGH16a], the Fourier filters inherently allow for a high number of modes without requiring a large number of parameters. The quality of the approximation of the density generally increases with increasing number of coefficients. As a key advantage in real-time applications, such as the bulk material sorting task, a trade-off between computation time and accuracy can be flexibly adjusted, even between two consecutive steps during run time. Another advantage, which we address in detail in Section 7.1.2, is that the Fourier coefficients can be used to easily integrate knowledge about the orientations of bulk material particles into the association decision of the multitarget tracker.

Unlike some of the filters in [O24], calculating integrals is necessary neither online nor offline in any of the Fourier filters. In contrast to the early Fourier-based approaches for the phase-locked loop problem, the IFF and SqFF are in $O(N \log N)$ for N coefficients when the topology-aware identity model with additive noise is used as the system model. Further, no assumptions about the densities are made, and we can not only use all classes of densities introduced in Section 5.2.1 but also arbitrary densities as long as they can be evaluated N times. The likelihood functions can be arbitrary, and the measurement space does not need to be periodic and can be, e.g., $\mathbb{R}^d$. Unlike the Fourier-based filters in [BSH06a, BSH06b], the applicability of the IFF and the SqFF is not limited to special cases. Further, unlike all previously proposed filters based on Fourier series, the IFF and SqFF can be used to deal with arbitrary nonlinear system models when the transition density is given [O8]. In this case, the run time of the Fourier filters increases to $O(N^2)$ for time-invariant transition densities and to $O(N^2 \log N)$ for time-variant ones.

For hypertoroidal manifolds, the IFF and SqFF clearly exceed the previous state of the art. Unlike the filters for the torus presented in [KGDH14, O22], the Fourier filters support approximating almost arbitrary densities and allow for high numbers of modes. Further, the particle filter is the only alternative for $d \geq 3$. Thus, the IFF and SqFF are the only filters that provide continuous approximations of the prior and posterior probability density functions. The key advantage of the ISHF and SqSHF over previously proposed filters for the sphere is that the approximation quality can be improved by increasing the number of parameters. Further, the ISHF and SqSHF are applicable to densities with several modes on $\mathbb{S}^2$. With a complexity of $O(N(\log N)^2)$ for N coefficients, the filters are efficient to compute.

Some limitations apply to the filters proposed. First, the theoretical applicability of the IFF and SqFF to arbitrary-dimensional estimation problems is limited by the need to use more coefficients for higher dimensions. If we use the minimum of 3 coefficients per dimension as required by our implementation, we obtain 3^d coefficients. For current standard computers, the dimension of the estimation problem should not be much higher than 10. Second, the Fourier filters are better suited to densities with few discontinuities. However, since trigonometric moments can also be derived for probability mass functions on the hypertorus, the IFF and the SqFF can also be used to approximate densities described by Dirac delta distributions. However, if the delta distributions represent a continuous density, knowledge about this density may be required to choose a suitable number of coefficients for the Fourier filters.

6.1 Basics of Fourier Series and Spherical Harmonics

In this section, we provide a brief overview of the orthogonal basis functions used to represent densities on the circle $\mathbb{S}^1$, the hypertorus $\mathbb{T}^d$, and the sphere $\mathbb{S}^2$. Further important properties are introduced in the sections on the respective filters.

Fourier Series and Trigonometric Polynomials Fourier series on circular domains can be based on two different systems of functions. The system

$$\mathcal{B}^{\text{Real}} = \left\{\frac{1}{2},\ \cos(x),\ \sin(x),\ \cos(2x),\ \sin(2x),\ \ldots\right\}$$

is called the (real) trigonometric system, whereas the system consisting of the complex exponential functions

$$\mathcal{B}^{\text{Complex}} = \left\{\mathrm{e}^{ikx} : k \in \mathbb{Z}\right\}$$

is called the complex trigonometric system [Zyg03, Volume I, Section I.4]. We shall refer to functions of the trigonometric systems as basis functions because the trigonometric systems are orthogonal and complete [Zyg03, Volume I, Section I.6]. Some authors also require basis functions to be normalized and use the term basis to denote a complete orthonormal sequence [KS13, Section 2.6.1].

The formal definitions of Fourier series [KS13, Definition 2.2.3], [Zyg03, Volume 1, Section I.3] allow for the use of various systems of basis functions, such as the trigonometric systems and the spherical harmonic functions described in this section. However, the term Fourier series is also frequently used (e.g., [PM06, Section 4.1], [Zyg03, Volume I, Section I.4]) to refer to the special case of trigonometric Fourier series, which we define in the next paragraph. In this thesis and our publications dealing with circular or hypertoroidal manifolds [O11, O8, O6], we use the shorthand term Fourier series for trigonometric Fourier series and their higher-dimensional generalizations.

A series involving functions of the real trigonometric system weighted by real-valued coefficients a_k and b_k in the form of

$$f^{\text{Real}}(x) = \frac{1}{2}a_0 + \sum_{k=1}^{\infty} (a_k \cos(kx) + b_k \sin(kx))$$

is called a (real) Fourier series [Zyg03, Volume I, Section I.4]. The series of the form

$$f^{\text{Complex}}(x) = \sum_{k=-\infty}^{\infty} c_k \mathrm{e}^{ikx} \tag{6.1}$$

involving complex-valued coefficients c_k is called a complex Fourier series [Zyg03, Volume I, Section I.4].

While a trigonometric polynomial can be evaluated on the entire real line $\mathbb{R}$, only a 2π interval of $\mathbb{R}$ is usually considered when dealing with 2π-periodic functions. For the sake of compatibility with our notation and conventions of directional statistics, we always use the interval $[0, 2\pi)$ in our definitions and assume that all functions we use are defined on this interval.

When performing a Fourier series expansion, a 2π-periodic function f is represented as a Fourier series. The required coefficients are calculated according to [Zyg03, Volume I, Section I.4]

$$a_k = \frac{1}{\pi} \int_0^{2\pi} f(x) \cos(kx)\, dx \ , \qquad b_k = \frac{1}{\pi} \int_0^{2\pi} f(x) \sin(kx)\, dx$$

for the real Fourier series and according to

$$c_k = \frac{1}{2\pi} \int_0^{2\pi} f(x) \mathrm{e}^{-ikx} dx \tag{6.2}$$

for the complex Fourier series. Due to the periodicity of the sine, cosine, and complex exponential functions, the integral can be calculated for any 2π interval of f if the function is defined as a periodic function on the entire real line. In our application, we only approximate real functions, and for these, c_{-k} is equal to $\bar{c}_k$ (the complex conjugate of c_k) [Zyg03, Volume I, Section I.1], [PM06, Section 4.1].

In our filters, we only employ finite numbers of coefficients. A (real) trigonometric polynomial of order $k_{\max}$ is defined as [Zyg03, Volume I, Chapter I.1], [Rud87, Section 4.23]

$$s_{k_{\max}}^{\text{Real}}(x) = \frac{1}{2} a_0 + \sum_{k=1}^{k_{\max}} (a_k \cos(kx) + b_k \sin(kx)) \ .$$

For a complex trigonometric polynomial, the symmetric partial sum

$$s_{k_{\max}}^{\text{Complex}}(x) = \sum_{k=-k_{\max}}^{k_{\max}} c_k \mathrm{e}^{ikx} \tag{6.3}$$

of (6.1) is used. The value $k_{\max} \in \mathbb{N}$ is called the order of the trigonometric polynomial [Zyg03, Volume I, Section I.1]. In our library [O13], both the complex and real representation can be used for estimation problems on the unit circle. To simplify the explanations in this thesis, we focus on complex trigonometric polynomials.

Generalization for Hypertori The complex trigonometric Fourier series defined above can be generalized to higher dimensions. The system

$$\mathcal{B}^{\text{Multidimensional}} = \{\mathrm{e}^{i(k_1 x_1 + k_2 x_2 + \dots + k_d x_d)} : \underline{k} \in \mathbb{Z}^d\}$$

is orthogonal and complete over the d-dimensional hypercube $[-\pi, \pi]^d$ [Zyg03, Volume II, Chapter XVII] and thus also the $[0, 2\pi)^d$ domain that we interpret as a hypertorus. For brevity, we rewrite the sum in the exponent using a dot product according to $\mathrm{e}^{i(\underline{k}\cdot\underline{x})}$. The corresponding Fourier series is given by [Zyg03, Volume II, Chapter XVII]

$$f(\underline{x}) = \sum_{\underline{k}\in\mathbb{Z}^d} c_{\underline{k}} \mathrm{e}^{i(\underline{k}\cdot\underline{x})}$$

and the Fourier coefficients can be calculated according to [Zyg03, Volume II, Chapter XVII]

$$c_{\underline{k}} = \left(\frac{1}{2\pi}\right)^d \int\limits_{[0,2\pi)^d} f(\underline{x}) \mathrm{e}^{-i(\underline{k}\cdot\underline{x})} \, d\underline{x} \; . \tag{6.4}$$

This definition only differs in the factor $1/(2\pi)^d$ from that of the trigonometric moment given in (5.12). For practical applications, we again limit ourselves to symmetric partial sums of the d-dimensional Fourier series.

An important property required for deriving likelihoods from measurement noise densities is the time shifting property [Zyg03, Volume I, Chapter II] that we generalize to the multidimensional case. If $c_{\underline{k}}$ is the Fourier coefficient with index $\underline{k}$ of $f(\underline{x})$, the Fourier coefficient $c_{\underline{k}}^{\text{shifted}}$ for $f(\underline{x}+\underline{u})$ can be calculated according to

$$c_{\underline{k}}^{\text{shifted}} = c_{\underline{k}} \mathrm{e}^{i(\underline{k}\cdot\underline{u})} \; . \tag{6.5}$$

Spherical Harmonics For Fourier series on $\mathbb{S}^2$, the trigonometric Fourier series cannot be trivially extended as in the hypertoroidal case. A common complete orthonormal sequence for the square-integrable functions on $\mathbb{S}^2$ is given by the spherical harmonic functions [KS13, Section 7.3.3], which are also called spherical harmonics for brevity. Spherical harmonics are well researched as they are of interested in a variety of fields, such as computer graphics [BGK95, RH01], chemistry [Chi76], physics [BL84, AW12], weather modeling [WHM13], and medical imaging [YHS$^+$07]. In this thesis, we focus on the complex spherical harmonics, which are more prevalent in the literature than the real spherical harmonics [KS13, Section 7.4.3], [Chi76, Chapter 4].

The basis functions Y_l^m are indexed by the degree $l \in \mathbb{N}_0$ and order $m \in \{-l, -l+1, \dots, l-1, l\}$. The formula for the complex basis functions are given by [KS13, Section 7.3.3]

$$Y_l^m(\theta, \phi) = N_l^m P_l^m(\cos(\theta))\mathrm{e}^{im\phi} \tag{6.6}$$

with the normalization constant

$$N_l^m = \sqrt{\frac{2l+1}{4\pi}\frac{(l-m)!}{(l+m)!}}$$

and the Legendre function using the Rodrigues' formula

$$P_l^m(x) = \begin{cases} \dfrac{(-1)^m}{2^l\, l!}(1-x^2)^{m/2}\dfrac{d^{l+m}}{dx^{l+m}}(x^2-1)^l & m \in \mathbb{Z}_0^+ \\ (-1)^m \dfrac{(l+m)!}{(l-m)!}P_l^{-m}(x) & m \in \mathbb{Z}^- \backslash \{0\} \ , \end{cases}$$

which includes the Condon–Shortley phase. The Condon–Shortley phase is an additional term that causes the sign to alternate with increasing m for $m > 0$. In some publications, e.g., [BFB97], the term is included in the definition of the spherical harmonics instead of in the definition of the Legendre function. There are also conventions that do not include it at all [KS13, Section 7.4.1].

For each degree l, there are $2l + 1$ basis functions. In Figure 6.1, we illustrate the real spherical harmonics up to degree 3. The spherical harmonic expansion based on the basis functions defined in (6.6) is given by [KS13, Section 7.3.5]

$$f(\theta, \phi) = \sum_{l=0}^{\infty} \sum_{m=-l}^{l} c_l^m Y_l^m(\theta, \phi) \ .$$

The Fourier coefficients of a Fourier series expansion based on spherical harmonics, also simply called spherical harmonic coefficients, are given by

$$c_l^m = \int_0^{2\pi} \int_0^{\pi} f(\theta, \phi) \overline{Y_l^m(\theta, \phi)} \sin(\theta) \, d\theta \, d\phi \ .$$

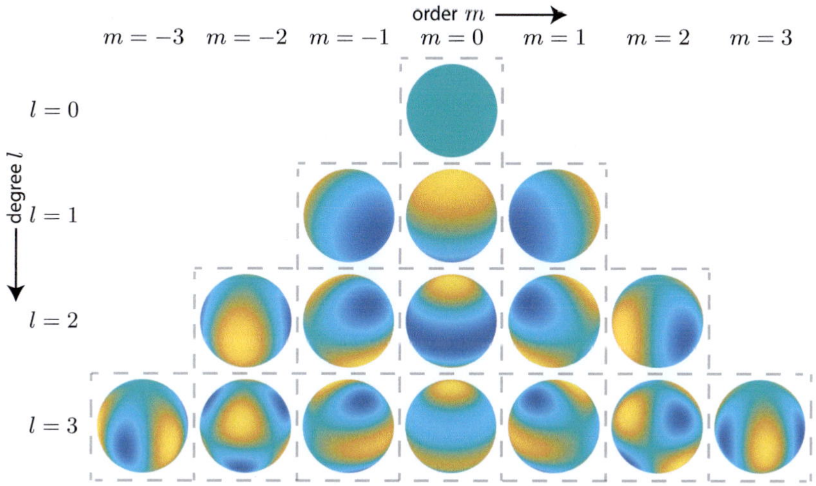

Figure 6.1.: Real spherical harmonic functions up to degree 3 (adapted version of an illustration from [O2]).

For practical purposes, we limit ourselves to a sum with the maximum degree L. In other words, the partial sum

$$s_L(\theta, \phi) = \sum_{l=0}^{L} \sum_{m=-l}^{l} c_l^m Y_l^m(\theta, \phi) \ ,$$

involving a total of $N = (L+1)^2$ spherical harmonic coefficients is used. When approximating real functions using complex spherical harmonics, only the coefficients of nonnegative order need to be determined because the coefficients of negative order can be derived from the coefficients of positive order.

Until this point, we have parameterized the points on the unit sphere by the two angles θ and ϕ. As explained in Chapter 5, $\mathbb{S}^2$ can be embedded in $\mathbb{R}^3$. In this case, we can parameterize the points on the unit sphere using a three-dimensional vector $\underline{x}$ of unit norm in Cartesian coordinates.

The convention to convert spherical coordinates to Cartesian coordinates that we use is [KS13, Section 7.2.1]

$$\underline{x} = \left[\sin(\theta)\cos(\phi) \quad \sin(\theta)\sin(\phi) \quad \cos(\theta)\right]^\top .$$

For the conversion of Cartesian coordinates to spherical coordinates, we can use the system of equations

$$\begin{aligned}
\cos(\phi) &= \frac{x_1}{\sqrt{x_1^2 + x_2^2}} , \\
\sin(\phi) &= \frac{x_2}{\sqrt{x_1^2 + x_2^2}} , \\
\cos(\theta) &= x_3 ,
\end{aligned}$$

which is uniquely defined for $\phi \in [0, 2\pi)$ and $\theta \in [0, \pi]$. It is also possible to use the atan2 to arrive at more implementation-friendly formulae. In the remainder of this thesis, we use the parameterization based on the three-dimensional vector. This parameterization is the common parameterization for densities on the sphere, such as the von Mises–Fisher density.

6.2 Filters for Circular Manifolds

In this section, we explain the IFF and the SqFF for circular manifolds. In our explanation, we employ different representations of functions, which are illustrated in Figure 6.2. One way to represent a function is based on its function values on equidistant grid points. Using so-called sampling (not to be confused with stochastic or deterministic sampling of density functions), continuous-time analog signals are represented by a sequence of numbers [Uns00]. In this context, the continuous-time signal is assumed to be periodic and the samples are obtained at different points in time. The time in the context of sampling should not be confused with the time index of our filter. For improved comprehensibility, we adapt the terminology of sampling theory to match the rest of our paper. We replace the term signal with function and state the function is evaluated at different points on a grid instead of sampled at different points in time. It is commonly assumed that the function can be written as a finite sum of sine and cosine functions, i.e., a trigonometric polynomial. When using equidistant grid points, the sampling theorem [Uns00] gives a lower bound for the minimum number of grid points required to reconstruct the original function, e.g., using a cardinal series. In a cardinal series (also called cardinal function [Whi15]), the function values on the grid are multiplied with cardinal sine functions [Uns00]. The weighted sum of the cardinal sine functions is then a continuous function again.

The discrete Fourier transform (DFT) [DM84, Chapter 2] can be used to derive complex Fourier coefficients. If the sampling theorem is fulfilled, the values obtained by applying a DFT to the function values on the grid only deviate from the Fourier coefficients by a known constant. Due to this close relationship, we shall refer to algorithms to derive the Fourier coefficients from function values on a grid simply as DFTs.

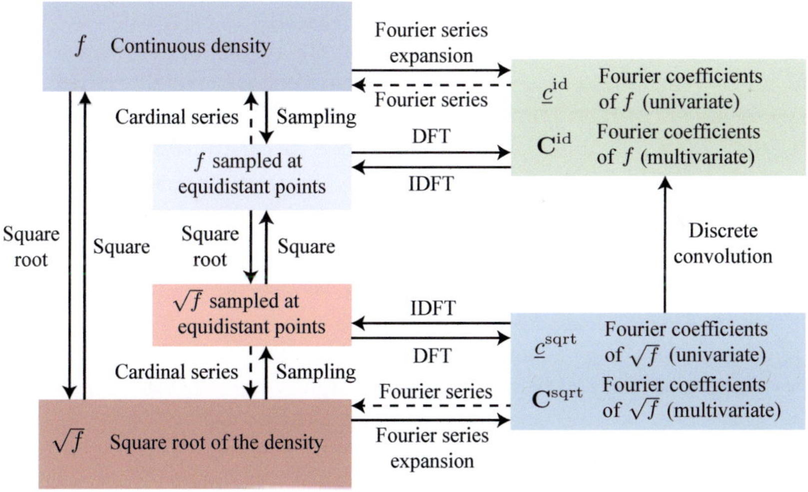

Figure 6.2.: Representations of periodic functions employed in this thesis and ways to transform one representation into another. The dashed lines indicate that the continuous functions obtained may not be identical to the original function if only a finite number of Fourier coefficients or grid points are used.

A popular approach to calculate Fourier coefficients using function values on an equidistant grid was presented in [CT65]. It has a complexity of $O(N \log N)$ and has since become popular for calculating the DFT. It is currently referred to as the fast Fourier transform [DV90]. Thus, even if no closed-form (or at least analytic) expressions can be given for the Fourier coefficients of a density, we can approximate the function in $O(N \log N)$ when the cost of each function evaluation is independent of the number of Fourier coefficients.

The trigonometric polynomial with the determined Fourier coefficients can be used as an approximation of the original function. An exact formula for the original function is only obtained if the sampling theorem is fulfilled. To determine as many function values on an equidistant grid as we have Fourier coefficients, the inverse discrete Fourier transform (IDFT) can be employed (the coefficient vector can be padded with zeros if more values are desired). An efficient way to implement the IDFT is to employ the inverse fast Fourier transform, which is also in $O(N \log N)$. Using an IDFT is more efficient than evaluating the trigonometric polynomial at all N grid points as the evaluation of the trigonometric polynomial is dependent on the number of coefficients. The effort to evaluate a trigonometric polynomial with N coefficients for N arbitrary input values is in $O(N^2)$. The methods to obtain Fourier coefficients and values of the function on a grid can be applied similarly for the square root of the function.

Obtaining the square root of a function is easy when the function is known and vice versa. The same holds for the function values on a grid. To obtain the Fourier coefficients of a function based on the Fourier coefficients of the square root of the function, a discrete convolution can be used. The discrete convolution of two Fourier coefficient vectors (or more generally, tensors) corresponds to the multiplication of the functions described by the trigonometric polynomials. Thus, the coefficient vector, matrix, or tensor only has to be convolved with itself.

However, when the Fourier coefficients of a function are given, there is, to our knowledge, no easy way to directly obtain the Fourier coefficients of the square root of the function. When we need to obtain the Fourier coefficients of the square root of the function based on the Fourier coefficients of the original function, we use the only way permitted in the diagram in Figure 6.2 to approximate the coefficients. We first perform an IDFT to obtain the function values on a grid. Then, we calculate the square root of these function values. Afterward, a DFT is used to obtain an approximation of the Fourier coefficients. We consider an easy example that shows that this is generally an approximation.

Assume we are given the Fourier coefficient vector $\underline{c} = [\frac{1}{4\pi}, \frac{1}{2\pi}, \frac{1}{4\pi}]^\top$, which describes the trigonometric polynomial $\frac{1}{2\pi}(1 + \cos(x))$. When we apply an IDFT to $\underline{c}$, we obtain three values of the function. This number of values is sufficient to reconstruct the function. However, when we take the square root of the function values, we obtain three function values of $\sqrt{\frac{1}{2\pi}(1 + \cos(x))}$. For this function, the three values do not fulfill the sampling theorem. Thus, the Fourier coefficients obtained from these values via a DFT are generally only an approximation.

It would also be possible to, for example, approximate the logarithm of the density. However, approximating the logarithm of a density can lead to problems, e.g., for densities with values of zero or close to zero. For values approaching zero, the logarithm diverges to $-\infty$, and for the input value of zero, it is undefined. In this thesis, we thus focus on approximating the density or its square root using Fourier coefficients. To differentiate between the two representations, we use the upper index "id" to denote Fourier coefficients of the density, whereas we use the upper index "sqrt" for Fourier coefficients of the square root of the density.

In the remainder of this section, we first address how to represent densities using Fourier series. Afterward, we explicate how to perform update and prediction steps. We first regard the prediction step for simple system models and then describe a more general form in Section 6.2.4.

6.2.1 Approximating Densities on the Circle

We start with the Fourier coefficient of index 0 when representing the density directly. Because

$$\mathrm{e}^{ikx} = \cos(kx) + i\sin(kx) \ ,$$

we know that

$$\forall k \in \mathbb{Z}\backslash\{0\} : \int_0^{2\pi} \mathrm{e}^{ikx} \, dx = 0 \; . \tag{6.7}$$

Hence, the integral of a trigonometric polynomial over any 2π interval is

$$\int_0^{2\pi} \sum_{k=-k_{\max}}^{k_{\max}} c_k \mathrm{e}^{ikx} \, dx = 2\pi c_0 \; .$$

Thus, if we directly approximate a univariate density,

$$c_0^{\mathrm{id}} = \frac{1}{2\pi}$$

because the integral must be 1 to ensure the normalization of the density. For most densities of practical relevance, the other coefficients c_k^{id} converge to 0 for $|k| \to 0$. Some notes on the convergence of the coefficients and a way to obtain bounds for their sizes are provided in Appendix A.

The Fourier coefficients for the IFF have a close relationship to trigonometric moments as

$$\forall k \in \mathbb{Z}^{-}\backslash\{0\} : c_k^{\mathrm{id}} = \frac{1}{2\pi} m_{-k} \; .$$

Combined with the knowledge that $c_{-k} = \overline{c}_k$ and $c_0^{\mathrm{id}} = \frac{1}{2\pi}$, it is easy to derive formulae for the Fourier coefficients of univariate densities if the formulae for the trigonometric moments are known. Due to this close relationship, the Fourier filters, in particular the IFF, respects multiple trigonometric moments. In contrast, the assumed density filter given in [ARCB09] only focuses on the first trigonometric moment.

As explained at the beginning of this section, the Fourier coefficients of the square root can, in general, not be trivially derived from the Fourier coefficients or trigonometric moments of the actual density. Therefore, it is useful to have formulae that do not involve integrals for the Fourier coefficients of the square root of common densities. In Appendix B.1, we provide closed-form or analytic expressions for most of the parametric densities that were introduced in Section 5.2.1.

If no closed-form solution is available for a density, the Fourier coefficients can be obtained by calculating the integrals in (6.2) using numerical integration ($f(x)$ has to be replaced with $\sqrt{f(x)}$ for the approximation of the square root). A fast approximation can be obtained by evaluating the function on an equidistant grid and then performing a DFT in $O(N \log N)$.

6.2.2 Update Step

To implement the update step of a recursive Bayesian estimator (as explained in Section 5.1), we need to implement a multiplication of the prior density with the likelihood followed by a normalization. We now explain how these operations can be implemented for the IFF and SqFF. Alternative update steps for both filters are explained in Appendix C.1.

Update Step of the IFF

The operations that need to be performed for an update step based on the prior density and the likelihood function are illustrated in Figure 6.3a. The corresponding operations on the Fourier coefficient vectors are illustrated in Figure 6.3b. To multiply two trigonometric polynomials, we can use the fact that the multiplication of two functions corresponds to a discrete convolution of the Fourier coefficient vectors. Thus, to calculate the Fourier coefficient vector $\breve{\underline{c}}_t^{\mathrm{e,id}}$ representing the exact unnormalized multiplication result[1]

$$\breve{f}_t^{\mathrm{e}}(x_t|\hat{\underline{z}}_1, \ldots, \hat{\underline{z}}_t) = f_t^{\mathrm{P}}(x_t|\hat{\underline{z}}_1, \ldots, \hat{\underline{z}}_{t-1}) f_t^{\mathrm{L}}(\hat{\underline{z}}_t|x_t)$$

based on the Fourier coefficient vectors $\underline{c}_t^{\mathrm{p,id}}$ and $\underline{c}_t^{\mathrm{L,id}}$ of f_t^{P} and f_t^{L}, we compute the discrete convolution

$$\mathring{\underline{c}}_t^{\mathrm{e,id}} = \underline{c}_t^{\mathrm{p,id}} * \underline{c}_t^{\mathrm{L,id}} .$$

[1] Even in the circular case, we always denote the measurements as vectors because the measurements may be higher dimensional than the state.

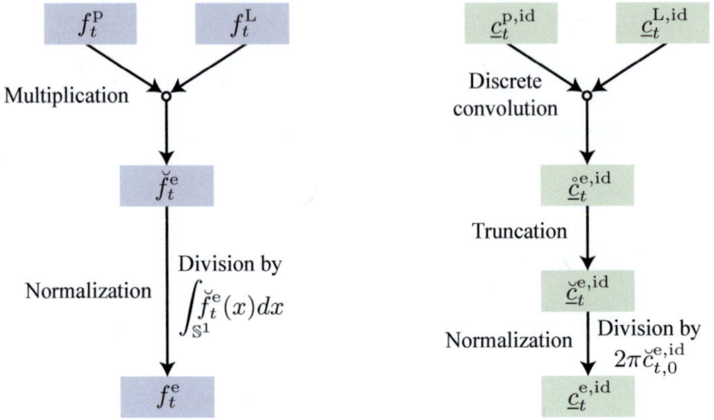

(a) Operations performed on the continuous densities.

(b) Operations for the Fourier coefficients.

Figure 6.3.: Update step of the IFF.

If we have a topology-aware system model with additive noise (e.g., the identity model (5.1) or a nonlinear model (5.2)) and the noise terms for the individual time steps are independent and identically distributed (i.i.d.), we do not need to transform f_t^{L} in every time step. We can transform the likelihood once for $\hat{z} = 0$ and then shift it according to the actual measurement $\hat{z}_t$ by employing (6.5) in every time step.

The discrete convolution is in $O(N \log N)$. In our approximation of the Fourier series using a trigonometric polynomial with N terms, we implicitly assume that all coefficients of higher order are 0. When performing the discrete convolution, additional entries with indices lower than $-k_{\max}$ and higher than $k_{\max}$ can become nonzero. We use $\underline{\mathring{c}}_t^{\mathrm{e,id}}$ to denote the convolution result to emphasize that the vector is longer than the original vectors and describes an unnormalized density. To avoid a steady increase in the number of coefficients, which would result in increased storage and computational requirements, we perform a parameter reduction.

In our Fourier filters, the parameter reduction is realized in the form of a truncation. This means we discard the coefficients of higher orders to obtain a trigonometric polynomial of order $k_{\max}$ again. In our illustration of the operations performed on the Fourier coefficients in Figure 6.3b, we use $\underline{\breve{c}}_t^{\mathrm{e,id}}$ to denote the vector of the correct length that is the result of the truncation. For practical implementations, the convolution should be combined with the truncation, i.e., elements of the result that are discarded should not be calculated at all.

To obtain Fourier coefficients representing a normalized density, we perform a normalization. As explained in Section 6.2.1, the integral of a trigonometric polynomial over $[0, 2\pi)$ only depends on the zeroth coefficient. For a function to integrate to 1, the zeroth coefficient must be $\frac{1}{2\pi}$. A function given as a trigonometric polynomial can be scaled by multiplying all the coefficients by the desired factor. This is evident from the formula of the trigonometric polynomial (6.3). We divide all the coefficients by $2\pi\breve{c}_{t,0}^{\mathrm{e,id}}$ and call the result $\underline{c}_t^{\mathrm{e,id}}$. Since $c_{t,0}^{\mathrm{e,id}} = \frac{1}{2\pi}$ holds, the end result $\underline{c}_t^{\mathrm{e,id}}$ describes a normalized density.

Update Step of the SqFF

No major changes are required for the SqFF. We provide an overview of the approach in Figure 6.4. The illustration can be used to quickly grasp the differences to the update step of the IFF sketched in Figure 6.3.

For brevity, we omit all the measurements obtained before the current time step t in the arguments of f_t^{e}, f_t^{P}, and f_t^{L} in the derivation. For the SqFF, we need to derive the Fourier coefficients for the square root of the posterior density. Thus, we need to obtain the Fourier coefficients for the right-hand side of

$$\sqrt{f_t^{\mathrm{e}}(x_t)} = \sqrt{\frac{f_t^{\mathrm{P}}(x_t) f_t^{\mathrm{L}}(\hat{\underline{z}}_t|x_t)}{\int_{\Omega_x} f_t^{\mathrm{P}}(x_t) f_t^{\mathrm{L}}(\hat{\underline{z}}_t|x_t) dx_t}} \,.$$

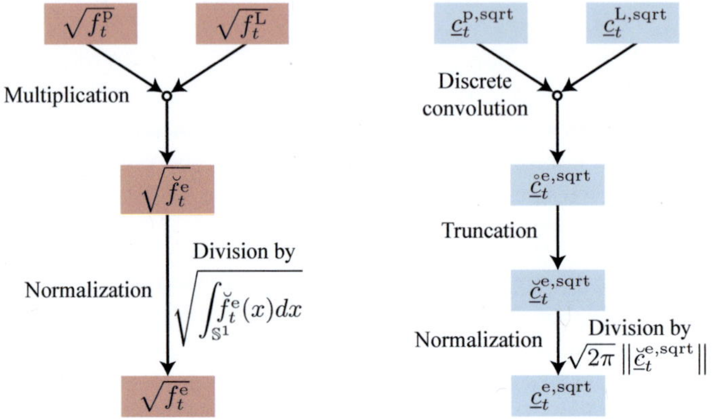

(a) Operations performed on the continuous densities.

(b) Operations for the Fourier coefficients.

Figure 6.4.: Update step of the SqFF.

As

$$\frac{f_t^{\mathrm{P}}(x_t) f_t^{\mathrm{L}}(\underline{\hat{z}}_t|x_t)}{\int_{\Omega_x} f_t^{\mathrm{P}}(x_t) f_t^{\mathrm{L}}(\underline{\hat{z}}_t|x_t) dx_t} = s f_t^{\mathrm{P}}(x_t) f_t^{\mathrm{L}}(\underline{\hat{z}}_t|x_t)$$

for some constant $s > 0$,

$$\begin{aligned}\sqrt{\frac{f_t^{\mathrm{P}}(x_t) f_t^{\mathrm{L}}(\underline{\hat{z}}_t|x_t)}{\int_{\Omega_x} f_t^{\mathrm{P}}(x_t) f_t^{\mathrm{L}}(\underline{\hat{z}}_t|x_t) dx_t}} &= \sqrt{s}\sqrt{f_t^{\mathrm{P}}(x_t) f_t^{\mathrm{L}}(\underline{\hat{z}}_t|x_t)} \\ &\propto \sqrt{f_t^{\mathrm{P}}(x_t) f_t^{\mathrm{L}}(\underline{\hat{z}}_t|x_t)} = \sqrt{f_t^{\mathrm{P}}(x_t)}\sqrt{f_t^{\mathrm{L}}(\underline{\hat{z}}_t|x_t)}\end{aligned}$$

holds. As s is the reciprocal of the integral over the unnormalized posterior density, we know that we have to normalize the result using the square root of the integral of the actual unnormalized density $\breve{f}_t^{\mathrm{e}}$ and not $\sqrt{\breve{f}_t^{\mathrm{e}}}$. All required operations are illustrated in Figure 6.4a.

For the Fourier coefficients, we can implement the multiplication similarly as for the IFF and only have to adjust the normalization. First, we calculate the Fourier coefficient vector

$$\underline{\mathring{c}}_t^{\mathrm{e,sqrt}} = \underline{c}_t^{\mathrm{p,sqrt}} * \underline{c}_t^{\mathrm{L,sqrt}}$$

describing the unnormalized and non-truncated result. Instead of obtaining the truncated result $\underline{\check{c}}_t^{\mathrm{e,sqrt}}$ using a separate truncation step (as illustrated in Figure 6.4b), better performance can be achieved by integrating the truncation into the convolution by not calculating any coefficients with indices $k : |k| > k_{\mathrm{max}}$. While it is irrelevant if the truncation or the normalization is performed first in the IFF, it is important to truncate first in the SqFF. The truncation operation can void the normalization of the density as all elements of the vector influence the integral of the square of the function represented by the coefficients.

To integrate over a density represented by a trigonometric polynomial approximating its square root, we use the fact that the function can be multiplied by itself by performing a convolution. To calculate the integral over $[0, 2\pi)$, we only require the zeroth coefficient $\check{c}_{t,0}^{\mathrm{e,id}}$ that can be calculated according to

$$\check{c}_{t,0}^{\mathrm{e,id}} = \sum_{k=-k_{\mathrm{max}}}^{k_{\mathrm{max}}} \check{c}_{t,k}^{\mathrm{e,sqrt}} \check{c}_{t,-k}^{\mathrm{e,sqrt}} = \sum_{k=-k_{\mathrm{max}}}^{k_{\mathrm{max}}} |\check{c}_{t,k}^{\mathrm{e,sqrt}}|^2 = \left\| \underline{\check{c}}_t^{\mathrm{e,sqrt}} \right\|^2 .$$

Thus, the integral of the function represented by $\underline{\check{c}}_t^{\mathrm{e,sqrt}}$ over $[0, 2\pi)$ is $2\pi \|\underline{\check{c}}_t^{\mathrm{e,sqrt}}\|^2$. The same formula can also be derived using the Parseval relation [KS13, Section 2.7.1] (also called Parseval's formula [Zyg03, Volume I, Section II.1, Theorem 1.12]). By calculating

$$\underline{c}_t^{\mathrm{e,sqrt}} = \frac{1}{\sqrt{2\pi} \left\| \underline{\check{c}}_t^{\mathrm{e,sqrt}} \right\|} \check{c}_t^{\mathrm{e,sqrt}} ,$$

we can ensure that the squared norm of the new vector $\underline{c}_t^{\mathrm{e,sqrt}}$ is $1/(2\pi)$, which ensures the normalization of the density.

6.2.3 Prediction Step for the Topology-Aware Identity Model with Additive Noise

To realize a prediction step for the topology-aware identity model with additive noise, operations corresponding to the topology-aware convolution (5.8) of the original densities must be implemented. Alternative prediction steps for the identity model with additive noise are described in Appendix C.2.

Prediction Step of the IFF

As illustrated in Figure 6.5, we can use the fact that the Fourier coefficients for the topology-aware convolution of two functions can be obtained using a Hadamard (element-wise) product of the coefficient vectors followed by a multiplication with 2π [Str07, Section 4.4]. This means the Fourier coefficient vector representing the convolution result can be calculated according to

$$\underline{c}_{t+1}^{\mathrm{p,id}} = 2\pi(\underline{c}_t^{\mathrm{e,id}} \circ \underline{c}_t^{\boldsymbol{w},\mathrm{id}}) \ ,$$

in which $\circ$ denotes the Hadamard product. The prediction operation for the topology-aware identity model with additive noise is thus in $O(N)$.

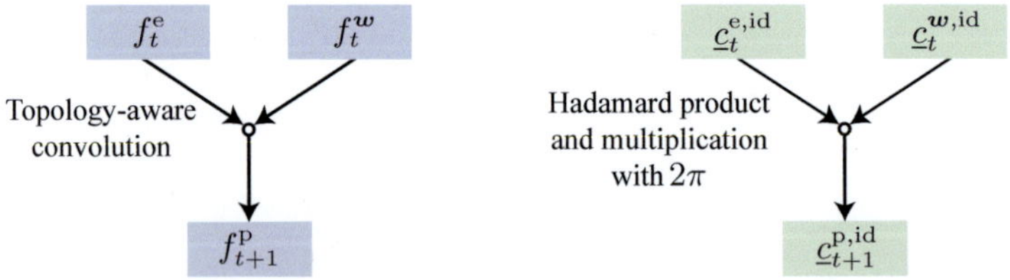

(a) Operations performed on the continuous densities.

(b) Operations for the Fourier coefficients.

Figure 6.5.: Prediction step of the IFF for the topology-aware identity model with additive noise.

Prediction Step of the SqFF

While the prediction step of the IFF is simple, the prediction step of the SqFF is a comparatively expensive and complicated operation. The result of our operations should be the Fourier coefficients of

$$\sqrt{f_{t+1}^{\mathrm{p}}(x_{t+1})} = \sqrt{(f_t^{\mathrm{e}} * f_t^{\boldsymbol{w}})(x_{t+1})} \ .$$

We cannot directly perform a convolution because we would obtain the Fourier coefficients of $\sqrt{f_t^{\mathrm{e}}} * \sqrt{f_t^{\boldsymbol{w}}}$, but in general,

$$\sqrt{(f_t^{\mathrm{e}} * f_t^{\boldsymbol{w}})(x_{t+1})} \neq \left(\sqrt{f_t^{\mathrm{e}}} * \sqrt{f_t^{\boldsymbol{w}}}\right)(x_{t+1}) \ .$$

Therefore, we proceed as illustrated for the densities in Figure 6.6a. We first calculate f_t^{e} and $f_t^{\boldsymbol{w}}$ from their square roots. Then, we perform a topology-aware convolution and determine the square root of the result.

To implement these steps based on the Fourier coefficients, we start by performing discrete convolutions of the Fourier coefficient vectors, as illustrated in Figure 6.6b. The intermediate results

$$\underline{\check{c}}_t^{\mathrm{e,id}} = \underline{c}_t^{\mathrm{e,sqrt}} * \underline{c}_t^{\mathrm{e,sqrt}}$$

and

$$\underline{\check{c}}_t^{\boldsymbol{w}\mathrm{,id}} = \underline{c}_t^{\boldsymbol{w}\mathrm{,sqrt}} * \underline{c}_t^{\boldsymbol{w}\mathrm{,sqrt}}$$

represent the normalized densities f_t^{e} and $f_t^{\boldsymbol{w}}$ but the vectors are longer than the original vectors $\underline{c}_t^{\mathrm{e,sqrt}}$ and $\underline{c}_t^{\boldsymbol{w}\mathrm{,sqrt}}$.

As in the IFF, the convolution can then be performed using the Hadamard product, i.e.,

$$\underline{\check{c}}_{t+1}^{\mathrm{p,id}} = 2\pi(\underline{\check{c}}_t^{\mathrm{e,id}} \circ \underline{\check{c}}_t^{\boldsymbol{w}\mathrm{,id}}) \ .$$

None of the vectors $\underline{\check{c}}_t^{\mathrm{e,id}}$, $\underline{\check{c}}_t^{\boldsymbol{w}\mathrm{,id}}$, and $\underline{\check{c}}_{t+1}^{\mathrm{p,id}}$ may be truncated without possibly voiding the nonnegativity of the density represented by $\underline{\check{c}}_{t+1}^{\mathrm{p,id}}$.

To obtain the Fourier coefficients of the square root of f_{t+1}^{p}, we proceed as explained at the beginning of Section 6.2. As we have the Fourier coefficients of the (correctly normalized) density f_{t+1}^{p}, we can first use an IDFT to obtain the function values of f_{t+1}^{p} on a grid. Using these, the function values of $\sqrt{f_{t+1}^{\mathrm{p}}}$ on a grid can be determined. Then, an IDFT is used to calculate the Fourier coefficient vector $\underline{\mathring{c}}_{t+1}^{\mathrm{p,sqrt}}$. The vector $\underline{\mathring{c}}_{t+1}^{\mathrm{p,sqrt}}$ may not represent a normalized density because the number of coefficients used may not be sufficient to accurately represent $\sqrt{f_{t+1}^{\mathrm{p}}}$. Further, the vector $\underline{\mathring{c}}_{t+1}^{\mathrm{p,sqrt}}$ is generally longer than desired, and thus, a truncation is performed. The density described by the truncation result $\underline{\check{c}}_{t+1}^{\mathrm{p,sqrt}}$ is still unnormalized. After one final normalization, performed as in the update step, the coefficient vector $\underline{c}_{t+1}^{\mathrm{p,sqrt}}$ representing the normalized result is obtained.

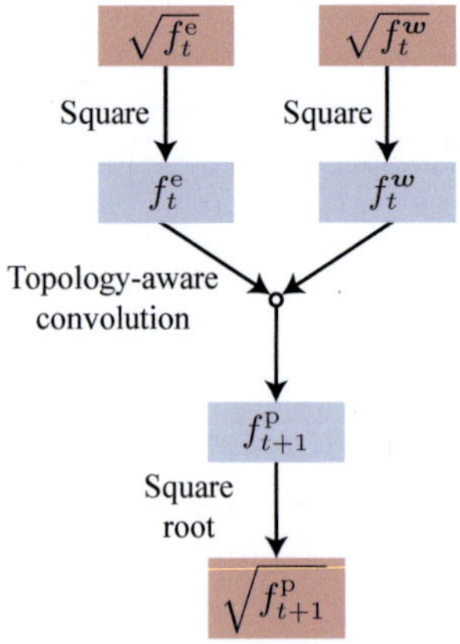

(a) Operations performed on the continuous densities.

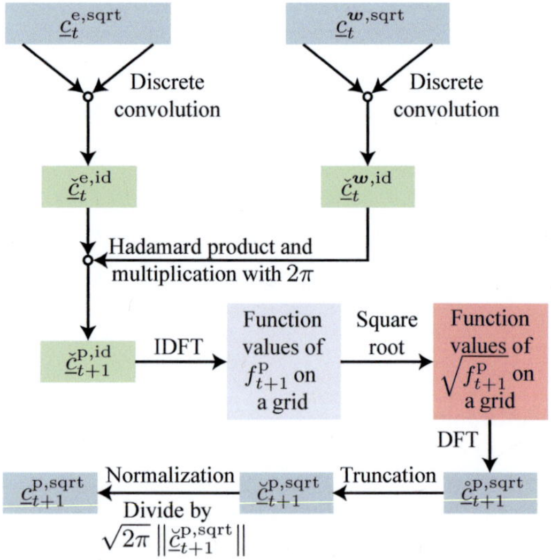

(b) Operations for the Fourier coefficients.

Figure 6.6.: Prediction step of the SqFF for the topology-aware identity model with additive noise.

Remark 2. Performing the truncation at the end is not the only possibility. We could truncate $\underline{c}_t^{\text{e,sqrt}}$ and $\underline{c}_t^{\boldsymbol{w},\text{sqrt}}$ initially to ensure that $\underline{\check{c}}_t^{\text{e,id}}$, $\underline{\check{c}}_t^{\boldsymbol{w},\text{id}}$, and $\underline{\check{c}}_{t+1}^{\text{p,id}}$ have the correct sizes. However, in this case, not all the coefficients obtained from the previous step would be used. Another way to perform the truncation is to calculate only half of the values on the grid of f_{t+1}^{P}. As long as all entries of $\underline{\check{c}}_{t+1}^{\text{p,id}}$ are used, all function values will be nonnegative. While the cardinal series based on the function values on the grid may have negative function values, this does not pose a problem as the function values on the grid are all nonnegative, which ensures that the square roots of function values on the grid are real numbers.

Remark 3. If multiple prediction steps are performed consecutively, it can make sense to continue with $\underline{\check{c}}_{t+1}^{\text{p,id}}$ and skip the calculation of $\underline{c}_{t+1}^{\text{p,sqrt}}$. Since the prediction step only involves a Hadamard product, the vector length never increases beyond $4k_{\text{max}} + 1$. However, one must pay attention to ensure that the vector $\underline{\check{c}}_t^{\boldsymbol{w},\text{id}}$ at the respective time step always represents a nonnegative function. This can be ensured, e.g., by calculating $\underline{\check{c}}_t^{\boldsymbol{w},\text{id}}$ via a discrete convolution of $\underline{c}_t^{\boldsymbol{w},\text{sqrt}}$ with itself. If the approximation of f_t^{L} is likewise ensured to be nonnegative and no truncations are performed, even an update step can be performed without voiding the nonnegativity. However, to truncate the coefficient vectors without voiding the nonnegativity, a transformation to the square root representation is required. The prediction step of the SqFF presented in this subsection ensures that all densities represented by the intermediate results (including the cardinal series of the function values on the grid) are nonnegative everywhere. An alternative prediction step in which this condition may be temporarily voided is described in Appendix C.

6.2.4 General Prediction Step

For the general prediction step, we assume that the transition density f_t^{T} is available. If the system model is given based on random variables instead, we assume that a derivation of f_t^{T}, as briefly discussed in Section 5.1, is possible. Having f_t^{T} at our disposal, we explain how the Chapman–Kolmogorov equation (5.4) can be realized in both representations.

General Prediction Step of the IFF

The Chapman–Kolmogorov equation consists of a multiplication

$$f_t^{\text{j}}(x_{t+1}, x_t|\hat{\underline{z}}_1, \dots, \hat{\underline{z}}_t) = f_t^{\text{T}}(x_{t+1}|x_t) f_t^{\text{e}}(x_t|\hat{\underline{z}}_1, \dots, \hat{\underline{z}}_t)$$

followed by a marginalization

$$f_{t+1}^{\text{p}}(x_{t+1}|\hat{\underline{z}}_1, \dots, \hat{\underline{z}}_t) = \int_{\mathbb{S}^1} f_t^{\text{j}}(x_{t+1}, x_t|\hat{\underline{z}}_1, \dots, \hat{\underline{z}}_t) \, dx_t \, .$$

We visualize all involved densities in Figure 6.7. In Figure 6.7a, we depict the density before the prediction step f_t^{e} and the prediction result f_{t+1}^{p}. In Figure 6.7b, we illustrate f_t^{e} in a three-dimensional plot with x_{t+1} on an additional axis. As f_t^{e} does not depend on x_{t+1}, there is zero variation along this dimension. This plot, however, makes it visually easier to grasp how the joint density is calculated. In Figure 6.7c, we give the transition density depending on x_{t+1} and x_t. The joint density f_t^{j} illustrated in Figure 6.7d is the product of the two functions illustrated in Figures 6.7b and 6.7c. A marginalization of the joint density yields the predicted density, as illustrated in Figure 6.7a. All steps performed are summarized in Figure 6.8a.

In Figure 6.8b, we give an overview of how these steps can be performed based on the Fourier coefficients. We treat f_t^{T} as a function of two input arguments and determine the Fourier coefficient matrix $\mathbf{C}_t^{\text{T,id}}$ thereof. If we use the same k_{max} along all dimensions for the approximation of f_t^{T}, we have a $(2k_{\text{max}} + 1) \times (2k_{\text{max}} + 1)$ matrix of coefficients. If f_t^{T} is time-invariant, the coefficient matrix only needs to be calculated once.

To calculate the coefficient matrix of f_t^{j}, we perform a discrete convolution. We shall assume that the first dimension of $\mathbf{C}_t^{\text{T,id}}$ corresponds to x_{t+1} and the second dimension to x_t. Then, the coefficient vector of f_t^{e} needs to be written as a $1 \times (2k_{\text{max}} + 1)$ vector. The convolution result corresponding to the coefficient matrix of f_t^{j} is then a $(2k_{\text{max}} + 1) \times (4k_{\text{max}} + 1)$ matrix and the index k_1 for the first dimension ranges from $-k_{\text{max}}$ to k_{max} and the index k_2 for the second dimension from $-2k_{\text{max}}$ to $2k_{\text{max}}$.

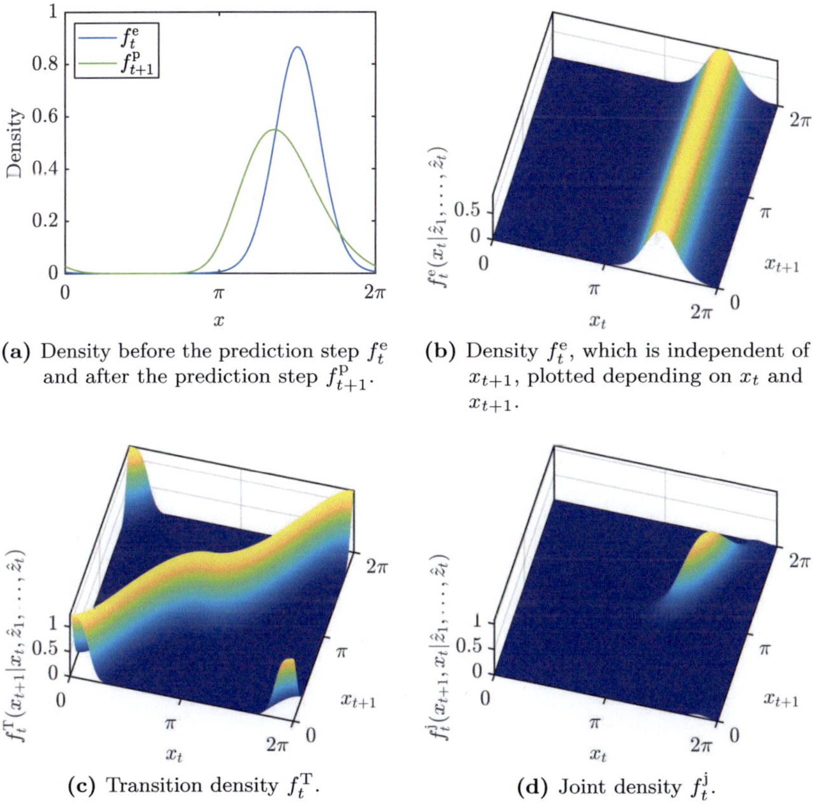

(a) Density before the prediction step f_t^{e} and after the prediction step f_{t+1}^{p}.

(b) Density f_t^{e}, which is independent of x_{t+1}, plotted depending on x_t and x_{t+1}.

(c) Transition density f_t^{T}.

(d) Joint density f_t^{j}.

Figure 6.7.: Visualization of the functions involved in the prediction step.

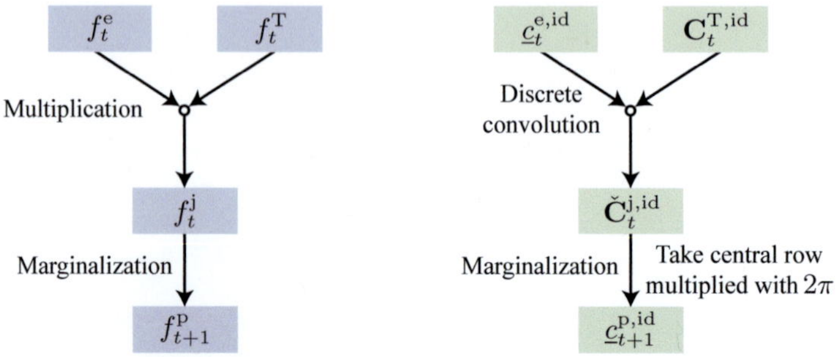

(a) Operations performed on the continuous densities.

(b) Operations for the Fourier coefficients.

Figure 6.8.: Prediction step of the IFF for nonlinear system models.

To marginalize x_t out of f_t^{j}, we first write out the trigonometric polynomial of f_t^{j}, yielding

$$\int_{\mathbb{S}^1} f_t^{\mathrm{j}}(x_{t+1}, x_t|\hat{\underline{z}}_1, \ldots, \hat{\underline{z}}_t)\, dx_t = \int_0^{2\pi} \sum_{k_1=-k_{\max}}^{k_{\max}} \sum_{k_2=-2k_{\max}}^{2k_{\max}} c_{[k_1,k_2]}^{\mathrm{j,id}} \mathrm{e}^{ik_1 x_{t+1}} \mathrm{e}^{ik_2 x_t} dx_t$$
$$= \sum_{k_1=-k_{\max}}^{k_{\max}} \mathrm{e}^{ik_1 x_{t+1}} \sum_{k_2=-2k_{\max}}^{2k_{\max}} c_{[k_1,k_2]}^{\mathrm{j,id}} \int_0^{2\pi} \mathrm{e}^{ik_2 x_t} dx_t \ .$$

Due to (6.7), the sum over k_2 can be reduced to the single term for $k_2 = 0$. We thus obtain

$$\int_{\mathbb{S}^1} f_t^{\mathrm{j}}(x_{t+1}, x_t|\hat{\underline{z}}_1, \ldots, \hat{\underline{z}}_t)\, dx_t = \sum_{k_1=-k_{\max}}^{k_{\max}} \mathrm{e}^{ik_1 x_{t+1}} c_{[k_1,0]}^{\mathrm{j,id}} \int_0^{2\pi} 1\, dx_t$$
$$= \sum_{k_1=-k_{\max}}^{k_{\max}} 2\pi c_{[k_1,0]}^{\mathrm{j,id}}\, \mathrm{e}^{ik_1 x_{t+1}} \ ,$$

which is a trigonometric polynomial that only depends on x_{t+1}.

Remark 4. For practical implementations, the whole procedure can be combined into a single step. Instead of calculating all $8k_{\max}^2 + 6k_{\max} + 1$ coefficients of f_t^{j}, we can just determine the $2k_{\max} + 1$ coefficients that are preserved during the marginalization and multiply them by 2π. This already significantly improves the run time. As can be derived using the formula for the discrete convolution, we can obtain the desired entries using a matrix–vector multiplication according to

$$\underline{c}_{t+1}^{\mathrm{p,id}} = \mathbf{C}_t^{\mathrm{T,id}} \operatorname{flip}(\underline{c}_t^{\mathrm{e,id}})^\top ,$$

in which flip indicates that the order of the entries of the vector is reversed. Since the Fourier coefficient vector describes a real function, the complex conjugate can be used instead of the flip operation. The effort of this vector–matrix multiplication is in $O(N^2)$. If a DFT is required in every time step to obtain the coefficient matrix $\mathbf{C}_t^{\mathrm{T,id}}$, the total effort is still in $O(N^2 \log N)$. However, if the Fourier coefficients of $f_t^{\mathrm{T,id}}$ can be calculated ahead of time (e.g., if the transition density is time-invariant) or if a closed-form formula is available for the coefficients, the prediction step is in $O(N^2)$ in this formulation.

General Prediction Step of the SqFF

For the SqFF, we approximate the square root of the transition density using a trigonometric polynomial. Because

$$\begin{aligned}\sqrt{f_t^{\mathrm{j}}(x_{t+1}, x_t|\hat{\underline{z}}_1, \ldots, \hat{\underline{z}}_t)} &= \sqrt{f_t^{\mathrm{T}}(x_{t+1}|x_t) f_t^{\mathrm{e}}(x_k|\hat{\underline{z}}_1, \ldots, \hat{\underline{z}}_t)} \\ &= \sqrt{f_t^{\mathrm{T}}(x_{t+1}|x_t)}\sqrt{f_t^{\mathrm{e}}(x_k|\hat{\underline{z}}_1, \ldots, \hat{\underline{z}}_t)} ,\end{aligned}$$

we can obtain the square root of the joint density by multiplying the square roots of f_t^{T} and f_t^{e}. As illustrated in Figure 6.9, the multiplication of f_t^{T} and f_t^{e} corresponds to a discrete convolution. The resulting Fourier coefficient matrix $\check{\mathbf{C}}_t^{\mathrm{j,id}}$ of $\sqrt{f_t^{\mathrm{j}}}$ is thus obtained using

$$\check{\mathbf{C}}_t^{\mathrm{j,sqrt}} = \underline{c}_t^{\mathrm{e,sqrt}} * \mathbf{C}_t^{\mathrm{T,sqrt}} .$$

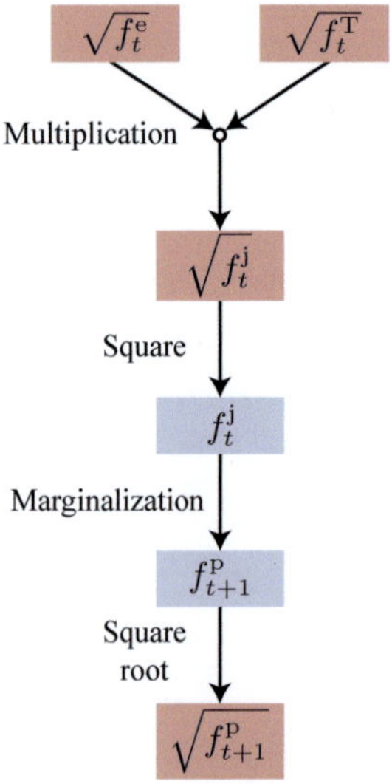

(a) Operations performed on the continuous densities.

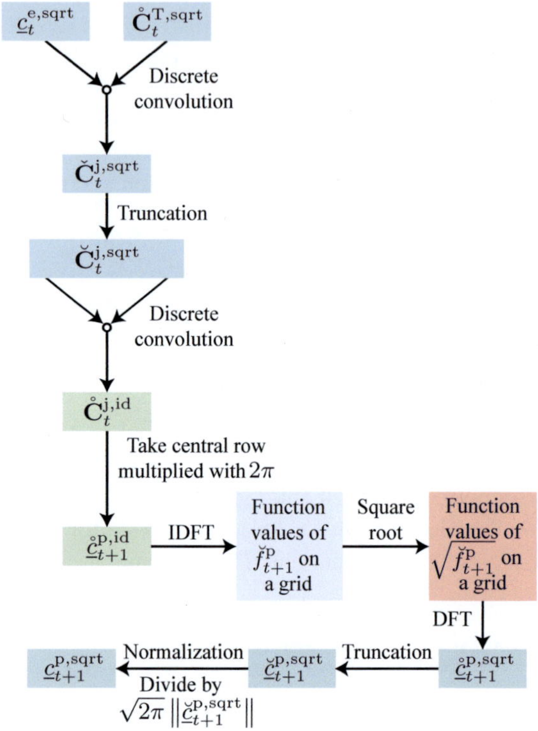

(b) Operations for the Fourier coefficients.

Figure 6.9.: Prediction step of the SqFF for nonlinear system models.

The dimensions of the vector $\underline{c}_t^{\mathrm{e,sqrt}}$ and the matrix $\mathbf{C}_t^{\mathrm{T,sqrt}}$ need to be as in the IFF. The coefficient matrix $\check{\mathbf{C}}_t^{\mathrm{j,sqrt}}$ represents a normalized density but it has more entries than $\mathbf{C}_t^{\mathrm{T,sqrt}}$. Since we are still in the square root representation at this point, we can truncate this intermediate result. While the truncation is optional, it can help reduce the computational time required for the next operations (and also for the discrete convolution as the discarded entries do not need to be determined). The result of the truncation is denoted $\breve{\mathbf{C}}_t^{\mathrm{j,sqrt}}$ to emphasize that it has the same size as $\mathbf{C}_t^{\mathrm{T,sqrt}}$ but may correspond to a density that is not normalized because the truncation may void the normalization. We do not normalize the density at this point because a normalization is not required for this intermediate result.

As

$$\begin{aligned}\sqrt{f_{t+1}^{\mathrm{p}}(x_{t+1}|\hat{\underline{z}}_1,\ldots,\hat{\underline{z}}_t)} &= \sqrt{\int_{\mathbb{S}^1} f_t^{\mathrm{j}}(x_{t+1},x_t|\hat{\underline{z}}_1,\ldots,\hat{\underline{z}}_t)\,dx_t} \\ &\neq \int_{\mathbb{S}^1} \sqrt{f_t^{\mathrm{j}}(x_{t+1},x_t|\hat{\underline{z}}_1,\ldots,\hat{\underline{z}}_t)}\,dx_t\,,\end{aligned}$$

we face a similar challenge as in the prediction step with the topology-aware identity model with additive noise. Therefore, we calculate the coefficient matrix $\mathring{\mathbf{C}}_t^{\mathrm{j,id}}$ representing the unnormalized joint density $\breve{f}_t^{\mathrm{j}}$ by performing a discrete convolution of $\breve{\mathbf{C}}_t^{\mathrm{j,sqrt}}$ with itself. We denote the result $\mathring{\mathbf{C}}_t^{\mathrm{j,id}}$ to emphasize that the density represented by $\mathring{\mathbf{C}}_t^{\mathrm{j,id}}$ is unnormalized and the number of coefficients in $\mathring{\mathbf{C}}_t^{\mathrm{j,id}}$ is higher than in $\mathbf{C}_t^{\mathrm{T,sqrt}}$.

By taking the central row and multiplying all entries with 2π, we can obtain the vector $\mathring{\underline{c}}_{t+1}^{\mathrm{p,id}}$ representing the unnormalized predicted density $\breve{f}_{t+1}^{\mathrm{p}}$. The vector $\mathring{\underline{c}}_{t+1}^{\mathrm{p,id}}$ is also longer than the original vector $\underline{c}_t^{\mathrm{e,sqrt}}$. Discarding the entries outside the central row is valid as the marginalization performed is (when disregarding numerical imprecisions) exact, and thus, no negative function values can be caused. As in the IFF, it is more efficient to not determine the entries outside the central row when performing the discrete convolution. As in the prediction step for the topology-aware identity model with additive noise, $\mathring{\underline{c}}_{t+1}^{\mathrm{p,id}}$ may not be truncated as doing so can void the nonnegativity of the density described by the coefficient vector. The rest of the steps are performed as in the prediction step for the topology-aware identity model with additive noise. Function values of $\breve{f}_{t+1}^{\mathrm{p}}$ on a grid are calculated using an IDFT, the square roots thereof are determined, and then a DFT is used to obtain the vector $\mathring{\underline{c}}_{t+1}^{\mathrm{p,sqrt}}$. After a truncation and a normalization, the vector $\underline{c}_{t+1}^{\mathrm{p,sqrt}}$ of the correct length describing the normalized prediction result is obtained.

Remark 5. In the explanation above, we calculated

$$\mathring{\mathbf{C}}_t^{\mathrm{j,id}} = \check{\mathbf{C}}_t^{\mathrm{j,sqrt}} * \check{\mathbf{C}}_t^{\mathrm{j,sqrt}} = \mathrm{trunc}\left(\underline{c}_t^{\mathrm{e,sqrt}} * \mathbf{C}_t^{\mathrm{T,sqrt}}\right) * \mathrm{trunc}\left(\underline{c}_t^{\mathrm{e,sqrt}} * \mathbf{C}_t^{\mathrm{T,sqrt}}\right),$$

in which trunc denotes a truncation. In this formulation, we can convolve the truncation result $\check{\mathbf{C}}_t^{\mathrm{j,sqrt}}$ with itself, and thus, we only require two discrete convolutions. The convolution of $\check{\mathbf{C}}_t^{\mathrm{j,sqrt}}$ with itself is the most expensive operation of the prediction step, resulting in a computational complexity of $O(N^2 \log N)$.

As an alternative approach that does not allow for a truncation of the intermediate results, we can calculate a coefficient matrix $\check{\mathbf{C}}_t^{\mathrm{j,id}}$ representing the joint density using the formula

$$\check{\mathbf{C}}_t^{\mathrm{j,id}} = \left(\underline{c}_t^{\mathrm{e,sqrt}} * \underline{c}_t^{\mathrm{e,sqrt}}\right) * \underbrace{\left(\mathbf{C}_t^{\mathrm{T,sqrt}} * \mathbf{C}_t^{\mathrm{T,sqrt}}\right)}_{\check{\mathbf{C}}_t^{\mathrm{T,id}}} .$$

While $\check{\mathbf{C}}_t^{\mathrm{j,id}}$ must not be truncated, $\check{\mathbf{C}}_t^{\mathrm{T,id}}$ only needs to be calculated once in the beginning if the transition density is time-invariant. The convolution of $\underline{c}_t^{\mathrm{e,sqrt}}$ with itself is in $O(N \log N)$. The remaining convolution of a vector with a matrix can then be calculated with a run time complexity of $O(N^2)$ as in the IFF, resulting in a total complexity of $O(N^2)$.

6.3 Filters for Hypertoroidal Manifolds

In this section, we describe the Fourier filters for hypertoroidal manifolds. As they are merely a generalization of the Fourier filters used in the circular case, we focus on the changes required and refer the reader to Section 6.2 for the rationale behind the individual steps. We follow the structure of the previous section and begin with the approximation of densities, continue with the update step, and then discuss both the prediction step for the topology-aware identity model with additive noise and the general prediction step based on transition densities.

6.3.1 Approximating Densities on the Hypertorus

When we approximate d-variate densities using Fourier series, we use coefficient tensors with the same length along all dimensions, i.e., each component of the vector-valued index vector $\underline{k}$ can attain all values from $-k_{\max}$ to $k_{\max}$. We thus have a d-dimensional tensor with $N = (2k_{\max}+1)^d$ coefficients.

As the integral formula (6.4) is particularly expensive for multidimensional functions, we focus on ways to approximate densities and likelihoods without a need for calculating integrals. A general way to approximate the densities is to use the d-dimensional DFT. Given N function values on a grid, N Fourier coefficients can be derived in $O(N \log N)$. However, evaluating the density on N grid points can be an expensive operation. For example, for the multivariate wrapped normal distribution (5.9), we know of no other approximation for arbitrary numbers of variates than truncating the series. Even if the partial sum described in Section 5.2.1 is used, the cost of evaluating the multivariate wrapped normal distribution grows exponentially with increasing dimension. In Appendix B.2, we provide a closed-form formula for the Fourier coefficients of the multivariate wrapped normal distribution.

Remark 6. The bivariate assumed density filter proposed in [KGDH14] is based on the trigonometric moment vector $\underline{m}_1$ as defined in (5.13) and a circular correlation coefficient. While the Fourier filters are not explicitly based on these quantities, the Fourier coefficients contain information about the trigonometric moments and the circular correlation. The moment vector $\underline{m}_1$ with scalar index consists of d trigonometric moments with vector-valued indices. Due to the close relationship of the Fourier coefficients to the trigonometric moments with vector-valued indices, all entries of $\underline{m}_1$ can be directly calculated from the Fourier coefficients. As many other correlation coefficients, the circular correlation used in [KGDH14] can be calculated from the Fourier coefficients.

6.3.2 Update Step

The operations of the update step are almost identical to the operations in the univariate case introduced in Section 6.2.2. All discrete convolutions are now d-dimensional, and the parameter reduction in the form of the truncation has to respect all dimensions in the multivariate case. A key difference to the update steps in the univariate case lies in the normalization step.

For the IFF, a normalization can be performed by dividing all entries of the coefficient tensor $\breve{\mathbf{C}}_t^{\mathrm{e,id}}$ by $(2\pi)^d \breve{c}_{t,\underline{0}}^{\mathrm{e,id}}$, with $\breve{c}_{t,\underline{0}}^{\mathrm{e,id}}$ being the coefficient with the index vector containing only zeros. In the hypertoroidal case, we have to divide all coefficients by $(2\pi)^d \breve{c}_{t,\underline{0}}^{\mathrm{e,id}}$ to ensure that the coefficient $c_{t,\underline{0}}^{\mathrm{e,id}}$ of the normalized result $\mathbf{C}_t^{\mathrm{e,id}}$ is $1/(2\pi)^d$. When $c_{t,\underline{0}}^{\mathrm{e,id}} = 1/(2\pi)^d$, the d-dimensional integral of the trigonometric polynomial over the hypertorus $\mathbb{T}^d$ is 1.

For the SqFF, we use the fact that the integral of the square of a function described by a Fourier coefficient tensor over $\mathbb{T}^d$ is equal to the sum of the squared entries of the tensor. We can either derive this using steps similar to those in the univariate case in Section 6.2.3 or by using the fact that the multidimensional trigonometric system is a complete orthogonal sequence of the separable Hilbert space (i.e., a Hilbert space with a countable orthogonal basis) $L^2(\mathbb{T}^d)$, allowing us to invoke the Parseval relation [KS13, Section 2.7.1]. The integral of the function represented by $\breve{\mathbf{C}}_t^{\mathrm{e,sqrt}}$ is thus $(2\pi)^d \|\breve{\mathbf{C}}_t^{\mathrm{e,sqrt}}\|_{\mathrm{F}}^2$ (the additional scaling factor $(2\pi)^d$ is necessary because our basis functions are not normalized in $L^2(\mathbb{T}^d)$). We use the shorthand $\|\breve{\mathbf{C}}_t^{\mathrm{e,sqrt}}\|_{\mathrm{F}}^2$ for the sum of the squared entries of the tensor. The lower index F is used because the operation can be seen as the Frobenius norm for tensor-valued arguments. By dividing all the coefficients by the square root of the integral, i.e., $\sqrt{(2\pi)^d}\|\breve{\mathbf{C}}_t^{\mathrm{e,sqrt}}\|_{\mathrm{F}}$, we can ensure that the squared Frobenius norm of the resulting coefficient tensor $\|\mathbf{C}_t^{\mathrm{e,sqrt}}\|_{\mathrm{F}}^2$ is $1/(2\pi)^d$. Thus, the density represented by $\mathbf{C}_t^{\mathrm{e,sqrt}}$ integrates to 1 when integrated over $\mathbb{T}^d$.

6.3.3 Prediction Step for the Topology-Aware Identity Model with Additive Noise

In the prediction step of the IFF, only two minor changes to the approach in the univariate are required. First, the Hadamard product is calculated of d-dimensional tensors instead of vectors. Second, the result has to be multiplied with $(2\pi)^d$ instead of 2π to ensure the normalization.

For the prediction step of the SqFF, the discrete convolution is now d-dimensional and the Hadamard product changes as in the IFF. We need to use a d-dimensional IDFT to obtain the values of f_{t+1}^{p} on a grid on $\mathbb{T}^d$. After taking the square root of all function values, a d-dimensional DFT is used to obtain the Fourier coefficient tensor $\mathring{\mathbf{C}}_{t+1}^{\text{p,sqrt}}$. We then truncate the tensor along all dimensions to obtain the Fourier coefficient tensor $\breve{\mathbf{C}}_{t+1}^{\text{p,sqrt}}$ representing an unnormalized density. After the normalization, which is performed as in the update step using a division by $\sqrt{(2\pi)^d}\|\breve{\mathbf{C}}_{t+1}^{\text{p,sqrt}}\|_{\text{F}}$, we obtain the Fourier coefficient tensor of the prediction result $\mathbf{C}_{t+1}^{\text{p,sqrt}}$.

6.3.4 General Prediction Step

For the multivariate variant of the general prediction step, all operations of the prediction step defined in Section 6.2.4 have to be adjusted to the higher dimensionality of the space. Both $\mathbf{C}_t^{\text{T,id}}$ and $\mathbf{C}_t^{\text{T,sqrt}}$ are now $2d$-dimensional, which means, e.g., that $\mathbf{C}_t^{\text{T,id}}$ is a four-dimensional tensor when f_t^{e} is bivariate and $\mathbf{C}_t^{\text{T,id}}$ is six-dimensional when f_t^{e} is trivariate. The $2d$-dimensional tensors have $(2k_{\text{max}}+1)^{2d}$ entries. The first d dimensions correspond to the d dimensions of $\underline{x}_{t+1}$, and the second d dimensions correspond to the d dimensions of $\underline{x}_t$. For the convolution of $\mathbf{C}_t^{\text{e,id}}$ and $\mathbf{C}_t^{\text{T,id}}$ to work correctly, $\mathbf{C}_t^{\text{e,id}}$ must then be reshaped into the form of a

$$\underbrace{1\times\cdots\times 1}_{d\text{ times}}\times\underbrace{(2k_{\text{max}}+1)\times\cdots\times(2k_{\text{max}}+1)}_{d\text{ times}}$$

tensor with the last d dimensions corresponding to the dimensions of $\underline{x}_t$.

The non-truncated convolution result is also a $2d$-dimensional tensor. For the IFF, the $2d$-dimensional discrete convolution of $\mathbf{C}_t^{\mathrm{e,id}}$ and $\mathbf{C}_t^{\mathrm{T,id}}$ only has to be followed by a truncation that corresponds to a marginalization of all dimensions describing $\underline{x}_t$. By calculating only the entries of the tensor with indices 0 for the last d dimensions and multiplying the result with $(2\pi)^d$, the convolution can be combined with the truncation.

For the SqFF, all steps are also the higher-dimensional analogues to the steps in the univariate case. First, a $2d$-dimensional discrete convolution of $\mathbf{C}_t^{\mathrm{T,sqrt}}$ and $\mathbf{C}_t^{\mathrm{e,sqrt}}$ (with the dimensions as described above) is calculated. Then, the result $\check{\mathbf{C}}_t^{\mathrm{j,sqrt}}$ is truncated along all $2d$ dimensions, yielding the tensor $\check{\mathbf{C}}_t^{\mathrm{j,sqrt}}$ describing the square root of a potentially unnormalized density. Afterward, a $2d$-dimensional convolution is used to obtain the coefficient tensor $\mathring{\mathbf{C}}_t^{\mathrm{j,id}}$ representing the joint density f_t^{j}. The marginalization is then performed as in the IFF. After the $2d$-dimensional IDFT, the square root is taken and a d-dimensional DFT is used to obtain the tensor $\mathring{\mathbf{C}}_{t+1}^{\mathrm{p,sqrt}}$. Afterward, $\mathring{\mathbf{C}}_{t+1}^{\mathrm{p,sqrt}}$ is truncated. Finally, we perform a normalization to calculate the tensor $\mathbf{C}_{t+1}^{\mathrm{p,sqrt}}$ describing a correctly normalized density from the result of the truncation $\check{\mathbf{C}}_{t+1}^{\mathrm{p,sqrt}}$. The normalization is performed by dividing all entries of $\check{\mathbf{C}}_{t+1}^{\mathrm{p,sqrt}}$ by $\sqrt{(2\pi)^d}\|\check{\mathbf{C}}_{t+1}^{\mathrm{p,sqrt}}\|_{\mathrm{F}}$.

When N is the number of coefficients in $\mathbf{C}_t^{\mathrm{e,id}}$, the computational complexity for performing the convolution of the two $2d$-dimensional tensors is in $O(N^2 \log N)$. However, as in the univariate case, this operation is not always required. For the IFF, an operation similar to the one explained in Remark 4 can be employed to perform the prediction step in $O(N^2)$. For the SqFF, we can proceed similarly as explained in Remark 5 if the transition density is time-invariant. The discrete convolution of $\mathbf{C}_t^{\mathrm{T,sqrt}}$ with itself is performed once at the beginning and the result is saved. The convolution of $\mathbf{C}_t^{\mathrm{e,sqrt}}$ with itself during run time is in $O(N \log N)$. Then, the convolution of the two tensors can be performed as in the IFF in $O(N^2)$. Thus, a complexity of $O(N^2)$ can also be attained for the SqFF for time-invariant transition densities.

6.4 Filters for the Unit Sphere

The spherical harmonics filters for the unit sphere are no straightforward generalizations of the filters for the unit circle, and thus, significant adaptations are required. As in the circular and hypertoroidal case, we present two variants. The first variant is the spherical harmonics identity filter (ISHF), which is based on directly approximating the density. The second variant is the spherical harmonics square root filter (SqSHF) [O2], in which the square root of the density is approximated. As in the filters for circular and hypertoroidal estimation problems, we ensure that the number of coefficients $N = (L+1)^2$ used to represent the densities is kept constant over time. For this, we ensure that the maximum degree L is not increased during prediction and update steps.

6.4.1 Approximating Densities on the Sphere

As in the hypertoroidal case, determining the spherical harmonic coefficients using numerical integration is computationally costly. In [DH94], the authors proved that if a function is band-limited (i.e., the coefficients are 0 for all degrees $l > L$), the function values on a finite set of grid points can be used to obtain all spherical harmonic coefficients. For this, an equiangular grid that is denser near the poles than on the equator is used and weights are employed to compensate for this. When the function is not band-limited, we only obtain an approximation of the coefficients. The effect is similar to the approximation error that occurs when using a DFT for functions on the circle or hypertorus that are not band-limited.

The fastest known solution that returns the (disregarding numerical imprecision) precise spherical harmonic coefficients is in $O(N(\log N)^2)$ [HRKM03]. Furthermore, fast approximations in $O(N \log N)$ exist [ST02][2]. The implementation of our filters is based on the spherical

[2] To avoid confusion, please note that in [ST02], N denotes the maximum degree and not the total number of coefficients.

harmonic transform implemented by the authors of [SDW06]. For azimuthally symmetric functions, meaning functions that are rotationally symmetric around the line going through the origin and $\begin{bmatrix}0 & 0 & 1\end{bmatrix}^\top$, all coefficients c_l^m with $m \neq 0$ are zero [KS13, Section 7.5.3]. Formulae for the spherical harmonic coefficients of the von Mises–Fisher distribution are provided in Appendix B.2.

In the hypertoroidal case, we have used that functions can be easily shifted based on their Fourier coefficients. For functions described by spherical harmonic coefficients, a rotation according to a rotation matrix can be implemented based on the spherical harmonic coefficients [BFB97][3]. However, straightforward implementations of this approach are costly. A different approach is more efficient when fast transformations are available. First, we generate function values on a grid using the inverse spherical harmonic transform. Then, we rotate the grid points. Finally, we apply a spherical harmonic transform on the function values that respects the new grid to obtain the spherical harmonic coefficients of the rotation result. For the hypertorus, the shifting operation is in $O(N)$. Thus, we were able to initially transform functions (e.g., the likelihood) once and shift them afterward in $O(N)$. Since the rotation operation for the spherical harmonic coefficients involves a spherical harmonic transform and its inverse, it can be less expensive to evaluate the functions on all grid points in every time step. Nonetheless, being able to rotate densities is useful for a system model introduced later.

[3] The paper addresses the rotation for real spherical harmonics. However, it is also possible to implement the approach for complex spherical harmonics.

6.4.2 Update Step

We again begin with the filter that directly works with the approximation of the density and then present the update step of the filter based on the square root of the density. Performing the update step using formulae that directly use the spherical harmonic coefficients is expensive. Therefore, we propose an update step that is an analogue to the alternative update step for the IFF and SqFF presented in Appendix C. As in the circular case, similar update steps are used for the two representations.

Update Step of the ISHF In theory, the spherical harmonic coefficients of the multiplication of two functions given by their spherical harmonic coefficients can be calculated directly using the coefficients of the individual functions. A multiplication approach merely based on the coefficients is introduced in Appendix D. While we do not use the formula presented in Appendix D, it allows for the insight that coefficients up to degree $2L$ may be required for representing the multiplication result when both the prior density and the likelihood are approximated using coefficients up to degree L. This insight will be useful for the prediction step of the SqSHF.

To obtain an efficient implementation, we proceed as in the alternative approach to the update step of the Fourier filters explained in Appendix C. As illustrated in Figure 6.10, we first invoke a fast inverse spherical harmonic transform and then perform a Hadamard product of the function values on the grid. Then, we have function values of the unnormalized product on a grid. Afterward, we use a fast transformation to obtain the spherical harmonic coefficients. A spherical harmonic transform of the likelihood is not required in this case. Using the fast transformations, the multiplication of the densities is in $O(N(\log N)^2)$ or $O(N \log N)$, depending on whether a precise or an approximate transformation is used. Further performance improvements can be achieved by staying in the grid representation when performing multiple update steps without prediction steps in between. As in the alternative update step for the Fourier filters described in Appendix C.1, we accept that the number of grid points may not be sufficient to represent the unnormalized posterior density $\breve{f}_t^{\mathrm{e}}$ even if the number of grid points was sufficient to precisely represent f_t^{P} and f_t^{L}. If both f_t^{P} and f_t^{L} can be represented precisely using spherical harmonics up to degree L, we could pad $\mathbf{C}_t^{\mathrm{p,id}}$ with zeros to degree $2L$ before applying the transformation. If a precise transformation is used, we would obtain sufficient grid points to precisely represent the unnormalized multiplication result $\breve{f}_t^{\mathrm{e}}$.

For the normalization, we consider how the integral over the spherical harmonic representation can be calculated. All spherical harmonics except Y_0^0 integrate to 0 when integrated over the whole unit sphere. Since Y_0^0 is $1/\sqrt{4\pi}$ everywhere, we can determine the integral by multiplying the coefficient of degree and order zero with $1/\sqrt{4\pi}$ and the surface area of the unit sphere 4π to calculate the integral. Thus, the integral of the multiplication result is $\sqrt{4\pi}\breve{c}_{t,0}^{\mathrm{e,id},0}$. By dividing all the coefficients by $\sqrt{4\pi}\breve{c}_{t,0}^{\mathrm{e,id},0}$, we can ensure that the coefficient $\breve{c}_{t,0}^{\mathrm{e,id},0}$ of the resulting matrix $\mathbf{C}_t^{\mathrm{e,id}}$ is $\sqrt{4\pi}$, which ensures that the density integrates to one.

Update Step of the SqSHF For the update step of the SqFF, we proceed similarly as for the ISHF. As illustrated in Figure 6.11, we first generate function values of $\sqrt{f_t^{\mathrm{P}}}$ on a grid using an inverse spherical harmonic transform. The square root of the likelihood $\sqrt{f_t^{\mathrm{L}}}$ is then evaluated at all grid points. The multiplication yields the function values of the square root of the unnormalized posterior density $\sqrt{\breve{f}_t^{\mathrm{e}}}$ on a grid.

For the normalization, we invoke the Parseval relation for spherical harmonics [KS13, Section 7.3.8] to know that the reconstructed density integrates to

$$\left\|\breve{\mathbf{C}}_t^{\mathrm{e,sqrt}}\right\|_{\mathrm{F}}^2 = \sum_{l=0}^{L}\sum_{m=-l}^{l}\left|c_{t,l}^{\mathrm{e,sqrt},m}\right|^2 .$$

To ensure the function is normalized, we thus only have to divide all the coefficients by $\|\breve{\mathbf{C}}_t^{\mathrm{e,sqrt}}\|_{\mathrm{F}}$.

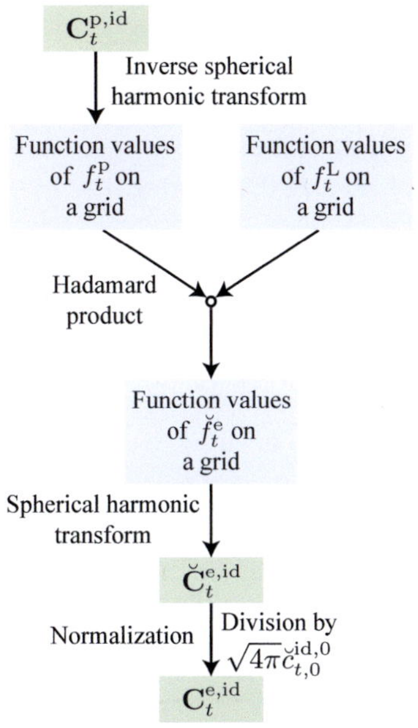

Figure 6.10.: Update step of the ISHF.

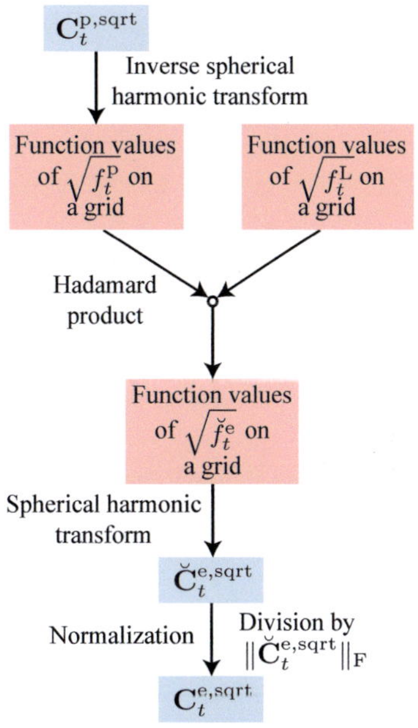

Figure 6.11.: Update step of the SqSHF.

6.4.3 Prediction Step

Because there is no established easier variant of the prediction step on $\mathbb{S}^2$, we start with the more general case to derive a simple prediction step for the spherical harmonics filter. However, we only use the general formulation using the transition density as our starting point and do not derive a prediction step for arbitrary transition densities as in Sections 6.2.4 and 6.3.4 because it would require, among others, a basis for $\mathbb{S}^2 \times \mathbb{S}^2$ to approximate the transition density. In $\mathbb{S}^2$, (5.4) becomes

$$f_{t+1}^{\mathrm{P}}(\underline{x}_{t+1}|\hat{\underline{z}}_1,\ldots,\hat{\underline{z}}_t) = \int_{\mathbb{S}^2} f_t^{\mathrm{T}}(\underline{x}_{t+1}|\underline{x}_t) f_t^{\mathrm{e}}(\underline{x}_t|\hat{\underline{z}}_1,\ldots,\hat{\underline{z}}_t)\, d\underline{x}_t \ .$$

It is not possible to define an easy model that simply adds a second random vector $\underline{\boldsymbol{w}}_t$ to $\underline{\boldsymbol{x}}_t$ as it is unclear how this addition would be realized on $\mathbb{S}^2$. This challenge is also reflected in the fact that there are multiple interpretations of the convolution on the unit sphere. Rather, there are different types of convolutions [KS13, Section 9], none of which is a perfect analogue to the convolution on a real vector space.

Prediction Step of the ISHF We shall now define an easy system model and derive requirements for suitable transition densities. To obtain an easy system model, we assume that all points $\underline{x}_{t+1}$ with an identical distance to $\underline{x}_t$ have the same probability density $f_t^{\mathrm{T}}(\underline{x}_{t+1}|\underline{x}_t)$. Under this assumption, the distance between $\underline{x}_t$ and $\underline{x}_{t+1}$ is sufficient to calculate the transition density.

A possible transition density that satisfies the assumption is based on the von Mises–Fisher density (5.10) and is given by

$$f_t^{\mathrm{T}}(\underline{x}_{t+1}|\underline{x}_t) = f_{\mathrm{VMF}}(\underline{x}_{t+1}; \underline{\mu} = \underline{x}_t, \kappa_t^{\mathrm{T}}) \ . \tag{6.8}$$

To validate that the von Mises–Fisher density fulfills the desired properties, we write out the formula for the density as

$$f_{\mathrm{VMF}}(\underline{x}_{t+1}; \underline{\mu} = \underline{x}_t, \kappa_t) = c(\kappa_t) \mathrm{e}^{\kappa_t \underline{x}_t^\top \underline{x}_{t+1}} \ .$$

As intended, this formula only depends on the distance between the two points $\underline{x}_t$ and $\underline{x}_{t+1}$ as $\underline{x}_t^\top \underline{x}_{t+1} = (\underline{x}_t \cdot \underline{x}_{t+1})$ is the cosine of the angular distance (5.17). As the arccosine is monotonically decreasing, the dot product without the arccosine is monotonically decreasing with increasing distance. Thus, the density decreases as the distance between $\underline{x}_t$ and $\underline{x}_{t+1}$ increases.

The transition density based on the von Mises–Fisher density thus has the commonly desired property that it favors points $\underline{x}_{t+1}$ that are closer to $\underline{x}_t$ over points that are further away. However, this property is not essential, and we could use any other density that is rotationally symmetric around the vector going through the origin and the mean direction, such as the Watson distribution [Wat65].

As in [THBM96], we are left with a function that only depends on the dot product between the two vectors. By considering the scalar result of the dot product as the input of a new function $h_0 \in L^2([-1,1])$, the convolution can be described using a function of scalar argument. This leads us to one of the types of convolutions on the sphere [KS13, Section 9.4] with

$$f_{t+1}^{\mathrm{P}}(\underline{x}_{t+1}|\hat{\underline{z}}_1,\ldots,\hat{\underline{z}}_t) = \sqrt{\frac{1}{2\pi}} \int_{\mathbb{S}^2} h_0(\underline{x}_{t+1} \cdot \underline{x}_t) f(\underline{x}_t)\, d\underline{x}_t \ .$$

The first step to finding a way to calculate the convolution using spherical harmonic coefficients is to interpret $h_0(\underline{x}_{t+1} \cdot \underline{x}_t)$ as an azimuthally symmetric function in $L^2(\mathbb{S}^2)$ [KS13, Section 9.4.1]. In the case of the von Mises–Fisher distribution, the azimuthally symmetric function can be written as

$$f_t^{\underline{\boldsymbol{w}}}(\underline{w}_t) = f_{\mathrm{VMF}}(\underline{w}_t; \underline{\mu} = \left[0,\, 0,\, 1\right]^\top, \kappa_t^{\mathrm{T}}) \ ,$$

which we shall refer to as our system noise density. Using the spherical harmonic coefficients $c_{t,l}^{\underline{\boldsymbol{w}},0}$ of degree l and order 0 of $f_t^{\underline{\boldsymbol{w}}}$ (all other coefficients are zero as $f_t^{\underline{\boldsymbol{w}}}$ is azimuthally symmetric [KS13, Section 7.5.3]), we can obtain the spherical harmonic coefficients $c_{t+1,l}^{\mathrm{p},m}$ of f_{t+1}^{P} according to [KS13, Section 9.4.1][4]

$$c_{t+1,l}^{\mathrm{p},m} = \sqrt{\frac{4\pi}{2l+1}} c_{t,l}^{\mathrm{e},m} c_{t,l}^{\underline{\boldsymbol{w}},0} \ .$$

Thus, the prediction step can be performed as illustrated in Figure 6.12.

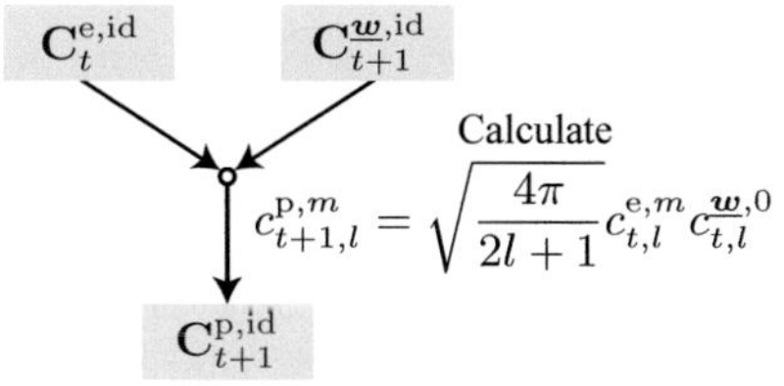

Figure 6.12.: Prediction step of the ISHF.

[4] It should be noted that this formula is essentially equivalent to the formulae obtained for convolutions that are defined differently, e.g., in [DH94, DP10]. These convolutions can be interpreted to involve an integral over $SO(3)$ [KS13, Section 9.3].

When the spherical harmonic coefficients of $f_t^{\boldsymbol{w}}$ and f_t^{e} are given, the effort to calculate the N spherical harmonic coefficients of f_{t+1}^{p} is thus in $O(N)$. If the spherical harmonic coefficients of $f_t^{\boldsymbol{w}}$ need to be calculated, the additional cost of $O(N(\log N)^2)$ for the transformation is the dominant term for the run time. However, faster run times could be achieved by employing a transformation that takes advantage of the azimuthal symmetry or by approximating the coefficients using the formula provided in Appendix B.2. Further, if the system noise term is i.i.d., it only has to be transformed once.

The model we just presented can be seen as an analogue to the random walk model on the real plane. We can also realize a prediction step for the more general model

$$f_t^{\mathrm{T}}(\underline{x}_{t+1}|\underline{x}_t) = f_{\mathrm{VMF}}(\underline{x}_{t+1}; \underline{\mu} = \mathbf{Q}_t \underline{x}_t, \kappa_t^{\mathrm{T}})$$

involving a rotation matrix $\mathbf{Q}_t \in SO(3)$, which was described in [KGH16b, Equation (6)]. To apply the additional rotation, we have to rotate the density f_t^{e} before the convolution or, equivalently, rotate the result f_{t+1}^{p}. The rotation can be performed as described in Section 6.4.1.

Prediction Step of the SqSHF For the square root variant of the prediction step illustrated in Figure 6.13, we first obtain the coefficients representing the actual density. Unlike in the hypertoroidal case, we cannot square the density using an easy operation on the coefficients. Therefore, we perform the squaring using transformations. As explained in Appendix D, if two functions are approximated up to degree L, coefficients up to degree $2L$ may be nonzero for the multiplication result. Likewise, when squaring a function, higher order coefficients are necessary to represent the precise result. To obtain a sufficient number of grid points, we first pad the coefficient matrices $\mathbf{C}_t^{\mathrm{e,sqrt}}$ and $\mathbf{C}_t^{\boldsymbol{w},\mathrm{sqrt}}$ with zeros to degree $2L$. Afterward, we perform the precise fast inverse spherical harmonic transform to obtain the function values of $\sqrt{f_t^{\mathrm{e}}}$ and $\sqrt{f_t^{\boldsymbol{w}}}$ on a grid. The individual function values are then squared.

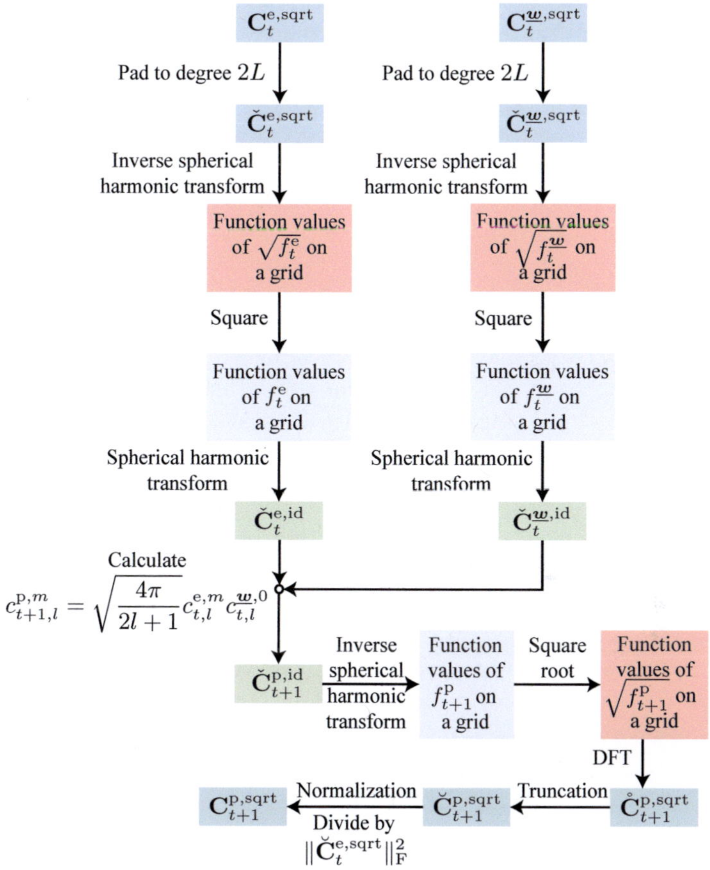

Figure 6.13.: Prediction step of the SqSHF.

Since we have used sufficient grid points to avoid introducing an approximation error in the squaring operation, we can then obtain the matrices $\check{\mathbf{C}}_t^{\mathrm{e,id}}$ and $\check{\mathbf{C}}_t^{\underline{\boldsymbol{w}},\mathrm{id}}$ representing the same densities as $\mathbf{C}_t^{\mathrm{e,sqrt}}$ and $\mathbf{C}_t^{\underline{\boldsymbol{w}},\mathrm{sqrt}}$ using an exact spherical harmonic transform. Due to the equality of the densities represented by the coefficient matrices, the densities described by $\check{\mathbf{C}}_t^{\mathrm{e,id}}$ and $\check{\mathbf{C}}_t^{\underline{\boldsymbol{w}},\mathrm{id}}$ are nonnegative on the entire domain. If the system noise is i.i.d., $\check{\mathbf{C}}_t^{\underline{\boldsymbol{w}},\mathrm{id}}$ can be reused. We then perform the convolution-like operation as for the ISHF. As the formula provides the exact result, the matrix $\check{\mathbf{C}}_{t+1}^{\mathrm{p,id}}$ also describes a nonnegative function. Using the inverse spherical harmonic transform, we obtain values of f_{t+1}^{p} on a grid. We then calculate the square root of these values and perform a spherical harmonic transform. Because the degree of the resulting approximation may not be sufficient to precisely represent the square root, an approximation error is introduced. The resulting matrix $\mathring{\mathbf{C}}_{t+1}^{\mathrm{p,sqrt}}$ contains coefficients up to degree $2L$ and may not represent a normalized density due to the approximation error. We first perform a truncation and then normalize the result afterward. Since the precise spherical harmonic transform is required to ensure the nonnegativity of the result, the prediction step of the SqSHF is in $O(N(\log N)^2)$.

6.5 Evaluations

In this section, we compare the proposed filters with alternative approaches in different scenarios. For the ISHF and SqSHF, a tracking scenario on the sphere is examined. For the IFF and SqFF, we consider three different bivariate and one trivariate scenario. We refer the reader to [O11] for an evaluation of the SqFF for circular scenarios. At least 3000 runs were performed for all filters for each scenario.

In each scenario, the respective system is simulated for multiple time steps. The filter results are evaluated at the last time step of each run. We only consider the quality at the last time step to reduce the influence of the initial prior density and to show the performance of the filters when they are in their typical predict–update cycles. The Fourier filters could be compared with each other based on the quality of the approximation of the posterior density. However, such an evaluation would not allow a comparison with the particle filter because there is no established way to obtain a continuous density from the samples of a particle filter on a hypertorus or unit sphere. Further, deriving an approximation of the ground truth of the posterior density using numerical integration would become very costly for multiple time steps because the integrals of the Chapman–Kolmogorov equation would have to be nested. Therefore, we limit ourselves to evaluating the quality of the point estimate of the state.

The point estimates of the filters using continuous densities are derived by calculating the mean direction of the density. For the particle filter, the particles are interpreted as weighted samples, of which the mean direction is determined. We use distance measures as explained in Section 5.2.3 to assess the accuracy of the estimates. The distance d_0 is used for the hypertoroidal scenarios, and d_{ang} is used for the spherical scenario. The individual distances are then combined into a single measure of error by taking the mean. Since we are taking an average over the error of multiple runs in a Bayesian estimation problem, the error will not approach 0 for increasing quality of the estimator. Rather, the error will approach the average error that an estimator would attain if it was able to calculate the mean direction based on the true posterior density.

We provide three plots for each scenario. In the first plot, we display the error depending on the number of coefficients or particles used. For simplicity, we refer to both the number of particles and the number of coefficients in the Fourier and spherical harmonics filters as the number of parameters. For the IFF and SqFF, we always use tensors with sizes of $2k_{\text{max}} + 1$ along all dimensions. For the ISHF and SqSHF, we vary the maximum degree L and always use all coefficients up to the specified degree. The number of coefficients N can thus be written according to $N = (2k_{\text{max}} + 1)^d$ for the hypertoroidal scenarios and $N = (L + 1)^2$ for the spherical scenario. On the axes of the plots, we show the total number of coefficients N. For the particle filter, we provide the number of particles used.

In the second plot, we present the run times for all configurations. For all filters, we use the Matlab implementations that we have made available as part of libDirectional [O13, O17]. All run times were measured on a laptop with an Intel Core i7-5500U processor, 12 GB of RAM, running Matlab 2018a on Windows 10. The run times given are the average run times per time step, including both the prediction and update step (no prediction step is performed at the last time step). The computational effort to initialize the filter, e.g., the time to approximate an i.i.d. system noise term using Fourier coefficients, is not included in the run time per time step.

In the third plot, we combine the information of the first two plots to provide a fair comparison of the approaches by plotting the error over run time. For the end user, the number of parameters is not crucial (assuming memory efficiency is not an issue) and only the error and the run time are of interest. This particularly holds true for real-time tasks as encountered in optical belt sorting.

6.5.1 Hypertoroidal Scenarios

We first describe three bivariate scenarios on the torus. The first scenario is based on the topology-aware identity model with additive noise as both the system and the measurement model. In the second scenario, we use a nonlinear measurement model. In the third scenario, a nonlinear system model is used. After the bivariate scenarios, we describe one trivariate scenario. For all scenarios on the hypertorus, the system was simulated for 10 time steps.

6.5.1.1 Bivariate Scenario with Topology-Aware Identity Models

The initial prior density used in this scenario is

$$\underline{\boldsymbol{x}}_0 \sim f_{\mathrm{WN}}\left(\underline{x}; \begin{bmatrix}1\\1\end{bmatrix}, \begin{bmatrix}1 & 0\\0 & 1\end{bmatrix}\right) .$$

As the system model, we use a topology-aware identity model with the i.i.d. additive noise term $\underline{\boldsymbol{w}}_t$ distributed according to

$$\underline{\boldsymbol{w}}_t \sim f_{\mathrm{WN}}\left(\underline{w}_t; \begin{bmatrix}0\\0\end{bmatrix}, \begin{bmatrix}4 & 3.6\\3.6 & 4\end{bmatrix}\right) .$$

The measurement model is also a topology-aware identity model with additive noise. The i.i.d. measurement noise $\underline{\boldsymbol{v}}_t$ is distributed according to a mixture of four wrapped normal distributions and can be described by

$$\begin{aligned}
\underline{\boldsymbol{v}}_t \sim \frac{1}{4}\Bigg(& f_{\mathrm{WN}}\left(\underline{v}_t; \begin{bmatrix}0.25\\0.25\end{bmatrix}, \mathbf{C}_t^{\underline{v}}\right) + f_{\mathrm{WN}}\left(\underline{v}_t; \begin{bmatrix}2\pi - 0.25\\0.25\end{bmatrix}, \mathbf{C}_t^{\underline{v}}\right) \\
& + f_{\mathrm{WN}}\left(\underline{v}_t; \begin{bmatrix}0.25\\2\pi - 0.25\end{bmatrix}, \mathbf{C}_t^{\underline{v}}\right) + f_{\mathrm{WN}}\left(\underline{v}_t; \begin{bmatrix}2\pi - 0.25\\2\pi - 0.25\end{bmatrix}, \mathbf{C}_t^{\underline{v}}\right)\Bigg) , \\
\mathbf{C}_t^{\underline{v}} = & \begin{bmatrix}1 & 0.5\\0.5 & 1\end{bmatrix} .
\end{aligned}$$

Run-time-wise, the scenario is well suited for the use of the Fourier filters. For the topology-aware identity model with i.i.d. additive noise terms, the system noise term and the likelihood only need to be transformed once. Only a shifting operation (6.5) is required for the coefficients of the likelihood to adapt them to the actual measurement. Due to the close spacing of the modes, the density is still unimodal. Therefore, it is also suited to the use of the bivariate wrapped normal filter, which we include in our analysis.

In our plot of the error over number of parameters in Figure 6.14a, we present the performance of the bivariate wrapped normal filter as a horizontal line because its number of parameters cannot be varied. Further, its results are a good baseline for the evaluation of the other filters. While the results of the bivariate wrapped normal filter are suboptimal, the estimation quality surpasses that of a particle filter with 2000 particles. The Fourier filters, however, achieve a better estimation quality than the bivariate wrapped normal filter using only 25 ($k_{\mathrm{max}} = 5$)

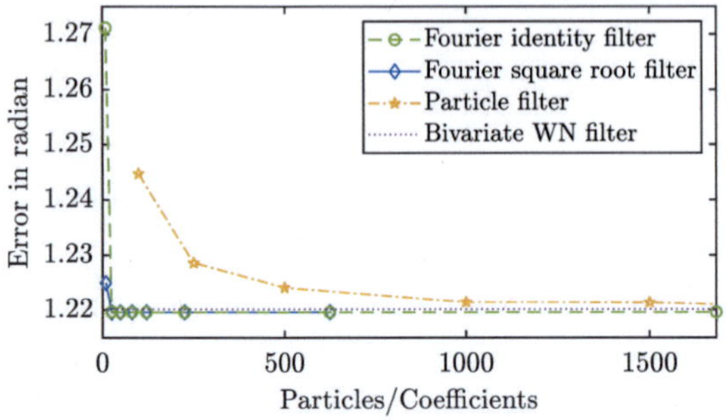

(a) Error over number of parameters. As no additional parameters can be used for the bivariate wrapped normal filter, its results are shown as a straight line.

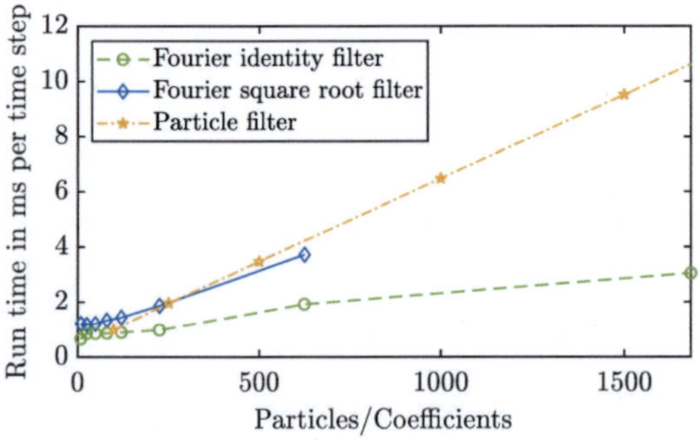

(b) Time over number of parameters.

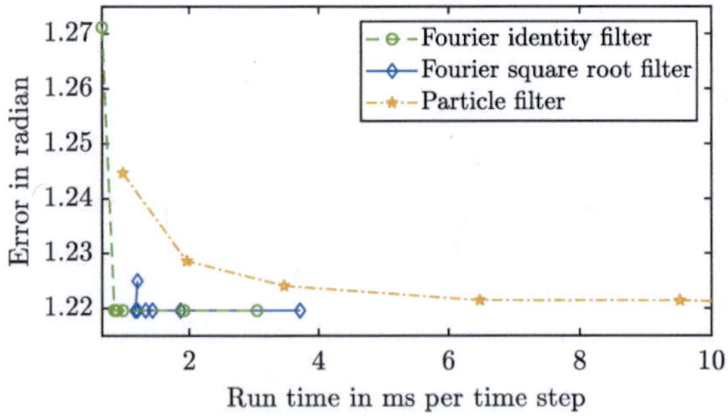

(c) Error over run time.

Figure 6.14.: Evaluation results for the bivariate scenario with identity models as the system and measurement models.

coefficients. The results of the Fourier filters do not change more than 10^{-4} when improving the number of coefficients beyond 25. This may indicate that the mean directions determined by the filters are almost identical to the mean direction of the true posterior density.

As presented in Figure 6.14b, the computation time per time step increases approximately linearly with the number of parameters for the Fourier filters and the particle filter. For 1681 ($k_{\text{max}} = 41$) coefficients, the Fourier coefficient matrices contain values in the order of 10^{-20} for the highest and lowest indices. We believe the implementation of the convolution in Matlab takes advantage of this, which explains why the computational effort of the IFF increases slower between $k_{\text{max}} = 25$ and $k_{\text{max}} = 41$ than between $k_{\text{max}} = 15$ and $k_{\text{max}} = 25$. To improve the clarity of the plots involving run times, we have omitted the bivariate wrapped normal filter, which had a run time of approximately 41 ms on average.

In our plot of the error over run time in Figure 6.14c, the superiority of the two Fourier filters over the particle filter is evident as a far better estimation quality is attained at equal run times. The IFF and SqFF are also superior to the bivariate wrapped normal filter, which was slow to achieve its results. As the particle filter neither surpasses the estimation quality nor the run time of the bivariate wrapped normal filter, we cannot compare the two filters on a run time basis using our current evaluation results. In this scenario, the IFF performs slightly better than the SqFF as the IFF needed less than one millisecond to attain a quality that the SqFF achieved in over one millisecond.

6.5.1.2 Bivariate Scenario with a Nonlinear Measurement Model

We now address a more difficult scenario with a nonlinear measurement model. In this scenario, the Fourier filters are expected to have longer run times as the Fourier coefficients for the likelihood have to be determined in every time step. In this scenario, two joint angles of a robotic arm, as illustrated in Figure 6.15, are estimated. The density of the initial state that is used to draw the initial true states and initialize the filters is given by

$$\underline{\boldsymbol{x}}_0 \sim f_{\mathrm{WN}}\left(\underline{x}_0; \begin{bmatrix}1\\1\end{bmatrix}, \begin{bmatrix}0.2 & 0\\0 & 0.2\end{bmatrix}\right) .$$

To estimate the joint angles, only one point on the end effector (shown in red) can be observed in a two-dimensional view from the side. We simulate the two-dimensional position measurements and perturb them by normally distributed noise. The perturbed measurements can thus potentially attain any value in $\mathbb{R}^2$. The measurement equation is given by

$$\underline{\boldsymbol{z}}_t = \begin{bmatrix}\cos(\boldsymbol{x}_{t,1})\\\sin(\boldsymbol{x}_{t,2})\end{bmatrix} l_1 + \begin{bmatrix}\cos(\boldsymbol{x}_{t,1}+\boldsymbol{x}_{t,2})\\\sin(\boldsymbol{x}_{t,1}+\boldsymbol{x}_{t,2})\end{bmatrix} l_2 + \underline{\boldsymbol{v}}_t .$$

For our simulation, we set $l_1 = 1.25$, $l_2 = 1.5$, and

$$\underline{\boldsymbol{v}}_t \sim \mathcal{N}\left(\underline{v}_t; \begin{bmatrix}0\\0\end{bmatrix}, \begin{bmatrix}0.2 & 0\\0 & 0.2\end{bmatrix}\right) .$$

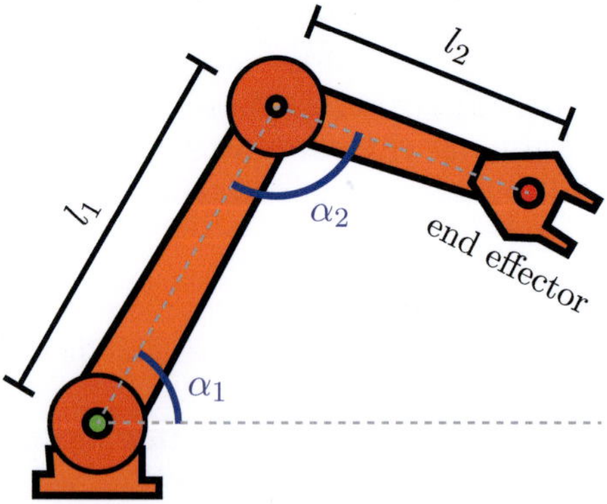

Figure 6.15.: Illustration of the robot arm simulated for the evaluation (from [O6]).

As the system model, we use a topology-aware identity model with the i.i.d. additive noise term

$$\underline{\boldsymbol{w}}_t \sim f_{\mathrm{WN}}\left(\underline{w}_t; \begin{bmatrix}0\\0\end{bmatrix}, \begin{bmatrix}0.2 & 0\\ 0 & 0.2\end{bmatrix}\right) .$$

In this scenario, the Fourier filters require more coefficients to achieve their optimal performance. Except for low numbers of parameters, the IFF and SqFF are superior to the particle filter for equal numbers of parameters (see Figure 6.16a). The run time plot in Figure 6.16b indicates that the SqFF is slower than the particle filter, while the IFF is faster for some configurations.

In our comparison of the error over run time in Figure 6.16c, we can see the particle performs well for low run times. However, the estimation quality of the Fourier filters with only 2 ms run time per step is unmatched even by a particle filter requiring more than 5 ms per time step. On a run time basis, the IFF performs better than the SqFF in this scenario.

6.5.1.3 Bivariate Scenario with a Nonlinear System Model

In this subsubsection, we consider another challenging scenario for the Fourier filters. Our system model is based on the function

$$a_\rho(\alpha) = \pi \cdot \left(\sin\left(\frac{\mathrm{sign}(\alpha - \pi)}{2} \frac{|\alpha - \pi|^\rho}{\pi^{\rho-1}}\right) + 1\right) , \tag{6.9}$$

which is a continuous bijection on $[0, 2\pi)$ for every parameter ρ. The function has first been used in [GKH15] and is illustrated for different parameters in Figure 6.17.

For our bivariate evaluation scenario, we use the topology-aware nonlinear system model with additive noise (5.3) given by

$$\underline{\boldsymbol{x}}_{t+1} = \begin{bmatrix}a_{1.5}(\boldsymbol{x}_{t,1})\\ a_{2.0}(\boldsymbol{x}_{t,2})\end{bmatrix} + \underline{\boldsymbol{w}}_t , \quad \underline{\boldsymbol{w}}_t \sim f_{\mathrm{WN}}\left(\underline{w}_t; \begin{bmatrix}0\\0\end{bmatrix}, \begin{bmatrix}1 & -0.3\\ -0.3 & 1.5\end{bmatrix}\right) .$$

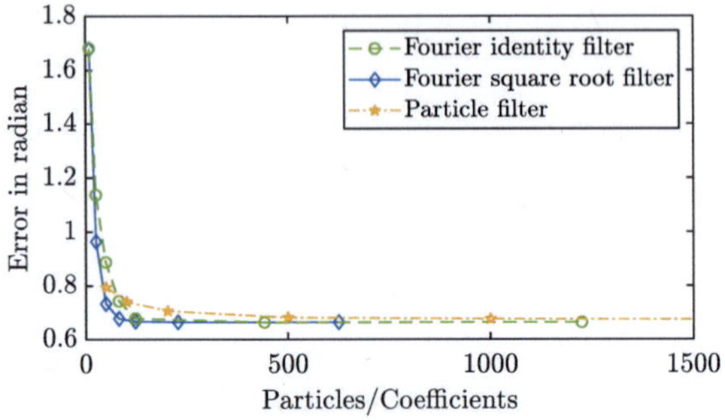

(a) Error over number of parameters.

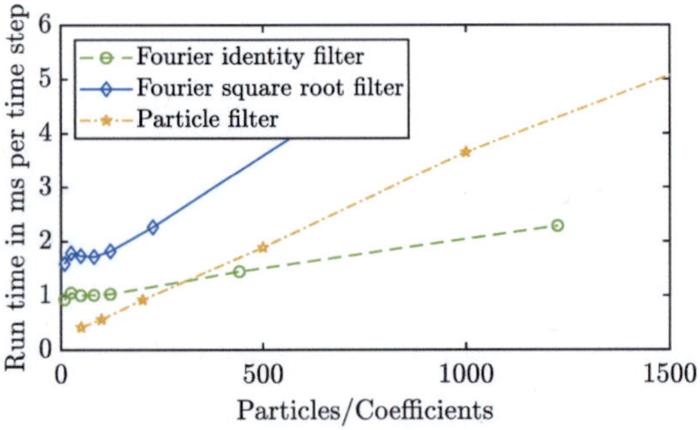

(b) Time over number of parameters.

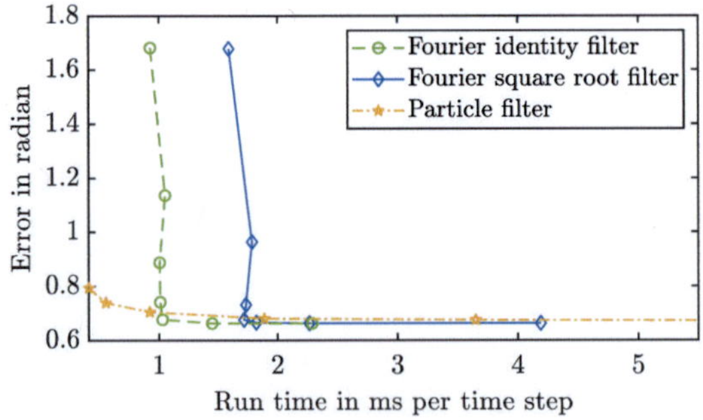

(c) Error over run time.

Figure 6.16.: Evaluation results for the bivariate scenario with a nonlinear measurement model.

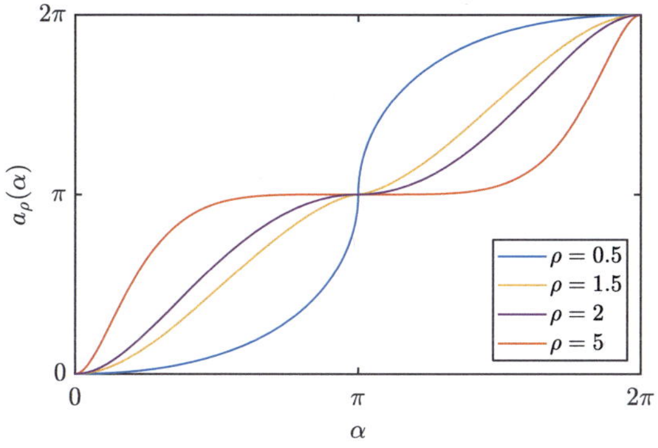

Figure 6.17.: Continuous bijection $a_\rho(\alpha)$ as defined in (6.9) for different values of ρ.

This system model requires the nonlinear prediction step of the Fourier filters as presented in Section 6.3.4. The initial state is drawn from a uniform distribution on the torus. For our measurement model, we use a topology-aware identity model with the i.i.d. additive noise term

$$\underline{\boldsymbol{v}}_t \sim f_{\mathrm{WN}}\left(\underline{v}_t; \begin{bmatrix}0\\0\end{bmatrix}, \begin{bmatrix}1 & 0.5\\0.5 & 1\end{bmatrix}\right) .$$

The evaluation results presented in Figure 6.18a indicate that the Fourier filters perform better than the particle filter on a per parameter basis. The increased run time of the general prediction step of the SqFF is apparent in the run times provided in Figure 6.18b. As the system model is time-invariant and the system noise is i.i.d., the Fourier coefficients of the transition density only have to be determined once. The IFF is much faster as only a d-dimensional part of the convolution result is required. For the SqFF, we use the approach described in Section 6.3.4 that yields a $2d$-dimensional tensor for the joint density as an intermediate result. The particle filter also requires more run time per particle than in the previous scenarios.

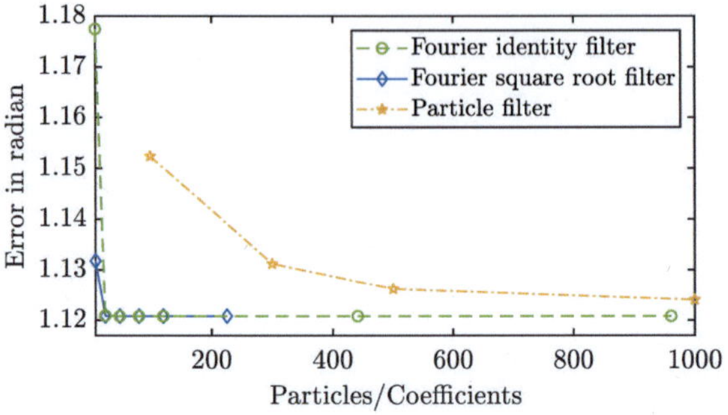

(a) Error over number of parameters.

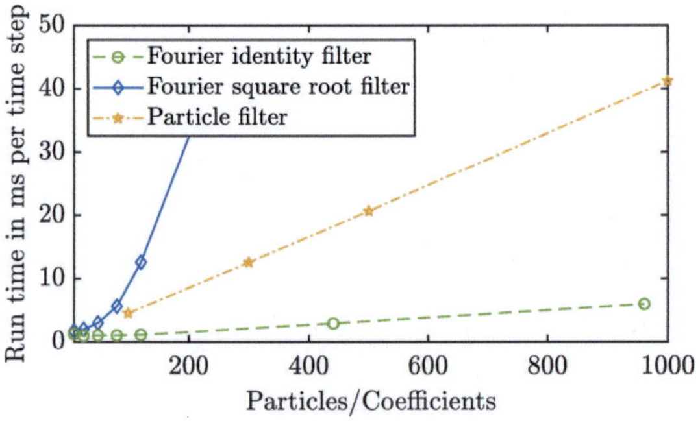

(b) Time over number of parameters.

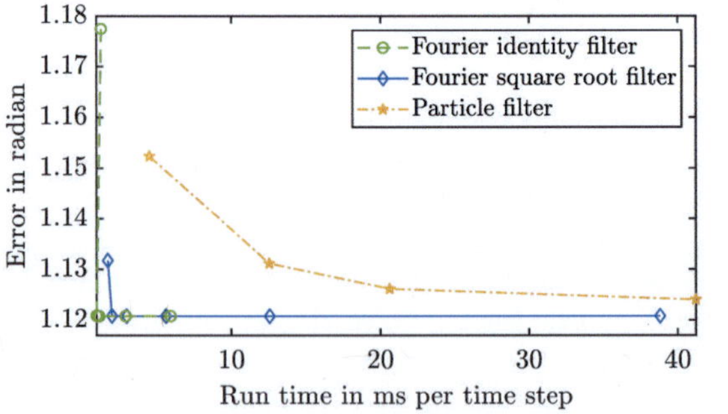

(c) Error over run time.

Figure 6.18.: Evaluation results for the bivariate scenario with a nonlinear system model.

In our comparison on a run time basis in Figure 6.18c, both Fourier filters are superior to the particle filter. Using less than 10 ms per time step, they reach a close to optimal performance that is not attained even by a particle filter using more than 40 ms per time step. While the SqFF is better than the IFF for the lowest parameterization of 9 coefficients, the IFF reaches its optimal estimation quality using less computation time.

6.5.1.4 Trivariate Scenario with Topology-Aware Identity Models

In our last scenario for the hypertorus, we evaluate the performance of the filters in a trivariate scenario. We use topology-aware identity models with i.i.d. additive noise terms as the system and measurement models. The state of the system and the filters are initialized according to

$$\underline{\boldsymbol{x}}_0 \sim f_{\mathrm{WN}}\left(\underline{x}_0; \begin{bmatrix}1\\1\\1\end{bmatrix}, \begin{bmatrix}1 & 0 & 0\\0 & 1 & 0\\0 & 0 & 1\end{bmatrix}\right) .$$

Both the system and measurement noise terms are distributed according to mixtures of trivariate wrapped normal distributions. The system noise used is

$$\begin{aligned}\underline{\boldsymbol{w}}_t \sim \frac{1}{2} f_{\mathrm{WN}}&\left(\underline{w}_t; \begin{bmatrix}0.5\\0.5\\0.5\end{bmatrix}, \begin{bmatrix}0.2 & 0.1 & 0.05\\0.1 & 0.15 & 0.03\\0.05 & 0.03 & 0.25\end{bmatrix}\right)\\ + \frac{1}{2} f_{\mathrm{WN}}&\left(\underline{w}_t; \begin{bmatrix}2\pi - 0.5\\2\pi - 0.5\\2\pi - 0.5\end{bmatrix}, \begin{bmatrix}0.2 & 0.1 & 0.05\\0.1 & 0.15 & 0.03\\0.05 & 0.03 & 0.25\end{bmatrix}\right)\end{aligned}$$

and the measurement noise is

$$\begin{aligned}\underline{\boldsymbol{v}}_t \sim \frac{1}{2} f_{\mathrm{WN}}&\left(\underline{v}_t; \begin{bmatrix}0.5\\0.5\\0.5\end{bmatrix}, \begin{bmatrix}0.25 & 0.05 & 0.03\\0.05 & 0.2 & 0.1\\0.03 & 0.1 & 0.15\end{bmatrix}\right)\\ + \frac{1}{2} f_{\mathrm{WN}}&\left(\underline{v}_t; \begin{bmatrix}2\pi - 0.5\\2\pi - 0.5\\2\pi - 0.5\end{bmatrix}, \begin{bmatrix}0.25 & 0.05 & 0.03\\0.05 & 0.2 & 0.1\\0.03 & 0.1 & 0.15\end{bmatrix}\right) .\end{aligned}$$

As illustrated in Figure 6.19a, the particle filter achieves a better estimation quality than the IFF when comparing configurations with equal numbers of parameters. We believe this is due to the particle filter's ability to place samples in regions of high probability density, which is advantageous in this trivariate scenario with relatively low noise. The SqFF is better than the IFF for equal numbers of parameters. This effect is less pronounced in the bivariate evaluation scenarios but makes a distinct difference in the trivariate scenario.

In the run times presented in Figure 6.19b, we see that the particle filter is considerably slower than the Fourier filters for equal numbers of parameters. The high run times of the particle filters are caused by the high computational effort involved in approximating the density of the trivariate wrapped normal distribution. In the Fourier filters, the trivariate wrapped normal distribution does not have to be evaluated at run time. For the IFF, the closed-form solution given in Appendix B.2 can be used. For the SqFF, the evaluation of the trivariate wrapped normal distribution is only required to transform the densities during the initialization.

Due to their superior run times, the Fourier filters outperform the particle filter when considering configurations of comparable run time in Figure 6.19c. While the SqFF achieves better results for low numbers of coefficients, the IFF achieves its close-to-optimal performance slightly faster than the SqFF.

6.5.2 Spherical Scenario

The evaluation scenario on the unit sphere is a tracking scenario on the sphere. The prior density used for the initialization of the filters and the generation of the initial state is a uniform distribution on the sphere. As our system model, we use the model given in (6.8) with $\kappa_t^{\mathrm{T}} = 7$ in every time step. Similar to the evaluation in [O2], each measurement only contains information about a single axis of the space $\mathbb{R}^3$ in which

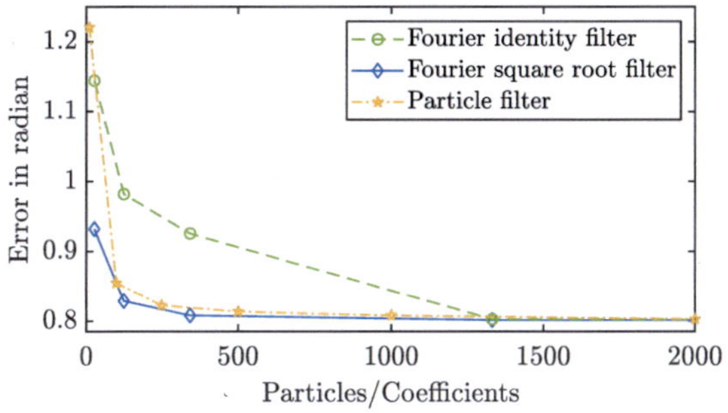

(a) Error over number of parameters.

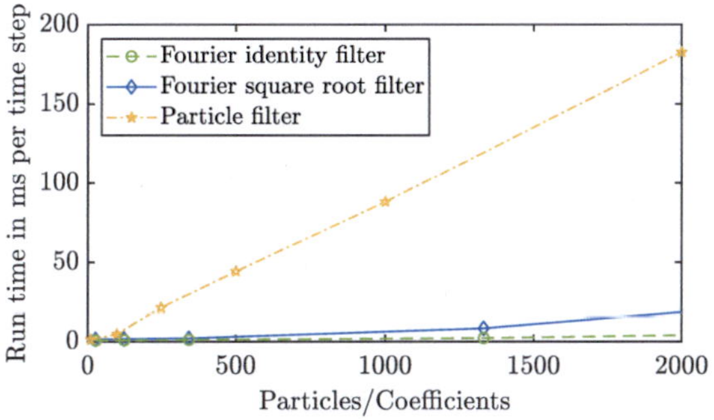

(b) Time over number of parameters.

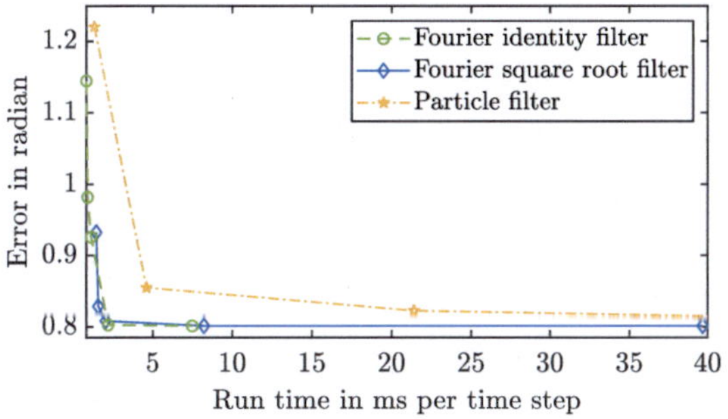

(c) Error over run time.

Figure 6.19.: Evaluation results for the trivariate scenario with topology-aware identity models.

the unit sphere is embedded. We use a time-variant measurement model according to

$$z_t = \begin{cases} x_{t,1} + v_t & \text{if } t \mod 3 = 0 \\ x_{t,2} + v_t & \text{if } t \mod 3 = 1 \\ x_{t,3} + v_t & \text{if } t \mod 3 = 1 \,, \end{cases}$$

with the normally-distributed measurement noise term $\boldsymbol{v}_t \sim \mathcal{N}(v; 0, 1)$. Unlike in the evaluation in [O2], only one measurement is obtained and processed in every time step. We evaluate the estimates of the filters at $t = 8$. We obtain a measurement at $t = 0$ and thus perform 9 update and 8 prediction steps in each run.

As illustrated in Figure 6.20a, the ISHF and SqSHF are clearly superior to the particle filter compared on a per parameter basis. For equal numbers of coefficients, the SqSHF is superior to the ISHF, which we have observed similarly for the SqFF and IFF in the hypertoroidal scenarios. As displayed in Figure 6.20b, the run times of the spherical harmonics filters are higher than those of the particle filter for equal numbers of parameters. The SqSHF is slower than the ISHF when comparing configurations with equal numbers of parameters. This was expected because more operations are required for the SqSHF. In the comparison of the filters on a run time basis in Figure 6.20c, both spherical harmonics filters clearly outperform the particle filter. Due to its much higher speed, the ISHF performs better than the SqSHF in this scenario.

6.6 Summary and Discussion

In the current and previous chapter, we addressed challenges in estimation on periodic manifolds and proposed novel filters. In Chapter 5, we explained the basics of nonlinear estimation and directional statistics. Then, we provided a historical overview of previously proposed filters for estimation problems on the circle, the hypertorus, and the unit sphere.

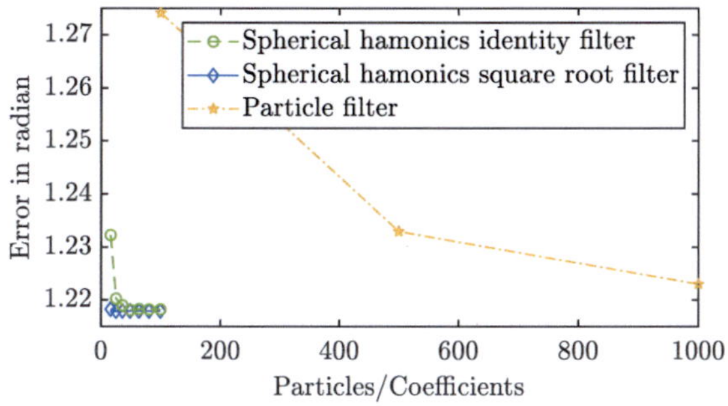

(a) Error over number of parameters.

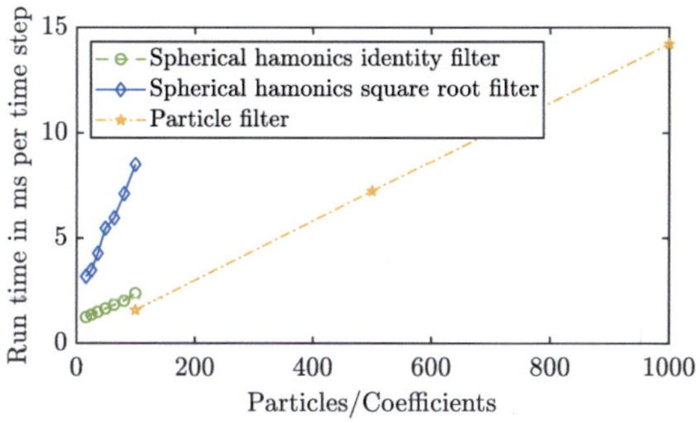

(b) Time over number of parameters.

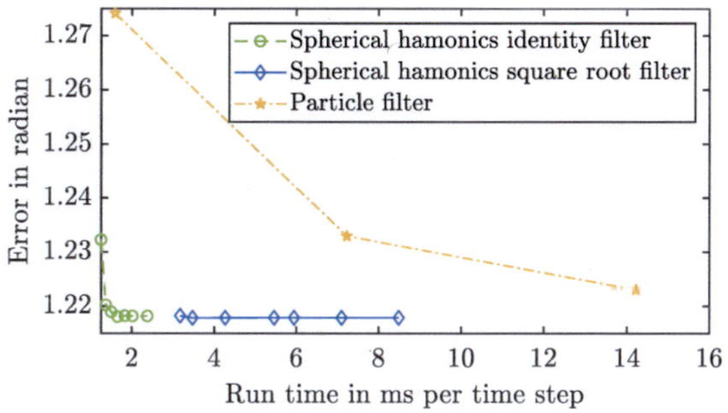

(c) Error over run time.

Figure 6.20.: Evaluation results for the tracking scenario on the sphere.

In the current chapter, we provided filters based on trigonometric polynomials and spherical harmonics. For the circle and the hypertorus, the IFF and SqFF were proposed. The ISHF and SqSHF were derived for the unit sphere. The IFF and ISHF are based on approximating the densities and likelihoods directly using Fourier or spherical harmonic coefficients. In the SqFF and SqSHF, approximations of the square roots of the functions are employed. For all topologies and all filters, the update step for arbitrary likelihoods was derived. Two predictions steps, both a simple and a very general one, were presented for the circle and the hypertorus. For the unit sphere, a simple system model was described and approaches to perform the prediction step were given.

The IFF and ISHF are faster and involve less complicated prediction steps than the SqFF and SqSHF. In contrast, the SqFF and SqSHF ensure that the density represented by the Fourier coefficients is always nonnegative. In our evaluation of their ability to estimate the mean direction, the SqFF and SqSHF performed better than the IFF and ISHF compared on a per coefficient basis. However, due to the higher speed of the IFF and ISHF, more coefficients can be used at comparable run times. Using more coefficients, the IFF and ISHF were able to outperform the SqFF and SqSHF in configurations of comparable run time.

Thus, despite the theoretical advantages of the SqFF and SqSHF, the IFF and ISHF may perform better if only the mean direction is to be estimated. However, the differences observed between the IFF and SqFF were only small. A larger difference in the run times was observed in the comparison of the ISHF with the SqSHF. For all topologies, the novel filters attained high-quality estimates at lower run times than a particle filter for periodic domains.

CHAPTER 7

Multitarget Tracking Supported by Directional Estimation

In Section 3.5.1, we explained the association process of our basic multitarget tracking algorithm. The derivation of the matrix used for the association is based on the assumption that the posterior densities and the measurement noises are Gaussian-distributed. In the tracking approach explained in Section 3.5.1, the association process is only based on information about the particles' positions.

As mentioned in Section 1.3.2, extensions to the association process have been proposed in related works. In [Dru00, Dru01], the author discusses the integration of additional features into multitarget tracking. For features on continuous domains, he suggests extending the state vectors used to track the positions of the targets by the feature data. Standard approaches to multitarget tracking relying on the assumption of Gaussian densities can then be applied to the extended state vector. However, the author implies that changes may be required if the densities involved are clearly non-Gaussian.

In this chapter, we integrate the orientations of the bulk material particles into the multitarget tracking algorithm for the bulk material sorting task. We only consider the angle around the vertical axis [O1], which can be derived from the image data for certain bulk materials. As explained in Chapter 5, Gaussian distributions should not be used to estimate orientations. Therefore, we begin with a new derivation of the association likelihood for state vectors that comprise both information about the position and the orientation of the particle. The required changes to the association process for including the orientations are given in the first section. We evaluate the novel approach against the previous approach without the orientation in the second section.

7.1 Adjusting the Association Process

To integrate the orientations into the association process, orientation measurements must be extracted and passed on to the respective components. If we treat the orientation as an additional feature, the changes to the processing chain can be performed as depicted in Figure 7.1. The changes to the original processing chain, given in Figure 3.3, are highlighted in red. The components that need to be adapted include the prediction step, the update step, and the calculation of the distances.

In the first subsection, we explicate what information can be derived about the particles' orientations based on two-dimensional image data. A derivation of a new matrix that can be used to maximize the association likelihood respecting both the positions and the orientations is provided in the second subsection.

7.1.1 Estimating Orientations of Bulk Material Particles Based on Image Data

Each particle of the bulk material is a three-dimensional object in a three-dimensional space. Full parameterizations of three-dimensional orientations, e.g, Euler angles, comprise at least three parameters. However, estimating the three-dimensional orientation based on two-dimensional images is nontrivial and would make the estimation problem quite complicated with little benefit over estimating a two-dimensional orientation. Therefore, we only estimate the orientation around the vertical axis, which can be extracted more easily from the two-dimensional image data.

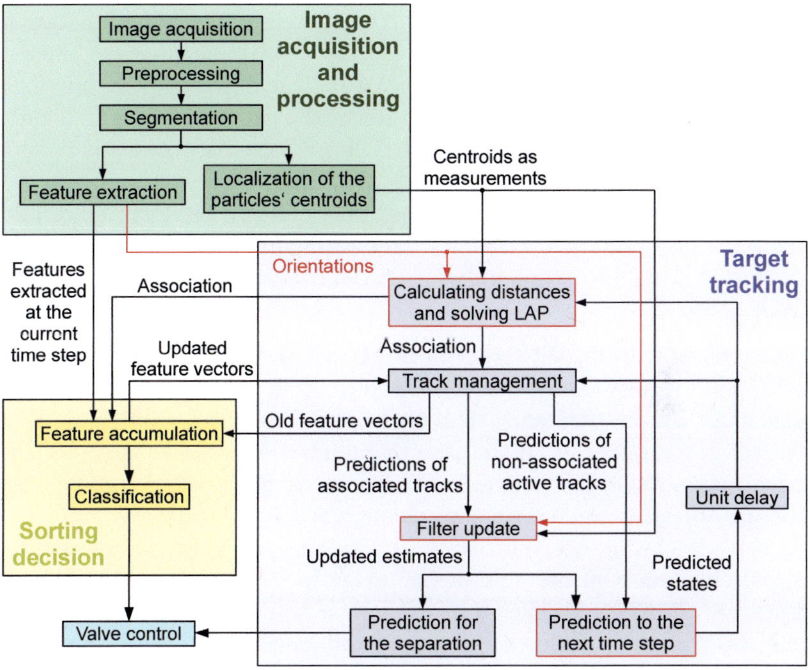

Figure 7.1.: Processing chain with integrated orientation estimation. In this diagram, we consider the orientation to be an additional feature.

Figure 7.2a presents a sample image containing cuboids that were used in the simulation for the evaluation described in Section 4.3. Based on the image data of each particle, an angle around the vertical axis can be extracted. However, for this bulk material, an image processing routine to extract the orientations may yield different results. Since the particles are 180 degree symmetric, the image data are ambiguous in regard to the orientation around the vertical axis. Further, while the cuboids shown in Figure 7.2a do not have square surfaces, errors in the image processing may lead to a result that, visually speaking, corresponds to a confusion of the long and the short edges. This can lead to an additional offset of 90 degrees. When assuming the errors to be distributed stochastically, the corresponding likelihood function is multimodal. An example of a noise density for a topology-aware identity measurement model with additive noise (5.2) is depicted in Figure 7.2c. Regarding the orientation around the vertical axis, there is less ambiguity in the cylinders displayed in Figure 7.2b. While the cylinders are also 180-degree symmetric, additional errors of ± 90 degrees are unlikely. An example of a possible noise density for the cylinders is given in Figure 7.2d. For some particles such as spheres, no meaningful orientation around the vertical axis can be extracted based on the contour of the particle viewed from above.

Since we only consider the orientation around the vertical axis, the estimation results can deteriorate if the particle rotates along a different axis than the vertical axis. For example, cuboids have different faces on which they can lie. If the face on which a cuboid lies changes, the orientation around the vertical axis extracted by the image processing may change abruptly. Such erroneous changes can have a negative influence on the association decision. However, judging based on our recordings of cuboids, such effects only occur rarely in the area recorded for the tracking. Further, problems in the extraction of the orientation may only arise if the visible orientation is influenced by the rotation. For example, when cylinders roll on their curved sides, this movement does not influence the angle around the vertical axis derived from the image data.

7.1.2 Association Likelihood for the Position and Orientation

To improve the associations, we estimate the orientation along with the particle's position. The state thus comprises not only the necessary components for the kinematic model (i.e., the position and velocity when using the CV model) but also the orientation of the particle as a scalar angle. In our mathematical description, we subdivide the state $\underline{x}$ of each particle into one part describing the position $\underline{x}^{\text{Pos}}$ and another part for the orientation x^{Ori}. Likewise, the measurement $\hat{\underline{z}}$ is subdivided into $\hat{\underline{z}}^{\text{Pos}}$ and $\hat{z}^{\text{Ori}}$. To avoid a more challenging estimation problem, we assume the two parts to be independent. For many bulk materials, the orientation of a particle does not influence the effect of the belt on the motion of the particle, and thus, this assumption is mostly accurate. However, for particles such as cylinders whose motions depend on their orientations, the assumption of independence clearly introduces an approximation.

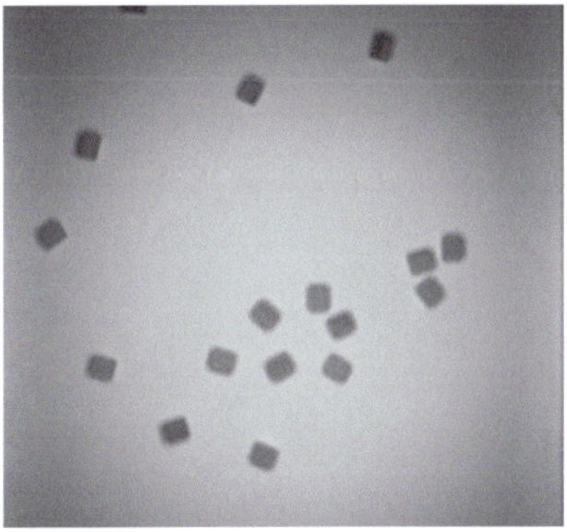

(a) Sample frame containing cuboids.

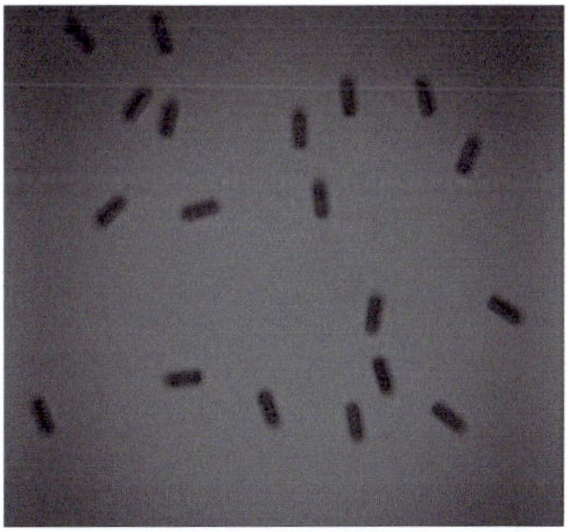

(b) Sample frame containing cylinders.

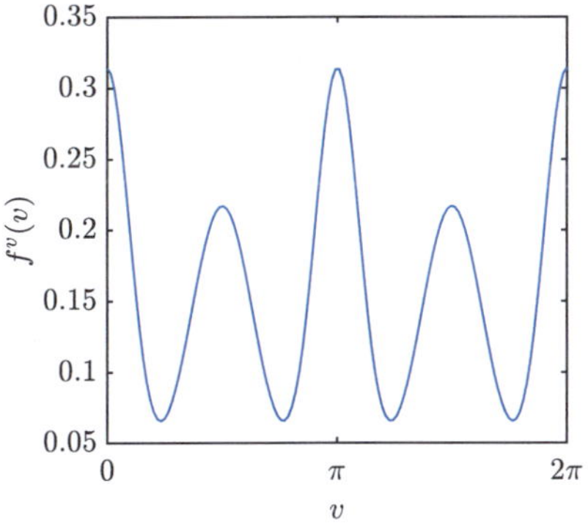

(c) Sample noise density for cuboids.

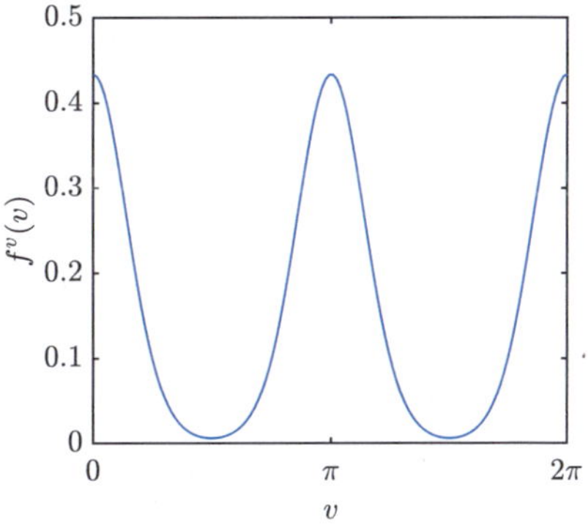

(d) Sample noise density for cylinders.

Figure 7.2.: Sample image data of wooden cylinders and cuboids recorded on TableSort and examples for possible measurement noise densities.

For deriving the association likelihood, we begin, as in Section 3.5.1, by formulating the likelihood as an integral according to

$$\ell(\hat{\underline{z}}|i) = \int_{\mathbb{R}^2\times[0,2\pi)} \ell(\hat{\underline{z}}, \underline{x}^i|i)\, d\underline{x}^i = \int_{\mathbb{R}^2\times[0,2\pi)} \ell(\hat{\underline{z}}^{\text{Pos}}, \hat{z}^{\text{Ori}}, \underline{x}^{\text{Pos},i}, x^{\text{Ori},i}|i)\, d\underline{x}^i \ .$$

Using the assumption that the position and the orientation are independent, we can rewrite the association likelihood as [O1]

$$\begin{aligned}\ell(\hat{\underline{z}}|i) &= \int_{\mathbb{R}^2} \ell(\hat{\underline{z}}^{\text{Pos}}, \underline{x}^{\text{Pos},i}|i)\, d\underline{x}^{\text{Pos},i} \int_{[0,2\pi)} \ell(\hat{z}^{\text{Ori}}, x^{\text{Ori},i}|i)\, dx^{\text{Ori},i} \\ &= \ell(\hat{\underline{z}}^{\text{Pos}}|i)\, \ell(\hat{z}^{\text{Ori}}|i) \ .\end{aligned}$$

By taking the negative logarithm of $\ell(\hat{\underline{z}}|i)$, we get

$$-\log \ell(\hat{\underline{z}}|i) = -\log \ell(\hat{\underline{z}}^{\text{Pos}}|i) - \log \ell(\hat{z}^{\text{Ori}}|i) \ .$$

As in Section 3.5.1, we now assume that we have n tracks and n measurements $\hat{z}^1, \ldots, \hat{z}^n$. The permutation τ of $\{1, \ldots, n\}$ that maximizes the likelihood

$$\ell(\hat{\underline{z}}^{\tau(1)}, \hat{\underline{z}}^{\tau(2)}, \ldots, \hat{\underline{z}}^{\tau(n)}|1, 2, \ldots, n) = \prod_{i=1}^{n} \ell(\hat{\underline{z}}^{\tau(i)}|i)$$

also minimizes

$$\begin{aligned}-\log \ell(\hat{\underline{z}}^{\tau(1)}, \hat{\underline{z}}^{\tau(2)}, \ldots, \hat{\underline{z}}^{\tau(n)}|1, 2, \ldots, n) &= -\sum_{i=1}^{n} \log \ell(\hat{\underline{z}}^{\tau(i)}|i) \\ &= -\sum_{i=1}^{n} \log \ell(\hat{\underline{z}}^{\text{Pos},\tau(i)}|i) - \sum_{i=1}^{n} \log \ell(\hat{z}^{\text{Ori},\tau(i)}|i) \ .\end{aligned}$$

To obtain the optimal solution for n tracks and n measurements, we formulate a linear assignment problem in the form of an $n \times n$ matrix. Instead of defining one matrix with the values of $-\log \ell(\hat{\underline{z}}^j|i)$ (with i and j in $\{1, \ldots, n\}$) as its entries, we generate two matrices that we can consider separately. The first matrix contains the relevant information about the negative logarithm of the association likelihood of the position component, while the second matrix is used for the orientation component. The LAP to be solved is described by the sum of the two matrices.

In Section 3.5.1, we performed further simplifications for normally distributed noise terms. These simplifications can also be used for the entries of the first matrix if the prior density and the likelihood of the position component are normally distributed. For arbitrary densities on the circle, the integrals required to determine $-\log \ell(\hat{z}^{\text{Ori},j}|i)$ for the second matrix cannot be simplified further. To obtain easier formulae for the second matrix, we consider two classes of densities. In Appendix E, we consider the case that all densities involved are von Mises densities. The presented formula can be used in combination with the von Mises filter, but an additional reformulation may be required for estimation problems involving multimodal densities, such as the one illustrated in Figure 7.2d. The second class of densities that we consider in the following paragraphs are densities represented by Fourier coefficients. After deriving the association likelihood for such densities, we provide more details on how the actual association matrix should be generated from the individual association matrices.

Association Likelihood for Densities Represented by Fourier Coefficients For densities represented by Fourier coefficients, the derivation of the association likelihood is more straightforward than for von Mises densities. A reformulation of the estimation problem as described in Appendix E.2 is also not necessary because trigonometric polynomials are inherently suited to approximating multimodal densities. We only address the calculation of the association likelihood when the density is approximated directly using a Fourier coefficient vector, which is the case in the IFF. Using the SqFF is preferable as negative association likelihoods may be obtained for the IFF. For the SqFF, the coefficient vector representing the density instead of its square root can be obtained using a discrete convolution. Based on the vector obtained, the same formula can be applied as for the IFF.

If $f^{\mathrm{p,Ori},i}(x^{\mathrm{Ori},i})$ denotes the prior density of the orientation component of track i (into which all measurements assigned to the track until $t-1$ have been integrated) and $f^{\mathrm{L,Ori},j}(\hat{z}^{\mathrm{Ori},j}|x^{\mathrm{Ori},i})$ the likelihood that the orientation component of measurement j stems from a particle with $x^{\mathrm{Ori},i}$ as its orientation component, the association likelihood $\ell(\hat{z}^{\mathrm{Ori},j}|i)$ is

$$\ell(\hat{z}^{\mathrm{Ori},j}|i) = \int_0^{2\pi} f^{\mathrm{p,Ori},i}(x^{\mathrm{Ori},i}) f^{\mathrm{L,Ori},j}(\hat{z}^{\mathrm{Ori},j}|x^{\mathrm{Ori},i})\, dx^{\mathrm{Ori},i} \ .$$

The Fourier coefficients vectors of $f^{\mathrm{L,Ori},j}$ and $f^{\mathrm{p,Ori},i}$ shall be called $\underline{c}^{\mathrm{L},j}$ and $\underline{c}^{\mathrm{p},i}$. The Fourier coefficient vector of the result of the multiplication of the prior density and the likelihood can be obtained according to

$$\underline{\breve{c}}^{\mathrm{e},i,j} = \underline{c}^{\mathrm{p},i} * \underline{c}^{\mathrm{L},j} \ .$$

To integrate over the Fourier series represented by $\underline{\breve{c}}^{\mathrm{e},i,j}$, we take the zeroth coefficient and multiply it by 2π. Since we only require the zeroth coefficient, we do not need to employ a discrete convolution. The formula for the zeroth coefficient

$$\breve{c}_0^{\mathrm{e},i,j} = \sum_{k=-k_{\max}}^{k_{\max}} c_k^{\mathrm{p},i}\, c_{-k}^{\mathrm{L},j}$$

can be formulated as a vector–vector multiplication according to

$$\breve{c}_0^{\mathrm{e},i,j} = (\underline{c}^{\mathrm{p},i})^\top \mathrm{flip}(\underline{c}^{\mathrm{L},j}) = (\underline{c}^{\mathrm{p},i})^\top \overline{\underline{c}}^{\mathrm{L},j} \ .$$

The last reformulation is possible because $\underline{c}^{\mathrm{L},j}$ describes a real function. Since we can determine the association likelihood according to $\ell(\hat{z}^{\mathrm{Ori},j}|i) = 2\pi\breve{c}_0^{\mathrm{e},i,j}$, we can take the logarithm thereof and invert the sign to efficiently calculate $-\log \ell(\hat{z}^{\mathrm{Ori},j}|i)$ for the entries of the association matrix for the orientation component.

Remark 7. Since we need to consider N Fourier coefficients for each of the n targets and m measurements, calculating the entries individually is in $O(nmN)$. To achieve good run times with our implementation, we stack the $1 \times N$ vectors $(\underline{c}^{\mathrm{p},i})^\top$ for all n targets into an $n \times N$ matrix. Similarly, we stack the $N \times 1$ vectors $\overline{\underline{c}}^{\mathrm{L},j}$ into an $N \times m$ matrix. The multiplication of the two matrices yields an $n \times m$ matrix containing all required association likelihoods. The association matrix for the orientation component can then be obtained by taking the negative logarithm of all entries.

Combined Association Matrix To combine the association matrix for the orientation containing $-\log \ell(\hat{z}^{\text{Ori},j}|i)$ with the association matrix for the position containing the squared Mahalanobis distances, a simple sum suffices if the factor $\frac{1}{2}$ in (3.5) is taken into account. Combining the two matrices via a simple sum is optimal in theory but may not be optimal in real-world applications. If the actual system or measurement noise does not match the noise assumed in the model, the association likelihood is higher or lower than the appropriate value. Since the particles' motions may be affected in ways that cannot be accounted for by the model (e.g., collisions in our bulk material tracking scenario), preventing such inaccuracies by refining the model parameters is not always possible. As deviations between the model and the true behavior may affect the position and orientation components differently, one of the two matrices may be given more weight than justified by the actual precision of the prediction. To counter such effects, the two matrices can be combined using an additional weighting factor. However, the effect of this weighting factor is dependent on whether the terms with an identical sum for all possible permutations (see Section 3.5.1) are disregarded.

To account for newly appearing particles and particles leaving the observable area, additional columns and rows are added as illustrated in Figure 3.4. The penalty terms in the additional cells, marked in red, green, and blue in Figure 3.4, need to be adjusted when both the positions and orientations are used to generate the association matrix. Suitable values for the penalty terms also need to respect whether the permutation-invariant optional terms are disregarded.

The association likelihood was only derived for von Mises densities and densities represented by Fourier coefficients. If the densities or likelihoods are not given in this form, the integral in $-\log \ell(\hat{z}^{\text{Ori},j}|i)$ can be solved numerically to obtain accurate entries for the association matrix. Alternatively, the Fourier coefficients of the prior density and the likelihood can be calculated, and then, the formula based on the Fourier coefficients can be used. If only point estimates can be derived from a filter, the orientations can still be used by replacing the negative logarithm of the likelihood with the distance (e.g., the cosine distance) between the point estimate and the measurement. This approach can also be employed if

$-\log \ell(\hat{z}^{\text{Ori},j}|i)$ cannot be calculated (e.g., due to time constraints). It is essential to reformulate the problem as a unimodal one as described in Appendix E.2 when using the distance-based approach. Further, when using a distance measure on the circle that does not respect the uncertainties, finding an appropriate weighting factor when combining the matrix for the orientation component with the matrix for the position component is essential. However, even with a suitable weighting factor, the implicit assumption when using a distance measure is that the uncertainties in the orientations are identical for all tracks and measurements. Therefore, if the distance-based approach is used, it should be used with caution.

7.2 Evaluation

If we evaluated the tracking performance based on only the accuracy of the temporal and spatial predictions as in Section 4.5, we would not respect that the associations also have an impact on the classification result. False associations can lead to incorrect data in the accumulated features, which can lead to errors in the classification and separation. Therefore, we introduce a measure of the reliability of the association decision that is tailored to our application. The evaluation scenario is described in the second subsection, and the evaluation results are presented in the last subsection.

7.2.1 Evaluation Criteria

To derive a meaningful measure of the association errors, we first consider the optimal case. When all association decisions are correct, there is a one-to-one correspondence between the tracks and the particles. This has two implications. First, only measurements of one particle are used in each track. Second, measurements that stem from the same particle are only used in a single track.

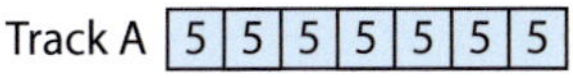

(a) A track without any errors (assuming no other track exists with measurements of particle 5).

(b) A track with an error of the first kind.

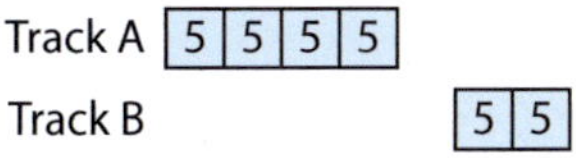

(c) Two tracks with an error of the second kind.

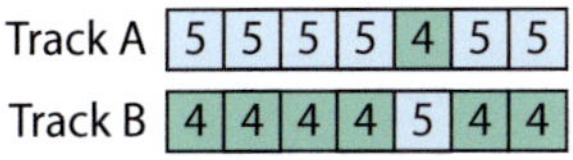

(d) Two tracks with a single wrongly assigned measurement that causes both kinds of errors.

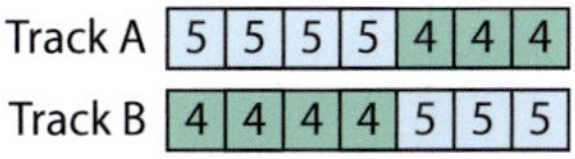

(e) Two tracks involving two particles that are confused from a certain time step on. This also causes both kinds of errors.

Figure 7.3.: Illustrations for the two types of association errors. Each number indicates the ID of the actual particle from which the measurement stems. At most, measurements of two particles (4 and 5) are depicted.

In Figure 7.3a, we visualize a single track to which 7 measurements of a particle with ID 5 were associated. If no additional measurements stem from the particle with ID 5, this is an optimal and error-free result. We define two types of errors that lead to deviations from this optimal result. We refer to an error as error of the first kind when measurements of different particles are used in a single track. An example is depicted in Figure 7.3b. An error is called error of the second kind when multiple tracks contain measurements of a single particle, as illustrated in Figure 7.3c. The errors often coincide. When two particles collide, the measurements of the neighboring tracks can be confused in one time step. An example of the resulting associations is shown in Figure 7.3d. It can also occur that the two particles are consistently confused from a certain time step on. Each track then starts following a different particle than at its initialization. We illustrate this in Figure 7.3e. While the two types of errors often coincide, errors of the individual kinds can also occur in isolation. For example, an error of the second kind occurs in isolation if a track is discontinued because the particle is not detected in one time step and a new track is initiated in the next time step. Such errors can be significantly reduced by the use of track scores. It is also possible that an error of the first kind occurs in isolation, e.g., when a track following a particle that has disappeared starts following a particle that has newly entered the field of view.

Errors of the first kind are only counted once per track and errors of the second kind only once per particle. Thus, a track containing measurements of three different particles only counts as a single error of the first kind. Likewise, if measurements of a single particle are used by three different tracks, this only counts as a single error of the second kind.

7.2.2 Evaluation Description

For a reliable evaluation, we require knowledge about which measurement stems from which particle. Therefore, we evaluate our approach based on a DEM simulation. In the simulation, all data about the individual particles are labeled with unique IDs. For each measurement we give to the tracking algorithm as input, we store the ID of the particle it is derived from. This information is only used to evaluate the tracking performance and is not used by the multitarget tracking algorithm.

The evaluation is based on a simulation of the TableSort system with a belt velocity of 1.15 m/s. The wooden cylinders described in Section 4.3 are used as the bulk material in the evaluation. The DEM simulation provides the orientations as full rotation matrices. We reduce the rotation matrices to the angles around the vertical axis to simulate measurements that could be encountered in real-world scenarios. The simulation data with 10 000 Hz are downsampled to 100 Hz for the evaluation. All positions of the particles on the belt are used. The simulation results comprise a total of 158 750 observations stemming from 4 427 particles.

To emulate the challenges of using real-world measurements that are never free of noise, we generate noisy measurements by adding artificial noise to the data obtained from the simulation. The position measurements are perturbed by an additive measurement noise $\underline{\boldsymbol{v}}_t^{\text{Pos}} \sim \mathcal{N}(\underline{v}_t^{\text{Pos}}; \underline{0}, \sigma^2 \mathbf{I}_{2\times 2})$. We consider four different scenarios, in which we employ standard deviations σ of 0.0003 m, 0.0005 m, 0.0008 m, and 0.001 m.

In the evaluation, we compare the multitarget tracking algorithm described in Chapter 3 that bases the association decisions only on the position component with the improved approach described in this chapter that incorporates the orientation component. In this evaluation, we use a constant velocity model, which is a suitable model for a belt velocity of 1.15 m/s. For the orientation component, an identity model with additive noise is used as the system model. For each particle, an IFF with 21 coefficients is employed to estimate its orientation. For the generation of the association matrix, the Fourier coefficients are used as described in the previous section. The parameters of the measurement noise used in the measurement model of the filter are set according to the parameters of the artificially introduced noise. Reasonable predefined values are used for the parameters of the noise terms in the system model. Some parameters, such as the penalty terms for the additional rows and columns of the association matrix and the weighting factor for the combination of the matrices for the position and orientation components, were determined experimentally.

7.2.3 Evaluation Results

In the evaluation results presented in Figure 7.4, the number of errors significantly increases with growing uncertainty. A higher quality of the association decisions can be achieved in the presence of high noise when using the orientation as an additional feature.

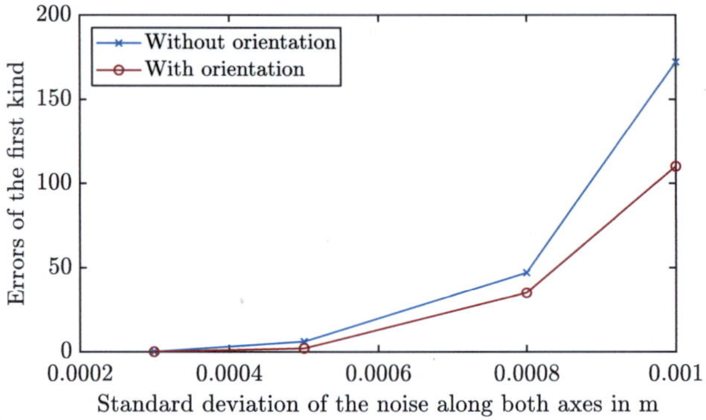

(a) Errors of the first kind.

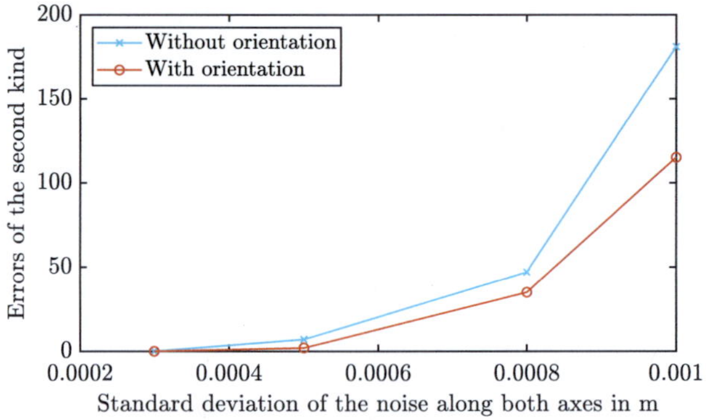

(b) Errors of the second kind.

Figure 7.4.: Errors of the first and second kind for the tracking approaches with and without the use of the orientation. No large difference between the number of errors of the first and second kind were observed in any configuration.

In the scenario involving measurement noise with a standard deviation of 0.0003 m, zero association errors were observed for both approaches. Error-free results were also obtained in experiments with even less noise. With increasing standard deviation, the number of errors increases significantly. For a standard deviation of 0.001 m, 181 errors of the second kind occurred when only the position component was considered for the association. The highest possible number of errors of the second kind is equal to the number of particles, i.e., 4 427 in our scenario. Thus, the number of errors is non-negligible. When also using the orientations, the number of errors also increases with growing uncertainty. For $\sigma = 0.0005$ m, all errors except two of both kinds could be prevented by using the orientation in the association decision. For $\sigma = 0.0008$ m, we achieved a reduction of the errors of over 25% and for $\sigma = 0.001$ m of over 35%. Eliminating all false associations using the orientation is not possible using our current models. Association errors often occur when particles collide. When cylinders collide, fast rotations that are not modeled by the motion model frequently occur. Such rotations will also lead to higher values in the association matrix for the orientation component.

Nonetheless, improvements of 25% and higher are valuable for improving the prediction accuracy and the reliability of the predictive tracking. Since each error can lead to an erroneous accumulation of features or imprecise predictions, integrating the orientation into the association process is expected to result in a higher sorting quality in real-world applications. Further, if the rate of false associations is high over multiple time steps, the multitarget tracking algorithm can break down completely. By reducing the number of false associations, the tracker can remain stable in the presence of higher measurement noise.

CHAPTER 8

Conclusion and Outlook

In this thesis, we have developed and evaluated approaches to improve the reliability of optical belt sorters. The improvements were achieved mainly using algorithmic innovations. In terms of changes to the hardware, it was only necessary to replace the line scan camera with an area scan camera and adapt the light source. Using simple image processing routines, the particles' centroids were extracted from the image data. By deriving a suitable multitarget tracking algorithm, we were able to accurately predict the particles' trajectories. The higher accuracy of our novel predictions can be used to separate the stream of bulk material more reliably. Moreover, the presented multitarget tracking algorithm allows accumulating visual features of the particles and thus facilitates the classification decision. In real-world sorting tasks, improvements to the classification and the separation entail a higher sorting quality.

When particles are densely clustered and the measurement uncertainty is high, false associations may occur even when using suitable motion models. The reliability of the associations can be improved by integrating additional features into the association decision. Therefore, we integrated the particles' orientations as an additional property that can be accurately estimated using techniques of recursive Bayesian estimation on periodic manifolds. In this context, two filters for circular manifolds were developed that can be used for almost arbitrary system and measurement models when the likelihoods and transition densities are given. The filters can be adapted well to the sorter's current workload because they offer a variable trade-off between estimation quality and run time. For jointly estimating the orientations of neighboring particles in future work, higher-dimensional variants of the filters were derived. First, the filters were generalized for arbitrary-dimensional hypertori. Second, adapted forms of the filters were proposed for the unit sphere.

In the first section, we summarize the key contributions of this thesis. Potential areas of future work are discussed in the second section.

8.1 Contributions

We divide the contributions of this thesis into two categories that we address consecutively. First, we briefly describe the features and properties of the proposed filters for periodic manifolds. Second, we provide a summary of the predictive tracking approach that was developed to improve optical belt sorters.

New Filters for Periodic Manifolds Classical filters for circular manifolds based on, e.g., wrapped normal distributions are limited by the underlying assumed density and mainly focus on the first trigonometric moment. In this thesis, we presented two filters based on Fourier series that allow approximating the posterior density using a variable number of parameters. Using sufficiently high numbers of parameters, almost arbitrary densities and likelihoods can be approximated accurately.

The proposed two Fourier filters, the Fourier identity filter and the Fourier square root filter, differ in whether the density or its square root is approximated using a trigonometric polynomial. While the Fourier square root filter provides a valid probability density function in each time step, the Fourier identity filter is faster when using the same number of parameters. Due to the close relationship between trigonometric moments and Fourier coefficients, the Fourier filters can consider different numbers of trigonometric moments. For both filters, we were able to efficiently implement Bayes' formula and the Chapman–Kolmogorov equation. For the update step, the computational effort never exceeds $O(N \log N)$ for N coefficients. The computational effort of the prediction step is in

$O(N^2)$ for time-invariant transition densities and in $O(N^2 \log N)$ for time-variant ones. For simple system models, the computational effort of the prediction step can be reduced to $O(N \log N)$ for both filters and even to $O(N)$ for the Fourier identity filter when the system noise is i.i.d.

Previously proposed assumed density filters are hard to generalize to hypertoroidal manifolds as, among others, a suitable correlation coefficient must be chosen and matched. In contrast, we were able to extend the Fourier filters in a straightforward manner by employing multidimensional Fourier series. The Fourier filters are, to our knowledge, the only filters yielding continuous densities that can be used for estimation problems on hypertoroidal manifolds with dimension three and higher. Their computational complexity does not directly depend on the dimensionality of the estimation problem and mainly depends on the number of Fourier coefficients used. However, generally, a higher number of Fourier coefficients should be used to accurately approximate densities in higher dimensions.

The concept of using orthogonal basis functions for recursive Bayesian estimation was also applied to filtering on the unit sphere. Spherical harmonics were employed to approximate the densities and likelihoods. For filtering on the unit sphere, the prediction and update steps had to be adapted. The prediction step had to be designed differently because there is no direct analogue to the identity model with additive noise on the sphere. By limiting ourselves to transition densities that treat all points at the same distance to the current state equally, we were able to derive a prediction step that is intuitive, theoretically sound, and allows for an efficient implementation. The prediction and update steps can both be performed in $O(N(\log N)^2)$.

Improvements to Optical Belt Sorting Using the newly introduced area scan camera, the predictions as to when and where each particle reaches the separation mechanism were improved. To generate accurate predictions, we tailored a multitarget tracking approach to the task of tracking bulk material particles on a conveyor belt. The proposed approach uses hard association decisions based on the most likely association of the measurements to the known tracks. As hard association decisions are used, the approach is suitable for accumulating the particles' visual features derived from the image data. We paid special attention to modeling the appearance of particles newly entering the field of view and the disappearance of particles leaving the field of view. By continuously refining our estimate of the initial velocity of the particles, the reliability of the judgment whether a particle has newly entered the field of view is improved over time.

Reliable associations of the measurements to the tracks are important both for highly accurate state estimates and predictions based thereon and for reliably accumulating each particle's visual features. To further improve the quality of the association decisions, we integrated the estimation of the orientations into the tracking. For this, we analyzed the association likelihood for states comprising linear and periodic quantities. For the general case, we provided a formula involving an integral. For real-time applications, a closed-form formula for the density representations used by the Fourier filters were derived. Integrating the orientations allowed for more reliable association decisions in the presence of significant measurement noise.

To plan the valve activations for the separation, the times and places at which the particles pass the separation mechanism are predicted based on continuous-time motion models. Accurate motion models are crucial to bridging the temporal gap between the particle's last observation and its arrival at the separation mechanism with high precision. We presented novel motion models that outperformed the classical constant velocity and constant acceleration models. For the motion along the transport direction, combining the estimate of the particle's current velocity with the acceleration behavior of previously observed particles yielded the best results. Orthogonal to the transport direction, we obtained the most accurate results for two of the three types of particles considered by combining the estimated velocity of the particle with the assumption that the particle's deceleration is similar to the deceleration of previously observed particles.

8.2 Future Research

In the context of bulk material sorting, there is a variety of ways to further improve the quality of the sorting result. For further enhancing the precision of the predictions derived using the multitarget tracking algorithm, focusing on optimizing the image processing component to improve the accuracy of the measurements may be rewarding. A promising extension would be a close integration of the image processing and tracking algorithms. For example, the image processing may benefit from information about the predictions of the particles' positions to, e.g., improve the segmentation of colliding particles. Another promising way to improve the detection of the particles would be to amend the background subtraction that is currently based on the assumption of a static background. Since the belt is seen periodically, it would be possible to maintain a model of its current appearance that includes the currently accumulated dirt. This model could then be used to reduce the number of false measurements.

To further enhance the reliability of the tracking algorithm and the precision of the predictions without any changes to the image processing routines, motion models that are even more accurate could be developed. New models could be derived by simplifying physical simulations or using data-driven machine learning approaches. To maximize the performance of the models, bulk materials could be divided into classes (e.g., based on their shape), and models could be developed for each individual class. As good results were obtained for motion models utilizing knowledge about previously observed particles, new motion models should also adapt to the precise bulk material during run time to further improve the prediction accuracy.

The estimates of the particles' states and the reliability of the tracking algorithm could be enhanced by jointly estimating the positions and orientations of neighboring particles. Particularly if the particles are in contact, estimating their states jointly is expected to improve the estimation quality. While a Kalman filter may be employed to estimate the positions, the orientations could be estimated jointly using the Fourier filters for hypertoroidal domains.

The reliability of the association decisions could be further enhanced by integrating additional properties that can be extracted from the image data into the association process. For example, popular features in image processing and visual tracking [SCC+14] could be used. Since we cannot expect to have accurate measurement models with stochastic noise for these features at our disposal, they may not integrate seamlessly into the current approach. However, as long as similarity scores can be derived, these could be transformed and combined with the association matrix containing the negative logarithms of the likelihoods to improve the association decisions.

Further, work on extracting additional knowledge about the particles from their trajectories [O20, O23] is ongoing. If, for example, the classes to separate differ in their acceleration behavior, the trajectories derived using the tracking algorithm could be used to enhance the classification or even enable classifying visually indistinguishable particles. Moreover, information about the physical properties of the particles that are relevant to subsequent processing steps could be derived.

Future work on the approach to use orthogonal basis functions for estimation problems on periodic manifolds could focus on improving the performance of the filters or making the approach applicable to additional filtering problems. In some applications, sparse representations of the Fourier coefficient vectors [KM12] could improve the performance of the Fourier filters. Sparse representations are particularly promising if prediction steps with the topology-aware identity model with additive noise are performed frequently as the operations involved do not change the sparsity of the Fourier coefficient tensor.

The spherical harmonics filters could be generalized to allow for arbitrary transition densities in the prediction step. This can, e.g., be useful if transitioning into certain parts of the sphere is less likely than transitioning into other parts. To implement the general prediction step for the unit sphere, the transition density needs to be approximated using orthogonal basis functions for $\mathbb{S}^2 \times \mathbb{S}^2$. A suitable basis could be derived based on the spherical harmonic functions.

Other domains to consider for estimation based on orthogonal basis functions include hyperspherical manifolds and the unit ball. For the former, the use of hyperspherical harmonics should be considered. For the latter, an orthogonal basis could be derived by regarding the unit ball as the Cartesian product of $\mathbb{S}^2$ and the interval $[0, 1]$. A suitable basis can then be generated by combining the spherical harmonic functions for $\mathbb{S}^2$ with a scaled Fourier basis for $[0, 1]$.

APPENDIX A

Notes on the Convergence of Fourier Series Approximations of Densities

In this appendix, we describe some basic convergence properties when approximating densities or the square roots of densities using trigonometric polynomials. We start by considering the approximation of the density directly. We know that every valid density f integrates to 1, and thus, $f \in L^1(\mathbb{S}^1)$, i.e., the density is integrable. Using the Riemann–Lebesgue lemma [BC49, Section II.1, Theorem 1], we obtain

$$\left|c_k^{\mathrm{id}}\right| \xrightarrow{|k|\to\infty} 0 \,.$$

We now assume that the density is square integrable on $[0, 2\pi)$, i.e., $f \in L^2(\mathbb{S}^1)$, which is a reasonable assumption in practice. In this case, the sum of the absolute values of the Fourier coefficients convergences, i.e.,

$$\sum_{k=-\infty}^{\infty} \left|c_k^{\mathrm{id}}\right| < \infty \,.$$

This can be proven using Bessel's inequality [Zyg03, Volume I, Section I.7]. We can thus invoke the theorem of Riesz–Fischer [Zyg03, Volume I, Chapter IV, Theorem 1.1] and conclude for the trigonometric polynomial $s_{k_{\max}}$ with all terms of the Fourier series from $-k_{\max}$ to $k_{\max}$ that

$$\int_0^{2\pi} \left|f(x) - s_{k_{\max}}(x)\right|^2 dx \xrightarrow{k_{\max}\to\infty} 0 \ .$$

In other words, $s_{k_{\max}}$ converges in $f \in L^2(\mathbb{S}^1)$.

For the approximation of the square root, we define $g = \sqrt{f}$. We know that $g \in L^2(\mathbb{S}^1)$ because the integral of g^2 is 1 due to the normalization of the density. Thus, we know

$$\sum_{k=-\infty}^{\infty} \left|c_k^{\text{sqrt}}\right| < \infty \ ,$$

which implies

$$\left|c_k^{\text{sqrt}}\right| \xrightarrow{|k|\to\infty} 0 \ .$$

If the convergence of c_k^{id} and c_k^{sqrt} to 0 did not hold, this would be unfavorable to approximations with limited numbers of coefficients because coefficients of arbitrary size could arise at arbitrarily large indices. However, the convergence properties provided so far do not guarantee good results in practice. Using only these, no statements can be made about the coefficients with indices $k : |k| > k_{\max}$ when we choose $k_{\max}$ based on, e.g., the available run time.

By introducing another assumption about the density, we can provide limits on the sizes of the entries c_k^{id}. In practice, we rarely encounter densities with infinitely many modes on $\mathbb{S}^1$. If the density does not diverge to ∞ for any point and only has a finite number of modes in $[0, 2\pi)$, the density function is a bounded variation function. For a density with M modes, we can give an upper bound for its total variation $T_f(0, 2\pi)$ [Rud87, Chapter 7] according to

$$T_f(0, 2\pi) \leq 2M \sup_x(f(x))$$

and for the total variation of its square root g according to

$$T_g(0, 2\pi) \leq 2M \sup_x(g(x)) \ .$$

If the function is also continuous on $(0, 2\pi)$, $s_{k_{\max}}$ converges uniformly, which is stronger than the convergence in $L^2(\mathbb{S}^1)$. This can be proven using the Dirichlet–Jordan theorem [GM07, Section 11.5.6, Theorem 11.91]).

The total variation can be used to bound the Fourier coefficients according to [Tai67]

$$\left|c_k^{\text{id}}\right| \leq T_f(0, 2\pi)\frac{2\pi}{|k|} \ , \qquad \left|c_k^{\text{sqrt}}\right| \leq T_g(0, 2\pi)\frac{2\pi}{|k|} \ .$$

For example, the maximum value of a von Mises distribution is always less than 4 for $\kappa \leq 100$. We thus know that

$$\left|c_{1000}^{\text{id}}\right| \leq T(0, 2\pi)\frac{2\pi}{1000} < 2 \cdot 4 \cdot \frac{2\pi}{1000} < 0.0503 \ .$$

Thus, we obtain at least a linear convergence for bounded variation functions. In our closed-form formulae for popular densities on the circle given in Appendix B.1, a superlinear convergence rate is obtained for most of the densities considered.

For the SqFF, we can provide an additional bound the Fourier coefficients with indices $k : |k| > k_{\max}$. As we have shown in Section 6.2.2,

$$\sum_{k=-\infty}^{\infty} |c_k|^2 = \|\underline{c}^{\text{sqrt}}\|^2 = \frac{1}{2\pi}$$

holds for valid densities. Thus, if the Fourier coefficients with indices $-k_{\max}$ to $k_{\max}$ have been calculated in a precise manner, the remaining Fourier coefficients for representing the square root of the density can be bounded according to

$$|c_k^{\text{sqrt}}| \leq \sqrt{\frac{1}{2\pi} - \sum_{k=-k_{\max}}^{k_{\max}} |c_k|^2} \quad \forall k \in \mathbb{Z} : |k| > k_{\max} \ .$$

APPENDIX B

Fourier Coefficients of Common Densities

In this appendix, we provide closed-form or analytic formulae for the Fourier coefficients of densities on periodic manifolds. We begin with densities on the circle. Afterward, formulae are given for one density on the hypertorus and one density on the unit sphere.

B.1 Densities on the Circle

In this part of the appendix, we consider the densities on the unit circle introduced in Section 5.2.1 and provide formulae for the Fourier coefficients of the densities and their square roots. For distributions that have the mean direction as a parameter, we only provide closed-form expressions for $\mu = 0$. The formulae for the coefficients of the density shifted by the actual mean direction can easily be derived by combining the formulae for $\mu = 0$ with the shifting operation (6.5). The formulae were first described by us in [O11].

Wrapped Normal Distribution For $\mu = 0$, the wrapped normal distribution reduces to

$$f_{\mathrm{WN}}(x; \mu = 0, \sigma) = \frac{1}{\sigma\sqrt{2\pi}} \sum_{j=-\infty}^{\infty} \exp\left(\frac{-(x + 2\pi j)^2}{2\sigma^2}\right) .$$

Using the formula for the trigonometric moments [Kur15, Section 2.2.4], we get

$$\forall k \in \mathbb{Z} : c_k^{\mathrm{id}} = \frac{1}{2\pi} \mathrm{e}^{-\sigma^2 k^2/2}$$

for the Fourier coefficients of the density. The coefficients decrease exponentially for $|k| \to \infty$. Thus far, we have not found an analytic expression for the Fourier coefficients of the square root of the density. However, a DFT can be used to obtain an approximation of the Fourier coefficients.

Von Mises Distribution For the von Mises distribution, we get

$$f_{\mathrm{VM}}(x; \mu = 0, \kappa) = \frac{\mathrm{e}^{\kappa \cos(x)}}{2\pi I_0(\kappa)}$$

as the formula for the density when the mean direction is set to zero. Using the formula for the trigonometric moments [Kur15, Section 2.2.4], we obtain the formula

$$\forall k \in \mathbb{Z} : c_k^{\mathrm{id}} = \frac{1}{2\pi I_0(\kappa)} I_{|k|}(\kappa)$$

for the Fourier coefficients, in which $I_{|k|}$ denotes the Bessel function of the first kind of order $|k|$.

To derive the Fourier coefficients of the square root of the density, we begin by writing out the formula

$$\sqrt{f_{\mathrm{VM}}(x; \mu = 0, \kappa)} = \sqrt{\frac{\mathrm{e}^{\kappa \cos(x)}}{2\pi I_0(\kappa)}} .$$

We can then expand the fraction via

$$\sqrt{\frac{\mathrm{e}^{\kappa\cos(x)}}{2\pi I_0(\kappa)}} = \frac{2\pi I_0(\kappa/2)}{2\pi I_0(\kappa/2)} \cdot \frac{\mathrm{e}^{\kappa/2\cdot\cos(x)}}{\sqrt{2\pi I_0(\kappa)}} = \frac{2\pi I_0(\kappa/2)}{\sqrt{2\pi I_0(\kappa)}} \cdot \frac{\mathrm{e}^{\kappa/2\cdot\cos(x)}}{2\pi I_0(\kappa/2)} \,.$$

Because the part in green is independent of x, we can move it in front of the integral used to determine the Fourier coefficients. The remaining part in blue is the formula for a von Mises density with $\kappa/2$ as its concentration parameter. Thus, we can use the formula for the Fourier coefficients of the von Mises distribution for $\kappa/2$ to determine the Fourier coefficients of the term in blue. Combining the two terms, we obtain

$$\forall k \in \mathbb{Z} : c_k^{\text{sqrt}} = \frac{2\pi I_0(\kappa/2)}{\sqrt{2\pi I_0(\kappa)}} \frac{1}{2\pi I_0(\kappa/2)} I_{|k|}(\kappa/2) = \frac{1}{\sqrt{2\pi I_0(\kappa)}} I_{|k|}(\kappa/2) \,.$$

To analyze the convergence of the Fourier coefficients for $|k| \to 0$, we regard the Bessel function [AS72, Section 9.6.10]

$$I_{|k|}(\kappa/2) = \left(\frac{\kappa}{4}\right)^{|k|} \sum_{m=0}^{\infty} \frac{(\frac{1}{16}\kappa^2)^m}{m!\,\Gamma(|k|+m+1)} \,.$$

While the term in front of the sum may (if $\kappa > 4$) increase exponentially, the terms summed decrease in the order of a factorial due to the gamma function in the denominator.

Circular Uniform Distribution As explained in Section 6.2.1, the coefficient c_0^{id} is always $\frac{1}{2\pi}$ when approximating a density directly. All other coefficients are zero because the density is a constant function. As can be easily derived using (6.2), the zeroth Fourier coefficient of the square root of the density c_0^{sqrt} is $1/\sqrt{2\pi}$ and all other coefficients are zero.

Wrapped Cauchy Distribution When the mean direction is set to zero, the density of the wrapped Cauchy distribution is given by

$$f_{\text{WC}}(x; \mu = 0, a) = \frac{1}{2\pi}\left(1 + 2\sum_{k=1}^{\infty} \mathrm{e}^{-ka}\cos(kx)\right) \,.$$

Again, we can determine the Fourier coefficients of the density using the trigonometric moments of the wrapped Cauchy distribution [Kur15, Section 2.2.4] to obtain

$$\forall k \in \mathbb{Z} : c_k^{\text{id}} = \frac{1}{2\pi} \mathrm{e}^{-|k|a} \, .$$

Using manual reformulations and the help of a computer algebra system, we were able to derive the formula

$$c_k^{\text{sqrt}} = \sqrt{\frac{1}{2\pi^3} \tanh\left(\frac{a}{2}\right)} \sum_{m=0}^{\infty} \frac{(\Gamma(\frac{1}{2}+m))^2 (\operatorname{sech}(\frac{a}{2}))^{2m}}{\Gamma(1-k+m)\Gamma(1+k+m)}$$

depending on the hyperbolic tangent $\tanh(\cdot)$ and the hyperbolic secant $\operatorname{sech}(\cdot)$ for the Fourier coefficients of the square root of the density. If the regularized generalized hypergeometric function [Wei] ${}_3\tilde{F}_2(\cdot,\cdot,\cdot)$ is available as a library function, we can rewrite the formula as

$$c_k^{\text{sqrt}} = \sqrt{\frac{1}{2\pi} \tanh\left(\frac{a}{2}\right)} \, {}_3\tilde{F}_2\left(\left[\frac{1}{2}, \frac{1}{2}, 1\right], [1-k, \, 1+k] \, , \left(\operatorname{sech}\left(\frac{a}{2}\right)\right)^2 \right) .$$

Wrapped Exponential Distribution For the wrapped exponential distribution, the formulae given in [JK04] can be used to obtain the real and complex parts of the trigonometric moments. Using these, we obtain

$$\forall k \in \mathbb{Z} : c_k^{\text{id}} = \frac{1}{2\pi} \frac{\lambda^2 - \lambda k i}{\lambda^2 + k^2}$$

for the Fourier coefficients. For the square root of the density, we derived the formula

$$\forall k \in \mathbb{Z} : c_k^{\text{sqrt}} = \frac{\sqrt{\lambda}}{\pi(\lambda + 2ki)} \frac{(\mathrm{e}^{\pi\lambda} - 1)}{\sqrt{\mathrm{e}^{2\pi\lambda} - 1}}$$

for the Fourier coefficients. In both cases, the Fourier coefficients converge linearly to 0 for $k \to \infty$.

B.2 Densities on Higher-Dimensional Manifolds

First, we introduce a formula for the Fourier coefficients of the multivariate wrapped normal distribution for hypertoroidal manifolds. Second, we address the Fourier coefficients of the von Mises–Fisher distribution with $\underline{\mu} = \begin{bmatrix} 0 & 0 & 1 \end{bmatrix}$. For the five-parameter Fisher–Bingham distribution, an analytic expression was derived in [AKK16], but it is not closed-form and involves infinite series.

Multivariate Wrapped Normal Distribution For all absolutely continuous densities, the characteristic function $\varphi_{\underline{\boldsymbol{x}}}$ of the random vector $\underline{\boldsymbol{x}}$ is given by [And03, Section 2.6.1],

$$\varphi_{\underline{\boldsymbol{x}}}(\underline{t}) = \mathrm{E}(\mathrm{e}^{i(\underline{t}\cdot\underline{\boldsymbol{x}})}) = \int_{\Omega_{\underline{\boldsymbol{x}}}} \mathrm{e}^{i(\underline{t}\cdot\underline{x})} f(\underline{x})\, d\underline{x} \; .$$

For vectors $\underline{t}$ comprising only integers, the formula only differs by a factor of $1/(2\pi)^d$ from the formula for the Fourier coefficient with index $-\underline{t}$.

We now derive the characteristic function of the multivariate wrapped normal distribution using the characteristic function of the (regular) multivariate normal distribution. We start by splitting the multidimensional integral for the characteristic function of the multivariate normal distribution into an infinite number of hypercubes, yielding

$$\begin{aligned}
\varphi_{\underline{\boldsymbol{x}}}(\underline{t}) &= \int_{\mathbb{R}^d} \mathrm{e}^{i(\underline{t}\cdot\underline{x})} \mathcal{N}(\underline{x}; \underline{\mu}, \mathbf{C})\, d\underline{x} \\
&= \sum_{\underline{j}\in\mathbb{Z}^d} \int_{[0,2\pi)^d} \mathrm{e}^{i(\underline{t}\cdot(\underline{x}+2\pi\underline{j}))} \mathcal{N}(\underline{x}+2\pi\underline{j}; \underline{\mu}, \mathbf{C})\, d\underline{x} \\
&= \sum_{\underline{j}\in\mathbb{Z}^d} \int_{[0,2\pi)^d} \mathrm{e}^{i(\underline{t}\cdot\underline{x})} \mathcal{N}(\underline{x}+2\pi\underline{j}; \underline{\mu}, \mathbf{C})\, d\underline{x} \; .
\end{aligned}$$

Then, we can swap the sum and the integral to obtain

$$\begin{aligned}\varphi_{\underline{\boldsymbol{x}}}(\underline{t}) &= \int_{[0,2\pi)^d} e^{i(\underline{t}\cdot\underline{x})} \sum_{\underline{j}\in\mathbb{Z}^d} \mathcal{N}(\underline{x} + 2\pi\underline{j}; \underline{\mu}, \mathbf{C})\, d\underline{x} \\ &= \int_{[0,2\pi)^d} e^{i(\underline{t}\cdot\underline{x})} f_{\mathrm{WN}}(\underline{x}; \underline{\mu}, \mathbf{C})\, d\underline{x}\ .\end{aligned}$$

Thus, the characteristic function of the multivariate wrapped normal distribution is equivalent to the characteristic function of the (regular) multivariate normal distribution.

We can now use the formula for the characteristic function of the multivariate wrapped normal distribution [Obe73, Table C] to obtain a closed-form formula for the Fourier coefficients of the multivariate wrapped normal distribution. By including the factor $1/(2\pi)^d$ and evaluating the characteristic function at $-\underline{k}$, we get

$$c_{\underline{k}}^{\mathrm{id}} = \frac{1}{(2\pi)^d}\varphi_{\underline{\boldsymbol{x}}}(-\underline{k}) = \frac{1}{(2\pi)^d} e^{-i(\underline{k}\cdot\underline{\mu})-(\underline{k}^\top\mathbf{C}\underline{k})/2}\ .$$

We have not found a closed-form formula for the Fourier coefficients of the square root of the density. However, if the expensive evaluation of the density function is to be avoided, one can calculate the Fourier coefficients of the density in $O(N)$ and then evaluate the function on an equidistant grid using an IDFT. Since this is equal to evaluating the truncated Fourier series at the grid points, it is not guaranteed that all function values are nonnegative. If all function values are nonnegative, we can calculate the square roots of the values and then perform a DFT to obtain an approximation of the Fourier coefficients of the square root of the multivariate wrapped normal density.

Von Mises–Fisher Distribution In [Seo06], the spherical harmonic coefficients of azimuthally symmetric von Mises–Fisher densities (i.e., von Mises–Fisher densities with $\mu = \begin{bmatrix} 0 & 0 & 1 \end{bmatrix}$) are discussed. Therein, the recursion relation

$$
\begin{aligned}
c_0^0 &= 1 \,, \\
c_1^0 &= \cosh \kappa - \frac{1}{\kappa} \,, \\
c_{l+1}^0 + c_l^0 &= \frac{e^{\kappa}}{2\sinh(\kappa)} - \frac{1}{\kappa} \sum_{m-0}^{l} (2m+1) c_m^0
\end{aligned}
$$

and a closed-form approximation of c_l^0 according to

$$
c_l^0 \approx \exp\left[-\frac{l(l+1)}{2\kappa} \right]
$$

for $\kappa \gg 1$ are given. All coefficients of order $m \neq 0$ are zero due to the azimuthal symmetry of the density.

APPENDIX C

Alternative Update and Prediction Steps

In this appendix, we provide alternative variants of the prediction step with additive noise and the update step for the unit circle. These variants provide interesting insights into how the prediction and update steps can be performed based on grid values. Using the alternative prediction and update steps, an alternative filter could be derived. Further, the alternative variant of the update step is used as the basis for the update step of the spherical harmonics filter. However, it is important to note that the formulae given do not yield the same results as the prediction and update steps presented in Section 6.2.2 and Section 6.2.3.

C.1 Update Step

The alternative update step for the IFF is sketched in Figure C.1a. As the first step, function values of f_t^{p} on a grid are derived from the Fourier coefficient vector $\underline{c}_t^{\mathrm{p,id}}$. Afterward, we evaluate f_t^{L} at the same grid points. We then calculate the Hadamard product of the vectors comprising the function values on the grid. After performing a DFT, we have a new coefficient vector $\underline{\breve{c}}_t^{\mathrm{e,id}}$, which is as long as $\underline{c}_t^{\mathrm{p,id}}$ but represents an unnormalized density. The end result is then obtained using a normalization that is performed as in the regular update step described in Section 6.2.2.

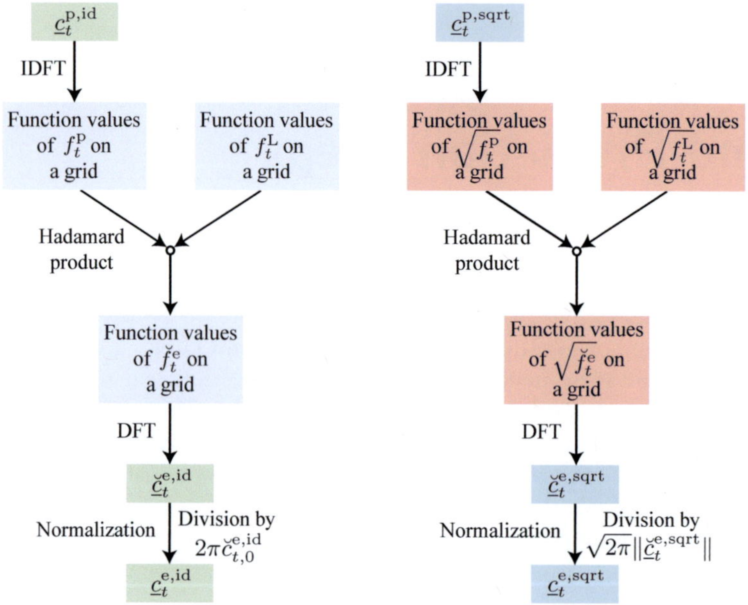

(a) Alternative update step for the IFF. **(b)** Alternative update step for the SqFF.

Figure C.1.: Alternative update steps for the IFF and SqFF.

There are some key differences to the regular update step. First, we do not need the correspondence between the multiplication of the functions and the discrete convolution of the coefficient vectors. This is useful for the spherical harmonics filters, since performing the operation based on the coefficients is much more elaborate. The second difference is that $\underline{c}_t^{\mathrm{L,id}}$ does not need to be derived from f_t^{L}. In the update step illustrated in Figure C.1a, we perform one IDFT and one DFT. In the regular update step, one DFT and one convolution are required. However, since all of these operations are in the same complexity class, this difference does not result in major differences in the run times. A third difference is that no truncation is required. As evident from the derivation of the regular update step, $4k_{\max}+1$ coefficients are required to represent the exact result of the multiplication of the trigonometric polynomials for f_t^{p} and f_t^{L}. In the alternative update step, we limit ourselves to $2k_{\max}+1$ grid points for the approximation of the coefficient vector $\underline{\breve{c}}_t^{\mathrm{e,id}}$. This means we accept that the function values of $\breve{f}_t^{\mathrm{e}}$ on the grid may not allow for a precise reconstruction of $\breve{f}_t^{\mathrm{e}}$. In both the regular and the alternative update step, an approximation error generally occurs unless f_t^{e} can be precisely represented using the considered $2k_{\max}+1$ Fourier coefficients. In the regular update step, an approximation error occurs when the likelihood f_t^{L} is represented using the coefficient vector $\underline{c}_t^{\mathrm{L,id}}$ that may not precisely describe f_t^{L}. An additional error occurs in the truncation step. In the alternative update step, an approximation error is introduced when we only calculate N function values of $\breve{f}_t^{\mathrm{e,id}}$ even though more would be required for an exact representation. This is usually the case as more grid points are required for $\breve{f}_t^{\mathrm{e,id}}$ than for f_t^{p} and f_t^{L}. Thus, the coefficient vector $\underline{\breve{c}}_t^{\mathrm{e,id}}$ is generally an approximation.

We can also provide an alternative variant of the update step for the SqFF, which is summarized in Figure C.1b. The alternative update step for the SqFF follows the same rationale as the alternative update step for the IFF. A key difference is that all approximation errors affect the approximation of the square root of the density. As the Fourier coefficient vector $\underline{c}_t^{\mathrm{p,sqrt}}$ describes a real function, all function values $\sqrt{f_t^{\mathrm{p}}}$ are real numbers. Further, f_t^{L} is a nonnegative function, and thus, all values of $\sqrt{f_t^{\mathrm{L}}}$ are real numbers. Consequentially, all values of $\sqrt{f_t^{\mathrm{e}}}$ are real-valued. Therefore, the trigonometric polynomial with the coefficient vector $\underline{\breve{c}}_t^{\mathrm{e,sqrt}}$ is a real function. Hence, the squared function values are guaranteed to be nonnegative.

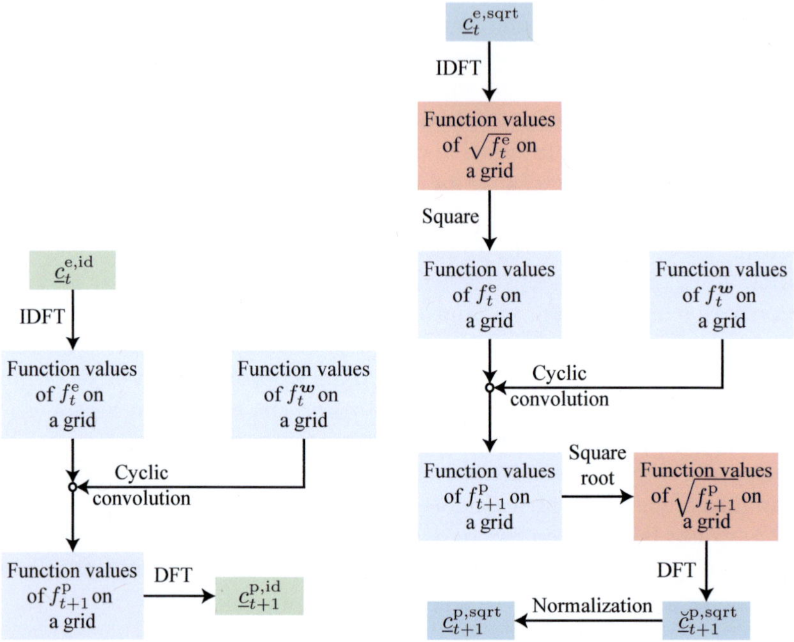

(a) Alternative prediction step for the IFF.

(b) Alternative prediction step for the SqFF.

Figure C.2.: Alternative prediction steps for the IFF and SqFF.

C.2 Prediction Step for the Topology-Aware Identity Model with Additive Noise

In Figure C.2a, we illustrate an alternative prediction step for the identity model with additive noise for the IFF. Using an IDFT, we determine the function values of f_t^{e} on a grid. We can directly evaluate $f_t^{\boldsymbol{w}}$ on the grid points and do not require its Fourier coefficients (if $\boldsymbol{w}_t$ is i.i.d., the function values only have to be calculated once). Afterward, we perform a cyclic convolution of the vectors containing the function values of f_t^{e}

and $f_t^{\boldsymbol{w}}$, which corresponds to a Hadamard product of the coefficient vectors [Yar10, Section 8.10.8]. As no additional Fourier coefficients are required to represent the result, performing the operation like this does not introduce an additional approximation error. If all function values of f_t^{e} generated using the IDFT are nonnegative, the function values of f_{t+1}^{p} will also be nonnegative. This is because the values of $f_t^{\boldsymbol{w}}$ on any grid are always nonnegative and the cyclic convolution only involves multiplications and summations, which yield nonnegative values if all input values are nonnegative. However, the cardinal series based on the function values on the grid may have negative function values. This also holds for the trigonometric polynomial with the coefficient vector $\underline{c}_{t+1}^{\mathrm{p,id}}$ derived using an IDFT. In the approach depicted in Figure C.2a, we assume that the cardinal series based on the function values of $f_t^{\boldsymbol{w}}$ on the grid is a normalized density. If this is not the case, the coefficient vector obtained via a DFT may not be normalized and an additional normalization step may be required.

The alternative update step for the SqFF is presented in Figure C.2b. We first obtain function values of $\sqrt{f_t^{\mathrm{e}}}$ on a grid using an IDFT. Then, we square the function values. Even when $\sqrt{f_t^{\mathrm{e}}}$ is perfectly described by $\underline{c}_t^{\mathrm{e,sqrt}}$, this step introduces an approximation error. As discussed previously, more coefficients, and thus also more grid points, are required to precisely represent the square of a function. We then evaluate $f_t^{\boldsymbol{w}}$ on a grid. Afterward, we calculate the cyclic convolution as in the IFF. An approximation error is introduced in the next step in which we calculate the square roots of the function values of f_{t+1}^{p} to obtain the function values of $\sqrt{f_{t+1}^{\mathrm{p}}}$ on a grid. Using a DFT, we can obtain a Fourier coefficient vector again. Due to the approximation errors, the resulting coefficient vector may not correspond to a normalized density. Therefore, a normalization is required.

The resulting coefficient vector $\underline{c}_{t+1}^{\mathrm{p,sqrt}}$ always represents a density that is nonnegative everywhere. While applying an IDFT to $\underline{c}_{t+1}^{\mathrm{p,sqrt}}$ may yield negative values, the values are squared, and thus, only positive values are obtained for f_t^{e}. The function values of $f_t^{\boldsymbol{w}}$ are always nonnegative because we directly calculate function values of a valid density. Hence, the cyclic convolution only yields nonnegative function values for f_{t+1}^{p}. Thus, all function values of $\sqrt{f_{t+1}^{\mathrm{p}}}$ on the grid are real. Thus, the trigonometric polynomial with the coefficient vector $\underline{c}_{t+1}^{\mathrm{p,sqrt}}$ is a real function and the reconstructed density is always nonnegative. However, as in the IFF, applying a DFT to the function values on the grid of f_t^{e}, $f_t^{\boldsymbol{w}}$, or f_{t+1}^{p} obtained as intermediate results would not necessarily result in Fourier coefficients of a trigonometric polynomial with only nonnegative function values.

It is also possible to skip the DFT and IDFT operations in Figures C.1a and C.2a to create a new filter, which is based on unnormalized function values on a grid and does not require DFTs and IDFTs. Whenever a valid normalized density is to be derived from the function values on the grid, we can proceed as follows. First, we calculate the square roots of the function values. As all function values on the grid are nonnegative, the square roots of the values are real-valued. Second, we perform a DFT to obtain the Fourier coefficients representing the square root of the density. Third, we perform a normalization based on the Fourier coefficients. As in the SqFF, the Fourier coefficients then represent a function that may have negative function values. By squaring the potentially negative function values, we obtain a valid approximation of the density. The Fourier coefficient vector representing the square root of the density can also be used to provide a flexible truncation operation. If the coefficient vector is padded with zeros or truncated, applying an IDFT to the new vector yields only real values. By squaring these values, nonnegative function values on a grid can be obtained. The nonnegative values can then be used in the next prediction or update step of the filter based on unnormalized function values on a grid. If the number of parameters was reduced by directly evaluating the function on a new grid using, e.g., a cardinal series, nonnegative function values could arise. However, the Fourier coefficient vector representing the square root of the density is not always required to reduce the number of parameters in a way that ensures the nonnegativity of the function values. An approach to parameter reduction that can be implemented directly based on a grid is to only preserve every qth ($q \in \mathbb{N}^+$) grid point and the corresponding function values.

APPENDIX D

Multiplying Functions on the Sphere Based on Their Spherical Harmonic Coefficients

A basis for deriving the spherical harmonic coefficients of the result of the multiplication of two spherical harmonic approximations is the equation [DH94, Theorem 2]

$$Y_{l_1}^{m_1} Y_{l_2}^{m_2} = \sum_{l_c=|l_1-l_2|}^{l_1+l_2} \sqrt{\frac{(2l_1+1)(2l_2+1)}{4\pi(2l_c+1)}} C_{0,0,0}^{l_1,l_2,l_c} C_{m_1,m_2,m_1+m_2}^{l_1,l_2,l_c} Y_{l_c}^{m_1+m_2}, \tag{D.1}$$

in which C is the Wigner symbol in the convention of [BL84, Equation (3.165)]. While calculating the Wigner symbol is costly, it is possible to precalculate the values. A simple way to use (D.1) to obtain the spherical harmonic coefficients of the multiplication result is as follows. We allocate a new coefficient matrix for the (unnormalized) multiplication result $\mathring{C}_l^{\mathrm{e,id}}$. The matrix, which is initialized with zeros, needs to be able to store coefficients up to degree $L_1 + L_2$ when L_1 and L_2 are the maximum degrees of the spherical harmonic approximations of the two functions. As in the Fourier filters, we always use the same number of coefficients for all functions, i.e., the matrix needs to be able to store coefficients up to degree $2L$.

To obtain the coefficients of the multiplication result, we consider all pairs of spherical harmonic basis functions with the corresponding spherical harmonic coefficients. Due to the possible applicability of the approach to the update step, we shall call the involved coefficient matrices $\mathbf{C}_t^{\text{p,id}}$, $\mathbf{C}_t^{\text{L,id}}$, and $\mathbf{C}_t^{\text{e,id}}$. We can use (D.1) to know that

$$c_{t,l_1}^{\text{e,id},m_1} Y_{l_1}^{m_1} c_{t,l_2}^{\text{L,id},m_2} Y_{l_2}^{m_2}$$
$$= \sum_{l_c=|l_1-l_2|}^{l_1+l_2} c_{t,l_1}^{\text{e,id},m_1} c_{t,l_2}^{\text{L,id},m_2} \sqrt{\frac{(2l_1+1)(2l_2+1)}{4\pi(2l_c+1)}}\, C_{0,0,0}^{l_1,l_2,l_c} C_{m_1,m_2,m_1+m_2}^{l_1,l_2,l_c} Y_{l_c}^{m_1+m_2}$$

holds. For all valid combinations of basis functions $Y_{l_1}^{m_1}$ and $Y_{l_2}^{m_2}$, we add

$$c_{t,l_1}^{\text{e,id},m_1} c_{t,l_2}^{\text{L,id},m_2} \sqrt{\frac{(2l_1+1)(2l_2+1)}{4\pi(2l_c+1)}}\, C_{0,0,0}^{l_1,l_2,l_c} C_{m_1,m_2,m_1+m_2}^{l_1,l_2,l_c}$$

to the entries of the preallocated matrix for degrees l_c from $|l_1 - l_2|$ to $l_1 + l_2$ and order $m_1 + m_2$.

If both functions are represented using $N = (L+1)^2$ coefficients, we have $N^2 = (L+1)^4$ combinations. For each combination, $O(L) = O(\sqrt{N})$ coefficients must be updated, resulting in a run time of $O(L^5) = O(N^{2.5})$ for this naïve implementation. While it may be possible to realize a more efficient implementation (similar to the fast discrete convolution for Fourier coefficient tensors), we know of no implementation with a computational effort of less than $O(N^{2.5})$ that yields the result without using a spherical harmonic transform.

APPENDIX E

Association Likelihood for von Mises Densities

In this appendix, we first derive a closed-form formula for the association likelihood for von Mises densities. The formula can be used as an approximation for other densities if they are unimodal and can be approximated well using von Mises densities. In the second part of this appendix, we provide a way to reformulate certain multimodal estimation problems. Such problems arise, e.g., in the bulk material tracking scenario when the orientations of the particles are ambiguous due to symmetries.

E.1 Derivation of the Association Likelihood

In Section 3.5.1, we have identified terms in $-\sum_{i=1}^{n} \log \ell(\hat{\underline{z}}^{\tau(i)}|i)$ that are independent of the permutation τ. Because such terms do not influence the result of the LAP solver, they can be disregarded when calculating the entries of the association matrix. For normal distributions, the only term that remains is the squared Mahalanobis distance scaled by $\frac{1}{2}$. In our derivation of the closed-form formula for the association matrix for von Mises densities, we also identify components that can be disregarded.

The involved von Mises densities are parameterized as follows. The prior density of the ith track is given by $f_{\text{VM}}(x^{\text{Ori},i}; \hat{\mu}^{\text{p},i}, \kappa^{\text{p},i})$, and the measurement likelihood of the jth measurement is $f_{\text{VM}}(\hat{z}^{\text{Ori},j}; x^{\text{Ori},i}, \kappa^{\boldsymbol{v},j})$. For these von Mises densities, we get

$$
\begin{aligned}
-\log \ell(\hat{z}^{\text{Ori},j}|i) &= -\log \int_0^{2\pi} f_{\text{VM}}(\hat{z}^{\text{Ori},j}; x^{\text{Ori},i}, \kappa^{\boldsymbol{v},j}) f_{\text{VM}}(x^{\text{Ori},i}; \hat{\mu}^{\text{p},i}, \kappa^{\text{p},i}) dx^{\text{Ori},i} \\
&= -\log \int_0^{2\pi} \frac{1}{2\pi I_0(\kappa^{\boldsymbol{v},j}) 2\pi I_0(\kappa^{\text{p},i})} \\
&\qquad \mathrm{e}^{\kappa^{\boldsymbol{v},j} \cos(\hat{z}^{\text{Ori},j} - x^{\text{Ori},i})} \mathrm{e}^{\kappa^{\text{p},i} \cos(x^{\text{Ori},i} - \hat{\mu}^{\text{p},i})} dx^{\text{Ori},i} \\
&= \log\left(2\pi I_0(\kappa^{\boldsymbol{v},j}) 2\pi I_0(\kappa^{\text{p},i})\right) \\
&\quad -\log \int_0^{2\pi} \mathrm{e}^{\kappa^{\boldsymbol{v},j} \cos(\hat{z}^{\text{Ori},j} - x^{\text{Ori},i})} \mathrm{e}^{\kappa^{\text{p},i} \cos(x^{\text{Ori},i} - \hat{\mu}^{\text{p},i})} dx^{\text{Ori},i} \,.
\end{aligned}
$$

We now take the sum over all negative logarithms of the likelihoods for an association decision that is described by the permutation τ. In this case, the measurement index is defined by the track index and the permutation according $j = \tau(i)$. Thus, we obtain

$$
\begin{aligned}
-\sum_{i=1}^{n} \log \ell(\underline{\hat{z}}^{\text{Ori},\tau(i)}|i) &= \sum_{i=1}^{n} \log\left(2\pi I_0(\kappa^{\boldsymbol{v},\tau(i)}) 2\pi I_0(\kappa^{\text{p},i})\right) \\
&\quad + \sum_{i=1}^{n} \underbrace{-\log \int_0^{2\pi} \mathrm{e}^{\kappa^{\boldsymbol{v},\tau(i)} \cos(\hat{z}^{\text{Ori},\tau(i)} - x^{\text{Ori},i})} \mathrm{e}^{\kappa^{\text{p},i} \cos(x^{\text{Ori},i} - \hat{\mu}^{\text{p},i})} dx^{\text{Ori},i}}_{\Delta:=} \,.
\end{aligned}
\tag{E.1}
$$

Because the value of

$$
\begin{aligned}
&\sum_{i=1}^{n} \log\left(2\pi I_0(\kappa^{\boldsymbol{v},\tau(i)}) 2\pi I_0(\kappa^{\text{p},i})\right) \\
&= \sum_{i=1}^{n} \log\left(2\pi I_0(\kappa^{\boldsymbol{v},\tau(i)})\right) + \sum_{i=1}^{n} \log\left(2\pi I_0(\kappa^{\text{p},i})\right) \\
&= \sum_{i=1}^{n} \log\left(2\pi I_0(\kappa^{\boldsymbol{v},i})\right) + \sum_{i=1}^{n} \log\left(2\pi I_0(\kappa^{\text{p},i})\right)
\end{aligned}
$$

is independent of τ, we can disregard the first sum on the right-hand side of (E.1).

As $f_{\text{VM}}(\hat{z}^{\text{Ori},j}; x^{\text{Ori},i}, \kappa^{\boldsymbol{v},j}) = f_{\text{VM}}(x^{\text{Ori},i}; \hat{z}^{\text{Ori},j}, \kappa^{\boldsymbol{v},j})$, the product in Δ is essentially a product of two unnormalized von Mises densities. To find a closed-form formula, we use the fact that the result of the multiplication of two von Mises densities is a (generally unnormalized) von Mises density. For the density obtained after the normalization, the parameters can be calculated depending on the means μ_1 and μ_2 and concentration parameters κ_1 and κ_2 according to [ARCB09]

$$C(\mu_1, \mu_2, \kappa_1, \kappa_2) = \kappa_1 \cos(\mu_1) + \kappa_2 \cos(\mu_2) \ , \tag{E.2}$$

$$S(\mu_1, \mu_2, \kappa_1, \kappa_2) = \kappa_1 \sin(\mu_1) + \kappa_2 \sin(\mu_2) \ , \tag{E.3}$$

$$\mu_{\text{Mult}}(\mu_1, \mu_2, \kappa_1, \kappa_2) = \text{atan2}(S(\kappa_1, \kappa_2, \mu_1, \mu_2), C(\kappa_1, \kappa_2, \mu_1, \mu_2)) \ ,$$

$$\kappa_{\text{Mult}}(\mu_1, \mu_2, \kappa_1, \kappa_2) = \sqrt{(C(\mu_1, \mu_2, \kappa_1, \kappa_2))^2 + (S(\mu_1, \mu_2, \kappa_1, \kappa_2))^2} \ .$$

We use these formulae for the input arguments $\mu_1 = \hat{z}^{\text{Ori},j}$, $\mu_2 = \hat{\mu}^{\text{p},i}$, $\kappa_1 = \kappa^{\boldsymbol{v},\tau(i)}$, and $\kappa_2 = \kappa^{\text{p},i}$ and omit the input arguments of C, S, μ_{Mult}, and κ_{Mult} for brevity from now on.

While a normalization is not desired in our case, we can use the formula for the parameters of the result of the update step to know that

$$\begin{aligned} &\exp\left(\kappa^{\boldsymbol{v},\tau(i)} \cos(\hat{z}^{\text{Ori},\tau(i)} - x^{\text{Ori},i})\right) \exp\left(\kappa^{\text{p},i} \cos(x^{\text{Ori},i} - \hat{\mu}^{\text{p},i})\right) \\ &\qquad = \lambda \exp\left(\kappa_{\text{Mult}} \cos(x^{\text{Ori},i} - \mu_{\text{Mult}})\right) \end{aligned} \tag{E.4}$$

holds for some constant $\lambda > 0$. To obtain λ, we use that the exponential function is positive on the entire real line, and thus, both the left-hand and the right-hand sides of (E.4) are positive. Since the entire function on the right-hand side of (E.4) is scaled by the same value, we can evaluate the left-hand side and the right-hand side without λ for an arbitrary input value and then determine by which factor the two values differ. Using zero as the input value, we get

$$\lambda = \frac{\exp\left(\kappa^{\boldsymbol{v},\tau(i)} \cos(\hat{z}^{\text{Ori},\tau(i)}) + \kappa^{\text{p},i} \cos(\hat{\mu}^{\text{p},i})\right)}{\exp\left(\kappa_{\text{Mult}} \cos(\mu_{\text{Mult}})\right)} \ . \tag{E.5}$$

Now, we inspect the argument of the exponential function in the denominator

$$\Gamma = \kappa_{\text{Mult}} \cos(\mu_{\text{Mult}}) \ .$$

We write $\cos(\mu_{\text{Mult}})$ depending on C and S defined in (E.2) and (E.3), yielding

$$\cos(\mu_{\text{Mult}}) = \cos(\text{atan2}(S, C)) \ .$$

We further use [Hem]

$$\cos(\text{atan}(\alpha)) = \frac{1}{\sqrt{1+\alpha^2}}$$

and consider all quadrants and borders of the quadrants of the atan2 separately to obtain

$$\cos(\mu_{\text{Mult}}) = \begin{cases} \cos(\text{atan}(S/C)) = \frac{1}{\sqrt{1+S^2/C^2}} = \frac{C}{\sqrt{C^2+S^2}} & C > 0,\ S > 0 \\ \cos(\pi + \text{atan}(S/C)) = -\frac{1}{\sqrt{1+S^2/C^2}} & \\ \qquad = \frac{-|C|}{\sqrt{C^2+S^2}} = \frac{C}{\sqrt{C^2+S^2}} & C < 0,\ S > 0 \\ \cos(-\pi + \text{atan}(S/C)) & \\ \qquad = \cos(\pi + \text{atan}(S/C)) = \frac{C}{\sqrt{C^2+S^2}} & C < 0,\ S < 0 \\ \cos(\text{atan}(S/C)) = \frac{C}{\sqrt{C^2+S^2}} & C > 0,\ S < 0 \\ \cos(0) = 1 = \frac{C}{\sqrt{C^2}} = \frac{C}{\sqrt{C^2+S^2}} & C > 0,\ S = 0 \\ \cos\left(\frac{\pi}{2}\right) = 0 = \frac{C}{\sqrt{C^2+S^2}} & C = 0,\ S > 0 \\ \cos(\pi) = -1 = \frac{C}{\sqrt{C^2}} = \frac{C}{\sqrt{C^2+S^2}} & C < 0,\ S = 0 \\ \cos\left(-\frac{\pi}{2}\right) = 0 = \frac{C}{\sqrt{C^2+S^2}} & C = 0,\ S < 0 \\ \text{undefined} & C = S = 0 \ . \end{cases}$$

Since $\cos(\text{atan2}(S, C))$ is defined for the same values and has the same function values as $C/\sqrt{C^2 + S^2}$,

$$\cos(\mu_{\text{Mult}}) = \frac{C}{\sqrt{C^2 + S^2}}$$

holds.

Thus, we can rewrite Γ as

$$\Gamma = \kappa_{\text{Mult}} \frac{C}{\sqrt{C^2 + S^2}} = \sqrt{C^2 + S^2} \frac{C}{\sqrt{C^2 + S^2}} = C \ .$$

By writing out C, we obtain

$$\Gamma = \kappa^{\boldsymbol{v},\tau(i)} \cos(\hat{z}^{\text{Ori},\tau(i)}) + \kappa^{\text{p},i} \cos(\hat{\mu}^{\text{p},i}) \ .$$

The right-hand side is precisely the argument of the exponential function in the numerator of (E.5). Hence, $\lambda = 1$.

Using this, we can write Δ as

$$\Delta = \int_0^{2\pi} \exp\left(\kappa_{\text{Mult}} \cos(x^{\text{Ori},i} - \mu_{\text{Mult}})\right) dx^{\text{Ori},i} \ .$$

This is an integral of a von Mises density without the normalization constant over $[0, 2\pi)$. Since the value of the integral is the reciprocal of the normalization constant, we obtain

$$-\log \Delta = -\log(2\pi I_0(\kappa_{\text{Mult}})) = -\log(2\pi) - \log(I_0(\kappa_{\text{Mult}})) \ .$$

The term $-\log(2\pi)$ can be discarded because it is independent of the permutation τ. Thus, only $-\log(I_0(\kappa_{\text{Mult}}))$ needs to be considered for the entries of the association matrix for the orientation component. To calculate the entries of the association matrix, we replace $\tau(i)$ by j and then calculate the negative logarithm of the concentration parameter κ_{Mult} for all combinations of indices i and j from 1 to n.

The formula can be used as an approximation if the densities and likelihoods can be approximated using von Mises densities. However, no reasonable approximation can be obtained when the mean direction is undefined, e.g., when the density is antipodally symmetric. For example, the noise distributions presented in Figures 7.2c and 7.2d do not have well-defined mean directions. To approximate the association likelihood based on the formula just presented, we describe a way to reformulate the estimation problem.

E.2 Adjusting the Estimation Problem for Visual Ambiguities

In Figure 7.2d, a von Mises mixture with two components is used to describe the measurement noise. The noise density was generated under the assumption that there are two sources of error. First, the extracted orientation is influenced by a von Mises-distributed noise term. Second, the image processing provides the resulting orientation or the orientation shifted by π with equal probability.

More formally, we can write the underlying measurement equation as

$$\boldsymbol{z}_t = (\boldsymbol{x}_t + \boldsymbol{v}_t + \pi \boldsymbol{r}_t) \mod 2\pi \tag{E.6}$$

with a von Mises-distributed noise term $\boldsymbol{v}_t$ and a uniformly distributed discrete random variable $\boldsymbol{r}_t$ with probability mass function

$$p_t^{\boldsymbol{r}}(0) = p_t^{\boldsymbol{r}}(1) = \frac{1}{2} \ .$$

This equation can also be used for, e.g., 120 or 90-degree symmetries by letting $\boldsymbol{r}_t$ take on additional values and scaling the random variable differently in the measurement equation.

Using the Fourier filters, even densities and likelihoods with multiple modes do not pose a problem for the estimator. However, for the von Mises filter, it is advantageous to reformulate the estimation problem as a unimodal one. While the orientation of a particle around the vertical axis is 2π-periodic, its absolute orientation may not be relevant to us. To improve the association decision, it is sufficient to focus on states that can be distinguished visually. Thus, we can formulate our problem as a π-periodic problem that considers states that are supposedly visually indistinguishable to be equal. The new measurement model is thus

$$\boldsymbol{z}_t^{\text{Symm}} = (\boldsymbol{x}_t^{\text{Symm}} + \boldsymbol{v}_t^{\text{Symm}}) \mod \pi \ . \tag{E.7}$$

Similarly, a π-periodic system model needs to be used for the prediction step. Using appropriate adjustments, filters for 2π-periodic manifolds can be used for the π-periodic estimation problem. To be able to use 2π-periodic filters, the measurements need to be multiplied by 2, which yields values in $[0, 2\pi)$. Further, the derived estimates need to be divided by 2 to obtain an estimate in $[0, \pi)$. For the Fourier filters, the system noise density and likelihood can simply be evaluated on a grid on $[0, \pi)$ to obtain appropriate coefficients using a DFT. To be able to apply the von Mises filter, the π-periodic system and measurement noise densities need to be scaled and approximated by 2π-periodic von Mises densities.

If the estimation problem is not formulated according to (E.7) but according to (E.6), suitable π-periodic system and measurement models have to be derived from the 2π-periodic models. Let us again consider a measurement noise density that is an antipodally symmetric mixture of two von Mises densities in the 2π-periodic formulation. To wrap this density on $[0, 2\pi)$ to a circle with circumference π, we add $f(x+\pi)$ to $f(x)$ for all $x \in [0, \pi)$ and obtain a normalized density on $[0, \pi)$. The problem can then be seen as a π-periodic problem in the form of (E.6). When appropriate π-periodic models have been derived, 2π-periodic filters can be applied by using the above described adjustments.

Bibliography

[AKK16] Yibeltal F. Alem, Zubair Khalid, and Rodney A. Kennedy. Spherical Harmonic Expansion of Fisher–Bingham Distribution and 3-D Spatial Fading Correlation for Multiple-Antenna Systems. *IEEE Transactions on Vehicular Technology*, 65(7):5695–5700, July 2016.

[AMGC02] M. Sanjeev Arulampalam, Simon Maskell, Neil Gordon, and Tim Clapp. A Tutorial on Particle Filters for Online Nonlinear/Non-Gaussian Bayesian Tracking. *IEEE Transactions on Signal Processing*, 50(2):174–188, 2002.

[And03] Theodore W. Anderson. *An Introduction to Multivariate Statistical Analysis*. Wiley-Interscience, Hoboken, New Jersey, USA, 3rd edition, 2003.

[ARCB09] Monir Azmani, Serge Reboul, Jean-Bernard Choquel, and Mohammed Benjelloun. A Recursive Fusion Filter for Angular Data. In *Proceedings of the 2009 IEEE International Conference on Robotics and Biomimetics (ROBIO 2009)*, December 2009.

[AS72] Milton Abramowitz and Irene A. Stegun. *Handbook of Mathematical Functions with Formulas, Graphs, and Mathematical Tables*. Dover, New York, 10th edition, 1972.

[AW12] George B. Arfken and Hans J. Weber. *Mathematical Methods for Physicists*. Academic Press, 7th edition, 2012.

[Bat81] Edward Batschelet. *Circular Statistics in Biology.* Mathematics in Biology. Academic Press, London, 1981.

[Bau15] Marcus Baum. Linear-time JPDAF Based on Many-2-Many Approximation of Marginal Association Probabilities. *Electronics Letters*, 51(19):1526–1528, 2015.

[BC49] Salomon Bochner and Komaravolu Chandrasekharan. *Fourier Transforms.* Princeton University Press, 1949.

[BCM70] Richard S. Bucy, S. Y. Cheng, and A. J. Mallinckrodt. A Design Study for an Optimal Non-Linear Receiver/Demodulator. Final Report. 1970.

[Ber09] Dimitri P. Bertsekas. *Encyclopedia of Optimization*, chapter Auction Algorithms, pages 128–132. Springer-Verlag, 2nd edition, 2009.

[BFB97] Miguel A. Blanco, M. Flórez, and M. Bermejo. Evaluation of the Rotation Matrices in the Basis of Real Spherical Harmonics. *Journal of Molecular Structure (Theochem)*, 419:19–27, 1997.

[BGK95] Christian Brechbühler, Guido Gerig, and Olaf Kübler. Parametrization of Closed Surfaces for 3-D Shape Description. *Computer Vision and Image Understanding*, 61(2):154–170, 1995.

[BH13] Marcus Baum and Uwe D. Hanebeck. The Kernel-SME Filter for Multiple Target Tracking. In *Proceedings of the 16th International Conference on Information Fusion (Fusion 2013)*, Istanbul, Turkey, July 2013.

[Bin74] Christopher Bingham. An Antipodally Symmetric Distribution on the Sphere. *The Annals of Statistics*, 2(6):1201–1225, November 1974.

[BL84] Lawrence C. Biedenharn and James D. Louck. *Angular Momentum in Quantum Physics.* Cambridge University Press, 1984.

[Bla04] Samuel S. Blackman. Multiple Hypothesis Tracking for Multiple Target Tracking. *IEEE Aerospace and Electronic Systems Magazine*, 19(1):5–18, Jan 2004.

[BM75] Richard S. Bucy and A. J. Mallinckrodt. An Optimal Phase Demodulator. *Stochastics*, 1(1-4):3–23, 1975.

[BMT+08] Wouter Boomsma, Kanti V. Mardia, Charles C. Taylor, Jesper Ferkinghoff-Borg, Anders Krogh, and Thomas Hamelryck. A Generative, Probabilistic Model of Local Protein Structure. *Proceedings of the National Academy of Sciences*, 105(26):8932–8937, 2008.

[Bov05] Alan C. Bovik. *Handbook of Image and Video Processing.* Academic Press, 2nd edition, 2005.

[BP99] Samuel Blackman and Robert Popoli. *Design and Analysis of Modern Tracking Systems.* 1999.

[BSDH09] Yaakov Bar-Shalom, Fred Daum, and Jim Huang. The Probabilistic Data Association Filter. *IEEE Control Systems*, 29(6):82–100, 2009.

[BSH06a] Dietrich Brunn, Felix Sawo, and Uwe D. Hanebeck. Efficient Nonlinear Bayesian Estimation Based on Fourier Densities. In *Proceedings of the 2006 IEEE International Conference on Multisensor Fusion and Integration for Intelligent Systems (MFI 2006)*, Heidelberg, Germany, September 2006.

[BSH06b] Dietrich Brunn, Felix Sawo, and Uwe D. Hanebeck. Nonlinear Multidimensional Bayesian Estimation with Fourier Densities. In *Proceedings of the 2006 IEEE Conference on Decision and Control (CDC 2006)*, San Diego, California, USA, December 2006.

[BSKG05] Yaakov Bar-Shalom, Thia Kirubarajan, and Cenk Gokberk. Tracking with Classification-Aided Multiframe Data Association. *IEEE Transactions on Aerospace and Electronic Systems*, 41(3):868–878, July 2005.

[CBR08] José A. Carta, Celia Bueno, and Penélope Ramírez. Statistical Modelling of Directional Wind Speeds Using Mixtures of von Mises Distributions: Case Study. *Energy Conversion and Management*, 49(5):897–907, May 2008.

[Chi76] Colin D. H. Chisholm. *Group Theoretical Techniques in Quantum Chemistry*. Academic Press, London, 1976.

[CHL+10] Yi-Shun Chen, Shu-San Hsiau, Hsuan-Yi Lee, Yau-Pin Chyou, and Chia-Jen Hsu. Size Separation of Particulates in a Trommel Screen System. *Chemical Engineering and Processing: Process Intensification*, 49(11), 2010.

[CP98] Alessandro Chiuso and Giorgio Picci. Visual Tracking of Points as Estimation on the Unit Sphere. *The Confluence of Vision and Control, Lecture Notes in Control and Information Science*, 237:90–105, 1998.

[CS79] Peter A. Cundall and Otto D. L. Strack. A Discrete Numerical Model for Granular Assemblies. *Géotechnique*, 29(1):47–65, 1979.

[CT65] James W. Cooley and John W. Tukey. An Algorithm for the Machine Calculation of Complex Fourier Series. *Mathematics of Computation*, 19(90):297–301, 1965.

[CWN+15a] Yu-Hui Chen, Dennis Wei, Gregory Newstadt, Marc DeGraef, Jeffrey Simmons, and Alfred Hero. Parameter Estimation in Spherical Symmetry Groups. *IEEE Signal Processing Letters*, 22(8):1152–1155, 2015.

[CWN+15b] Yu-Hui Chen, Dennis Wei, Gregory Newstadt, Marc DeGraef, Jeffrey Simmons, and Alfred Hero. Statistical Estimation and Clustering of Group-Invariant Orientation Parameters. In *Proceedings of the 18th International Conference on Information Fusion (Fusion 2015)*, Washington D. C., USA, July 2015.

[DF94] Rosa Di Felice. The Voidage Function for Fluid–Particle Interaction Systems. *International Journal of Multiphase Flow*, 20(1):153–159, 1994.

[DH94] James R. Driscoll and Dennis M. Healy, Jr. Computing Fourier Transforms and Convolutions on the 2-Sphere. *Advances in Applied Mathematics*, 15(2):202–250, 1994.

[DM84] Dan E. Dudgeon and Russell M. Mersereau. *Multidimensional Digital Signal Processing*. Prentice Hall, 1984.

[DP10] Ivan Dokmanic and Davor Petrinovic. Convolution on the n-Sphere With Application to PDF Modeling. *IEEE Transactions on Signal Processing*, 58(3):1157–1170, March 2010.

[Dru00] Oliver E. Drummond. Integration of Features and Attributes into Target Tracking. In *Proceedings of the SPIE, volume 4048, Signal and Data Processing of Small Targets 2000*, 2000.

[Dru01] Oliver E. Drummond. Feature-, Attribute-, and Classification-Aided Target Tracking. In *Proceedings of the SPIE, volume 4473, Signal and Data Processing of Small Targets 2001*, 2001.

[Dru03] Oliver E. Drummond. On Categorical Feature-Aided Target Tracking. In *Proceedings of the SPIE, volume 5204, Signal and Data Processing of Small Targets 2003*, 2003.

[Dur00] Jacques Duran. *Sands, Powders, and Grains: An Introduction to the Physics of Granular Materials*. Springer-Verlag, 2000.

[DV90] Pierre Duhamel and Martin Vetterli. Fast Fourier Transforms: A Tutorial Review and a State of the Art. *Signal Processing*, 19(4):259–299, 1990.

[FD04] Juan J. Fernández-Durán. Circular Distributions Based on Nonnegative Trigonometric Sums. *Biometrics*, 60(2):499–503, 2004.

[FGP15] Robert S. Fitzpatrick, Hylke J. Glass, and Richard D. Pascoe. CFD–DEM Modelling of Particle Ejection by a Sensor-Based Automated Sorter. *Minerals Engineering*, 79:176–184, 2015.

[FJY07] Maurice C. Fuerstenau, Graeme J. Jameson, and Roe-Hoan Yoon. *Froth Flotation: A Century of Innovation*. SME, 2007.

[Ger46] J. Geronimus. On the Trigonometric Moment Problem. *Annals of Mathematics*, 47(4):742–761, 1946.

[GK14] Jared Glover and Leslie P. Kaelbling. Tracking the Spin on a Ping Pong Ball with the Quaternion Bingham Filter. In *Proceedings of the 2014 IEEE Conference on Robotics and Automation (ICRA 2014)*, Hong Kong, China, 2014.

[GKH15] Igor Gilitschenski, Gerhard Kurz, and Uwe D. Hanebeck. Non-Identity Measurement Models for Orientation Estimation Based on Directional Statistics. In *Proceedings of the 18th International Conference on Information Fusion (Fusion 2015)*, Washington D.C., USA, July 2015.

[GKJH16] Igor Gilitschenski, Gerhard Kurz, Simon J. Julier, and Uwe D. Hanebeck. Unscented Orientation Estimation Based on the Bingham Distribution. *IEEE Transactions on Automatic Control*, 61(1):172–177, January 2016.

[GM07] Mariano Giaquinta and Giuseppe Modica. *Mathematical Analysis: Linear and Metric Structures and Continuity*. Birkhäuser, 2007.

[Hab11] Howard Haber. Physics 116A: Mathematical Methods in Physics I. Available online. http://scipp.ucsc.edu/~haber/ph116A/arg_11.pdf, 2011.

[Han13] Uwe D. Hanebeck. PGF 42: Progressive Gaussian Filtering with a Twist. In *Proceedings of the 16th International Conference on Information Fusion (Fusion 2013)*, Istanbul, Turkey, July 2013.

[HB15] Uwe D. Hanebeck and Marcus Baum. Association-Free Direct Filtering of Multi-Target Random Finite Sets with Set Distance Measures. In *Proceedings of the 18th International Conference on Information Fusion (Fusion 2015)*, Washington D.C., USA, July 2015.

[Hem] Thomas Hempel. Mathematische Grundlagen, trigonometrische Funktionen (in German). Available online. http://www.uni-magdeburg.de/exph/mathe_gl/trigonometrische_funktionen.pdf.

[HKK+18] Young J. Heo, Se J. Kim, Dayeon Kim, Keondo Lee, and Wan K. Chung. Super-High-Purity Seed Sorter Using Low-Latency Image-Recognition Based on Deep Learning. *IEEE Robotics and Automation Letters*, 2018.

[HRG+17] Lifeng He, Xiwei Ren, Qihang Gao, Xiao Zhao, Bin Yao, and Yuyan Chao. The Connected-Component Labeling Problem: A Review of State-of-the-Art Algorithms. *Pattern Recognition*, 70:25–43, 2017.

[HRKM03] Dennis M. Healy, Jr., D. N. Rockmore, P. J. Kostelec, and Sean S. B. Moore. FFTs for the 2-Sphere—Improvements and Variations. *Journal of Fourier Analysis and Applications*, 9(4):341–385, July 2003.

[Hug07] Gareth Hughes. *Multivariate and Time Series Models for Circular Data with Applications to Protein Conformational Angles*. Ph.D. thesis, The University of Leeds, 2007.

[HWS13] Dominik Höhner, Siegmar Wirtz, and Viktor Scherer. Experimental and Numerical Investigation on the Influence of Particle Shape and Shape Approximation on Hopper Discharge Using the Discrete Element Method. *Powder Technology*, 235:614–627, 2013.

[ILL10] Alberto Ibort, P. Linares, and José G. Llavona. On the Multilinear Trigonometric Problem of Moments. *Contemporary Mathematics*, 507:141–153, 2010.

[JK04] S. Rao Jammalamadaka and Tomasz J. Kozubowski. New Families of Wrapped Distributions for Modeling Skew Circular Data. *Communications in Statistics—Theory and Methods*, 33(9):2059–2074, 2004.

[JM80] Peter E. Jupp and Kanti V. Mardia. A General Correlation Coefficient for Directional Data and Related Regression Problems. *Biometrika*, 67(1):163–173, 1980.

[JS01] S. Rao Jammalamadaka and Ashis Sengupta. *Topics in Circular Statistics*. World Scientific, 2001.

[JU04] Simon J. Julier and Jeffrey K. Uhlmann. Unscented Filtering and Nonlinear Estimation. *Proceedings of the IEEE*, 92(3):401–422, March 2004.

[JV87] Roy Jonker and Anton Volgenant. A Shortest Augmenting Path Algorithm for Dense and Sparse Linear Assignment Problems. *Computing*, 38(4):325–340, 1987.

[JW77] Richard A. Johnson and Thomas Wehrly. Measures and Models for Angular Correlation and Angular–Linear Correlation. *Journal of the Royal Statistical Society B*, 39(2):222–229, 1977.

[Kal60] Rudolf E. Kalman. A New Approach to Linear Filtering and Prediction Problems. *Journal of Basic Engineering*, 82:35–45, 1960.

[Kay93] Steven Kay. *Fundamentals of Statistical Signal Processing: Estimation Theory*. Prentice Hall, 1993.

[KDH15] Gerhard Kurz, Maxim Dolgov, and Uwe D. Hanebeck. Nonlinear Stochastic Model Predictive Control in the Circular Domain. In *Proceedings of the 2015 American Control Conference (ACC 2015)*, Chicago, Illinois, USA, July 2015.

[KDJD03] H. U. R. Kattentidt, T. P. R. De Jong, and W. L. Dalmijn. Multi-Sensor Identification and Sorting of Bulk Solids. *Control Engineering Practice*, 11(1), 2003.

[Ken08] Hugh L. Kennedy. Controlling Track Coalescence with Scaled Joint Probabilistic Data Association. In *Proceedings of the 2008 International Conference on Radar*, September 2008.

[KGDH14] Gerhard Kurz, Igor Gilitschenski, Maxim Dolgov, and Uwe D. Hanebeck. Bivariate Angular Estimation Under Consideration of Dependencies Using Directional Statistics. In *Proceedings of the 53rd IEEE Conference on Decision and Control (CDC 2014)*, Los Angeles, California, USA, December 2014.

[KGH13] Gerhard Kurz, Igor Gilitschenski, and Uwe D. Hanebeck. Recursive Nonlinear Filtering for Angular Data Based on Circular Distributions. In *Proceedings of the 2013 American Control Conference (ACC 2013)*, Washington D.C., USA, June 2013.

[KGH14] Gerhard Kurz, Igor Gilitschenski, and Uwe D. Hanebeck. Nonlinear Measurement Update for Estimation of Angular Systems Based on Circular Distributions. In *Proceedings of the 2014 American Control Conference (ACC 2014)*, Portland, Oregon, USA, June 2014.

[KGH16a] Gerhard Kurz, Igor Gilitschenski, and Uwe D. Hanebeck. Recursive Bayesian Filtering in Circular State Spaces. *IEEE Aerospace and Electronic Systems Magazine*, 31(3):70–87, March 2016.

[KGH16b] Gerhard Kurz, Igor Gilitschenski, and Uwe D. Hanebeck. Unscented von Mises–Fisher Filtering. *IEEE Signal Processing Letters*, 23(4):463–467, April 2016.

[KGJH14] Gerhard Kurz, Igor Gilitschenski, Simon Julier, and Uwe D. Hanebeck. Recursive Bingham Filter for Directional Estimation Involving 180 Degree Symmetry. *Journal of Advances in Information Fusion*, 9(2):90–105, December 2014.

[KH15] Gerhard Kurz and Uwe D. Hanebeck. Toroidal Information Fusion Based on the Bivariate von Mises Distribution. In *Proceedings of the 2015 IEEE International Conference on Multisensor Fusion and Integration for Intelligent Systems (MFI 2015)*, San Diego, California, USA, September 2015.

[KH17] Gerhard Kurz and Uwe D. Hanebeck. Deterministic Sampling on the Torus for Bivariate Circular Estimation. *IEEE Transactions on Aerospace and Electronic Systems*, 53(1):530–534, February 2017.

[KM12] Stefan Kunis and Ines Melzer. A Stable and Accurate Butterfly Sparse Fourier Transform. *SIAM Journal on Numerical Analysis*, 50(3):1777–1800, 2012.

[KMvdO16] Stefan Kunis, H. Michael Möller, and Ulrich von der Ohe. Prony's Method on the Sphere. *arXiv preprint arXiv:1603.02020*, 2016.

[KPRvdO16] Stefan Kunis, Thomas Peter, Tim Römer, and Ulrich von der Ohe. A Multivariate Generalization of Prony's Method. *Linear Algebra and Its Applications*, 490:31–47, 2016.

[KS04] Karsten Kunze and Helmut Schaeben. The Bingham Distribution of Quaternions and Its Spherical Radon Transform in Texture Analysis. *Mathematical Geology*, 36:917–943, 2004.

[KS13] Rodney A. Kennedy and Parastoo Sadeghi. *Hilbert Space Methods in Signal Processing.* Cambridge University Press, 2013.

[Kuh55] Harold W. Kuhn. The Hungarian Method for the Assignment Problem. *Naval Research Logistics (NRL)*, 2(1-2):83–97, 1955.

[Kur15] Gerhard Kurz. *Directional Estimation for Robotic Beating Heart Surgery*, Ph.D. thesis, Karlsruhe Institute of Technology, 2015.

[Län07] Thomas Längle. Quality Control of Bulk Material in Factories of the Future. In *Proceedings of the 23rd ISPE International Conference on CAD/CAM, Robotics and Factories of the Future (Cars & FOF 2007)*, 2007.

[LC98] Erich L. Lehmann and George Casella. *Theory of Point Estimation.* Springer-Verlag, 2nd edition, 1998.

[LIHL09] Martin Liggins II, David Hall, and James Llinas. *Handbook of Multisensor Data Fusion: Theory and Practice.* CRC Press, 2nd edition, 2009.

[LJ03] X. Rong Li and Vesselin P. Jilkov. Survey of Maneuvering Target Tracking. Part I. Dynamic Models. *IEEE Transactions on Aerospace and Electronic Systems*, 39(4):1333–1364, 2003.

[LW75] James T. Lo and Alan Willsky. Estimation for Rotational Processes with One Degree of Freedom–Part I: Introduction and Continuous-Time Processes. *IEEE Transactions on Automatic Control*, 20(1):10–21, Feb 1975.

[Mah03] Ronald P. S. Mahler. Multitarget Bayes Filtering via First-Order Multitarget Moments. *IEEE Transactions on Aerospace and Electronic Systems*, 39(4):1152–1178, 2003.

[Mah07] Ronald P. S. Mahler. *Statistical Multisource-Multitarget Information Fusion.* Artech House, Inc., 2007.

[Mar81] Kanti V. Mardia. Directional Statistics in Geosciences. *Communications in Statistics—Theory and Methods*, 10(15):1523–1543, 1981.

[MHTS08] Kanti V. Mardia, Gareth Hughes, Charles C. Taylor, and Harshinder Singh. A Multivariate von Mises Distribution with Applications to Bioinformatics. *Canadian Journal of Statistics*, 36(1):99–109, 2008.

[MJ99] Kanti V. Mardia and Peter E. Jupp. *Directional Statistics.* John Wiley & Sons, 1999.

[MS07] Jens Maue and Peter Sanders. Engineering Algorithms for Approximate Weighted Matching. *Experimental Algorithms, Lecture Notes in Computer Science*, 4525:242–255, 2007.

[MTS07] Kanti V. Mardia, Charles C. Taylor, and Ganesh K. Subramaniam. Protein Bioinformatics and Mixtures of Bivariate von Mises Distributions for Angular Data. *Biometrics*, 63(2):505–512, 2007.

[Nor89] Kenneth Nordström. Some Further Aspects of the Löwner-Ordering Antitonicity of the Moore–Penrose Inverse. *Communications in Statistics—Theory and Methods*, 18(12):4471–4489, 1989.

[Obe73] Fritz Oberhettinger. *Fourier Transforms of Distributions and Their Inverses.* Academic Press, 1973.

[Obe74] John Oberteuffer. Magnetic Separation: A Review of Principles, Devices, and Applications. *IEEE Transactions on Magnetics*, 10(2):223–238, Jun 1974.

[PM06] John G. Proakis and Dimitris G. Manolakis. *Digital Signal Processing.* Prentice Hall, 4th edition, 2006.

[RH01] Ravi Ramamoorthi and Pat Hanrahan. An Efficient Representation for Irradiance Environment Maps. In *Proceedings of the 28th Annual Conference on Computer Graphics and Interactive Techniques*, 2001.

[RLB15] Matthias Richter, Thomas Längle, and Jürgen Beyerer. An Approach to Color-Based Sorting of Bulk Materials with Automated Estimation of System Parameters. *tm – Technisches Messen*, 82(3):135–144, 2015.

[RLB16] Matthias Richter, Thomas Längle, and Jürgen Beyerer. Knowing When You Don't: Bag of Visual Words with Reject Option for Automatic Visual Inspection of Bulk Materials. In *Proceedings of the 2016 23rd International Conference on Pattern Recognition (ICPR 2016)*, December 2016.

[Rud87] Walter Rudin. *Real and Complex Analysis.* Tata McGraw-Hill Education, 3rd edition, 1987.

[SC04] Paul Frank Singer and Amanda L. Coursey. Feature-Aided Tracking (FAT). In *Proceedings of the SPIE, volume 5428, Signal and Data Processing of Small Targets 2004*, 2004.

[SCC+14] Arnold W. M. Smeulders, Dung M. Chu, Rita Cucchiara, Simone Calderara, Afshin Dehghan, and Mubarak Shah. Visual Tracking: An Experimental Survey. *IEEE Transactions on Pattern Analysis and Machine Intelligence*, 36(7):1442–1468, July 2014.

[Sch17] Walter Schmidt. Statistische Methoden beim Gefügestudium krystalliner Schiefer. *Sitzungsberichte der Kaiserlichen Akademie der Wissenschaften in Wien – mathematisch-naturwissenschaftliche Classe*, 126:515–539, July 1917.

[SDW06] Frederik J. Simons, F. A. Dahlen, and Mark A. Wieczorek. Spatiospectral Concentration on a Sphere. *SIAM Review*, 48(3):504–536, 2006.

[Seo06] Kwang-Il Seon. Smoothing of an All-Sky Survey Map with a Fisher–von Mises Function. *Journal of the Korean Physical Society*, 48(3):331–334, March 2006.

[SH14] Jannik Steinbring and Uwe D. Hanebeck. Progressive Gaussian Filtering Using Explicit Likelihoods. In *Proceedings of the 17th International Conference on Information Fusion (Fusion 2014)*, Salamanca, Spain, July 2014.

[ST02] Reiji Suda and Masayasu Takami. A Fast Spherical Harmonics Transform Algorithm. *Mathematics of Computation*, 71(238):703–715, 2002.

[Str07] Gilbert Strang. *Computational Science and Engineering*. Wellesley-Cambridge Press, 2007.

[Tai67] Mitchell Taibleson. Fourier Coefficients of Functions of Bounded Variation. *Proceedings of the American Mathematical Society*, 18(4):766, 1967.

[THBM96] Max Tegmark, Dieter H. Hartmann, Michael S. Briggs, and Charles A. Meegan. The Angular Power Spectrum of BATSE 3B Gamma-Ray Bursts. *Astrophysical Journal*, 468:214–224, September 1996.

[TS13] Johannes Traa and Paris Smaragdis. A Wrapped Kalman Filter for Azimuthal Speaker Tracking. *IEEE Signal Processing Letters*, 20(12):1257–1260, 2013.

[TS14] Johannes Traa and Paris Smaragdis. Multiple Speaker Tracking With the Factorial von Mises–Fisher Filter. In *Proceedings of the IEEE International Workshop on Machine Learning for Signal Processing (MLSP 2014)*, September 2014.

[UEW07] Martin Ulmke, Ozgur Erdinc, and Peter Willett. Gaussian Mixture Cardinalized PHD Filter for Ground Moving Target Tracking. In *Proceedings of the 10th International Conference on Information Fusion (Fusion 2007)*, July 2007.

[Uns00] Michael Unser. Sampling—50 Years after Shannon. *Proceedings of the IEEE*, 88(4):569–587, April 2000.

[VR09] Cristina N. Vasconcelos and Bodo Rosenhahn. Bipartite Graph Matching Computation on GPU. In *Proceedings of the 7th International Conference on Energy Minimization Methods in Computer Vision and Pattern Recognition*, 2009.

[Wat56] Geoffrey S. Watson. Analysis of Dispersion on a Sphere. *Geophysical Journal International*, 7:153–159, August 1956.

[Wat65] Geoffrey S. Watson. Equatorial Distributions on a Sphere. *Biometrika*, 52(1–2):193–201, 1965.

[Wei] Eric W. Weisstein. Regularized Hypergeometric Function. From MathWorld—A Wolfram Web Resource. `http://mathworld.wolfram.com/RegularizedHypergeometricFunction.html`.

[Whi15] Edmund T. Whittaker. On the Functions Which are Represented by the Expansions of the Interpolation-Theory. *Proceedings of the Royal Society of Edinburgh*, 35:181–194, 1915.

[WHM13] Nils P. Wedi, Mats Hamrud, and George Mozdzynski. A Fast Spherical Harmonics Transform for Global NWP and Climate Models. *Monthly Weather Review*, 141(10):3450–3461, 2013.

[Wil74a] Alan S. Willsky. Fourier Series and Estimation on the Circle with Applications to Synchronous Communication—Part I: Analysis. *IEEE Transactions on Information Theory*, 20(5):584–590, 1974.

[Wil74b] Alan S. Willsky. Fourier Series and Estimation on the Circle with Applications to Synchronous Communication—Part II:: Implementation. *IEEE Transactions on Information Theory*, 20(5):577–583, 1974.

[WL75] Alan S. Willsky and James T. Lo. Estimation for Rotational Processes with One Degree of Freedom—Part II: Discrete-time Processes. *IEEE Transactions on Automatic Control*, 20(1):22–30, February 1975.

[Wot08] Hermann Wotruba. Stand der Technik der sensorgestützten Sortierung (in German). *BHM Berg- und Hüttenmännische Monatshefte*, 153:221–224, June 2008.

[Yar10] R. K. Rao Yarlagadda. *Analog and Digital Signals and Systems*. Springer-Verlag, New York, 2010.

[YHS+07] Peng Yu, Xiao Han, Florent Ségonne, Rudolph Pienaar, Randy L. Buckner, Polina Golland, P. Ellen Grant, and Bruce Fischl. Cortical Surface Shape Analysis Based on Spherical Wavelets. *IEEE Transactions on Medical Imaging*, 26(4):582–597, 2007.

[Zha00] Zhengyou Zhang. A Flexible New Technique for Camera Calibration. *IEEE Transactions on Pattern Analysis and Machine Intelligence*, 22(11):1330–1334, 2000.

[Zyg03] Antoni Zygmund. *Trigonometric Series*, volume 1 and 2. Cambridge University Press, 3rd edition, 2003.

Supervised and Co-Supervised Student Theses

[S1] Tobias Hornberger. *Ableitung von Bewegungsmodellen für Anwendungen in der Schüttgutsortierung mittels Machine Learning (in German)*. Master's thesis, Karlsruhe Institute of Technology, 2018.

[S2] Tobias Kronauer. *Featureunterstütztes Multi-Target-Tracking für optische Bandsortieranlagen unter Verwendung von maschinellem Lernen (in German)*. Master's thesis, Karlsruhe Institute of Technology, 2018.

[S3] Andrea Bittner. *Bewegungsanalyse von Schüttgut mittels instrumentierten Partikeln (in German)*. Master's thesis, Karlsruhe Institute of Technology, 2017.

[S4] Sergen Çiftçi. *Design und Entwicklung eines modularen Gerätes zur Validierung der optischen Sortierleistung (in German)*. Bachelor's thesis, Karlsruhe Institute of Technology, 2017.

[S5] Maximilian Schick. *Untersuchung von Algorithmen zum prädiktiven Tracking für Anwendungen in der Schuttgutsortierung (in German)*. Bachelor's thesis, Karlsruhe Institute of Technology, 2016.

[S6] Matthias Wagner. *Hochperformantes Multi-Object-Tracking mittels OpenCL im Kontext der optischen Schüttgutsortierung (in German)*. Master's thesis, Karlsruhe Institute of Technology, 2016.

[S7] Marcel Finger. *Echtzeitfähiges Multi-Target-Tracking für die optische Schüttgutsortierung (in German).* Master's thesis, Karlsruhe Institute of Technology, 2016.

[S8] Frederik Doll. *Konzeption, Planung, Konstruktion und Integration eines miniaturisierten, modularen Schüttgutsortierers (in German).* Master's thesis, Karlsruhe Institute of Technology, 2015.

[S9] Yassine Marrakchi. *Multi-Target-Tracking for Sorting Bulk Materials.* Master's thesis, Karlsruhe Institute of Technology, 2015.

Own Publications

[O1] Florian Pfaff, Gerhard Kurz, Christoph Pieper, Georg Maier, Benjamin Noack, Harald-Kruggel-Emden, Robin Gruna, Uwe D. Hanebeck, Siegmar Wirtz, Viktor Scherer, Thomas Längle, and Jürgen Beyerer. Improving Multitarget Tracking Using Orientation Estimates for Sorting Bulk Materials. In *Proceedings of the 2017 IEEE International Conference on Multisensor Fusion and Integration for Intelligent Systems (MFI 2017)*, Daegu, Republic of Korea, November 2017.

[O2] Florian Pfaff, Gerhard Kurz, and Uwe D. Hanebeck. Filtering on the Unit Sphere Using Spherical Harmonics. In *Proceedings of the 2017 IEEE International Conference on Multisensor Fusion and Integration for Intelligent Systems (MFI 2017)*, Daegu, Republic of Korea, November 2017.

[O3] Florian Pfaff, Benjamin Noack, and Uwe D. Hanebeck. Optimal Distributed Combined Stochastic and Set-Membership State Estimation. In *Proceedings of the 20th International Conference on Information Fusion (Fusion 2017)*, Xi'an, China, July 2017.

[O4] Florian Pfaff, Benjamin Noack, and Uwe D. Hanebeck. Information Form Distributed Kalman Filtering (IDKF) with Explicit Inputs. In *Proceedings of the 20th International Conference on Information Fusion (Fusion 2017)*, Xi'an, China, July 2017.

[O5] Florian Pfaff, Georg Maier, Mikhail Aristov, Benjamin Noack, Robin Gruna, Uwe D. Hanebeck, Thomas Längle, Jürgen Beyerer, Christoph Pieper, Harald Kruggel-Emden, Siegmar Wirtz, and Viktor Scherer. Real-Time Motion Prediction Using the Chromatic Offset of Line Scan Cameras. *at – Automatisierungstechnik, De Gruyter*, June 2017.

[O6] Florian Pfaff, Gerhard Kurz, and Uwe D. Hanebeck. Multivariate Angular Filtering Using Fourier Series. *Journal of Advances in Information Fusion*, 11(2):206–226, December 2016.

[O7] Florian Pfaff, Christoph Pieper, Georg Maier, Benjamin Noack, Harald Kruggel-Emden, Robin Gruna, Uwe D. Hanebeck, Siegmar Wirtz, Viktor Scherer, Thomas Längle, and Jürgen Beyerer. Simulation-Based Evaluation of Predictive Tracking for Sorting Bulk Materials. In *Proceedings of the 2016 IEEE International Conference on Multisensor Fusion and Integration for Intelligent Systems (MFI 2016)*, Baden-Baden, Germany, September 2016.

[O8] Florian Pfaff, Gerhard Kurz, and Uwe D. Hanebeck. Nonlinear Prediction for Circular Filtering Using Fourier Series. In *Proceedings of the 19th International Conference on Information Fusion (Fusion 2016)*, Heidelberg, Germany, July 2016.

[O9] Florian Pfaff, Christoph Pieper, Georg Maier, Benjamin Noack, Harald Kruggel-Emden, Robin Gruna, Uwe D. Hanebeck, Siegmar Wirtz, Viktor Scherer, Thomas Längle, and Jürgen Beyerer. Improving Optical Sorting of Bulk Materials Using Sophisticated Motion Models. *tm – Technisches Messen, De Gruyter*, 83(2):77–84, February 2016.

[O10] Florian Pfaff, Marcus Baum, Benjamin Noack, Uwe D. Hanebeck, Robin Gruna, Thomas Längle, and Jürgen Beyerer. TrackSort: Predictive Tracking for Sorting Uncooperative Bulk Materials. In *Proceedings of the 2015 IEEE International Conference on Multisensor Fusion and Integration for Intelligent Systems (MFI 2015)*, San Diego, California, USA, September 2015.

[O11] Florian Pfaff, Gerhard Kurz, and Uwe D. Hanebeck. Multimodal Circular Filtering Using Fourier Series. In *Proceedings of the 18th International Conference on Information Fusion (Fusion 2015)*, Washington D.C., USA, July 2015.

[O12] Florian Pfaff, Benjamin Noack, and Uwe D. Hanebeck. Data Validation in the Presence of Stochastic and Set-Membership Uncertainties. In *Proceedings of the 16th International Conference on Information Fusion (Fusion 2013)*, Istanbul, Turkey, July 2013.

[O13] Gerhard Kurz, Igor Gilitschenski, Florian Pfaff, Lukas Drude, Uwe D. Hanebeck, Reinhold Haeb-Umbach, and Roland Y. Siegwart. Directional Statistics and Filtering Using libDirectional. *Journal of Statistical Software*, May 2019.

[O14] Christoph Pieper, Florian Pfaff, Georg Maier, Harald Kruggel-Emden, Siegmar Wirtz, Benjamin Noack, Robin Gruna, Viktor Scherer, Uwe D. Hanebeck, Thomas Längle, and Jürgen Beyerer. Numerical Modelling of an Optical Belt Sorter Using a DEM–CFD Approach Coupled with a Particle Tracking Algorithm and Comparison with Experiments. *Powder Technology*, December 2018.

[O15] Georg Maier, Florian Pfaff, Christoph Pieper, Robin Gruna, Benjamin Noack, Harald Kruggel-Emden, Thomas Längle, Uwe D. Hanebeck, Siegmar Wirtz, Viktor Scherer, and Jürgen Beyerer. Application of Area-Scan Sensors in Sensor-Based Sorting. In *Proceedings of the 8th Conference on Sensor-Based Sorting & Control 2018 (SBSC 2018)*, Aachen, Germany, March 2018.

[O16] Gerhard Kurz, Florian Pfaff, and Uwe D. Hanebeck. Application of Discrete Recursive Bayesian Estimation on Intervals and the Unit Circle to Filtering on SE(2). *IEEE Transactions on Industrial Informatics*, 14(3):1197–1206, March 2018.

[O17] Gerhard Kurz, Igor Gilitschenski, Florian Pfaff, Lukas Drude, Uwe D. Hanebeck, Reinhold Haeb-Umbach, and Roland Y. Siegwart. Directional Statistics and Filtering Using libDirectional. *arXiv preprint: Computation (stat.CO)*, December 2017.

[O18] Georg Maier, Florian Pfaff, Matthias Wagner, Christoph Pieper, Robin Gruna, Benjamin Noack, Harald Kruggel-Emden, Thomas Längle, Uwe D. Hanebeck, Siegmar Wirtz, Viktor Scherer, and Jürgen Beyerer. Real-Time Multitarget Tracking for Sensor-Based Sorting. *Journal of Real-Time Image Processing*, November 2017.

[O19] Gerhard Kurz, Florian Pfaff, and Uwe D. Hanebeck. Discretization of SO(3) Using Recursive Tesseract Subdivision. In *Proceedings of the 2017 IEEE International Conference on Multisensor Fusion and Integration for Intelligent Systems (MFI 2017)*, Daegu, Korea, November 2017.

[O20] Georg Maier, Florian Pfaff, Florian Becker, Christoph Pieper, Robin Gruna, Benjamin Noack, Harald Kruggel-Emden, Thomas Längle, Uwe D. Hanebeck, Siegmar Wirtz, Viktor Scherer, and Jürgen Beyerer. Motion-Based Material Characterization in Sensor-Based Sorting. *tm – Technisches Messen, De Gruyter*, October 2017.

[O21] Christoph Pieper, Georg Maier, Florian Pfaff, Harald Kruggel-Emden, Robin Gruna, Benjamin Noack, Siegmar Wirtz, Viktor Scherer, Thomas Längle, Uwe D. Hanebeck, and Jürgen Beyerer. Numerical Modelling of the Separation of Complex Shaped Particles in an Optical Belt Sorter Using a DEM–CFD Approach and Comparison with Experiments. In *Proceedings of the 5th International Conference on Particle-Based Methods (PARTICLES 2017)*, Hannover, Germany, September 2017.

[O22] Gerhard Kurz, Florian Pfaff, and Uwe D. Hanebeck. Nonlinear Toroidal Filtering Based on Bivariate Wrapped Normal Distributions. In *Proceedings of the 20th International Conference on Information Fusion (Fusion 2017)*, Xi'an, China, July 2017.

[O23] Georg Maier, Florian Pfaff, Florian Becker, Christoph Pieper, Robin Gruna, Benjamin Noack, Harald Kruggel-Emden, Thomas Längle, Uwe D. Hanebeck, Siegmar Wirtz, Viktor Scherer, and Jürgen Beyerer. Improving Material Characterization in Sensor-Based Sorting by Utilizing Motion Information. In *Proceedings of the 3rd Conference on Optical Characterization of Materials (OCM 2017)*, Karlsruhe, Germany, March 2017.

[O24] Gerhard Kurz, Florian Pfaff, and Uwe D. Hanebeck. Discrete Recursive Bayesian Filtering on Intervals and the Unit Circle. In *Proceedings of the 2016 IEEE International Conference on Multisensor Fusion and Integration for Intelligent Systems (MFI 2016)*, Baden-Baden, Germany, September 2016.

[O25] Georg Maier, Florian Pfaff, Christoph Pieper, Robin Gruna, Benjamin Noack, Harald Kruggel-Emden, Thomas Längle, Uwe D. Hanebeck, Siegmar Wirtz, Viktor Scherer, and Jürgen Beyerer. Fast Multitarget Tracking via Strategy Switching for Sensor-Based Sorting. In *Proceedings of the 2016 IEEE International Conference on Multisensor Fusion and Integration for Intelligent Systems (MFI 2016)*, Baden-Baden, Germany, September 2016.

[O26] Jannik Steinbring, Christian Mandery, Florian Pfaff, Florian Faion, Tamim Asfour, and Uwe D. Hanebeck. Real-Time Whole-Body Human Motion Tracking Based on Unlabeled Markers. In *Proceedings of the 2016 IEEE International Conference on Multisensor Fusion and Integration for Intelligent Systems (MFI 2016)*, Baden-Baden, Germany, September 2016.

[O27] Christoph Pieper, Harald Kruggel-Emden, Siegmar Wirtz, Viktor Scherer, Florian Pfaff, Benjamin Noack, Uwe D. Hanebeck, Georg Maier, Robin Gruna, Thomas Längle, and Jürgen Beyerer. Numerical Investigation of Optical Sorting Using the Discrete Element Method. In *Proceedings of the 7th International Conference on Discrete Element Methods (DEM7)*, Dalian, China, August 2016.

[O28] Christoph Pieper, Georg Maier, Florian Pfaff, Harald Kruggel-Emden, Siegmar Wirtz, Robin Gruna, Benjamin Noack, Viktor Scherer, Thomas Längle, Jürgen Beyerer, and Uwe D. Hanebeck. Numerical Modeling of an Automated Optical Belt Sorter Using the Discrete Element Method. *Powder Technology*, July 2016.

[O29] Gerhard Kurz, Florian Pfaff, and Uwe D. Hanebeck. Kullback–Leibler Divergence and Moment Matching for Hyperspherical Probability Distributions. In *Proceedings of the 19th International Conference on Information Fusion (Fusion 2016)*, Heidelberg, Germany, July 2016.

[O30] Benjamin Noack, Florian Pfaff, Marcus Baum, and Uwe D. Hanebeck. State Estimation Considering Negative Information with Switching Kalman and Ellipsoidal Filtering. In *Proceedings of the 19th International Conference on Information Fusion (Fusion 2016)*, Heidelberg, Germany, July 2016.

[O31] Benjamin Noack, Florian Pfaff, and Uwe D. Hanebeck. Optimal Kalman Gains for Combined Stochastic and Set-Membership State Estimation. In *Proceedings of the 51st IEEE Conference on Decision and Control (CDC 2012)*, Maui, Hawaii, USA, December 2012.

[O32] Benjamin Noack, Florian Pfaff, and Uwe D. Hanebeck. Combined Stochastic and Set-Membership Information Filtering in Multisensor Systems. In *Proceedings of the 15th International Conference on Information Fusion (Fusion 2012)*, Singapore, July 2012.

[O33] Antonia Pérez Arias, Henning P. Eberhardt, Florian Pfaff, and Uwe D. Hanebeck. The Plenhaptic Guidance Function for Intuitive Navigation in Extended Range Telepresence Scenarios. In *Proceedings of the IEEE World Haptics Conference (WHC 2011)*, Istanbul, Turkey, June 2011.

Karlsruhe Series on Intelligent Sensor-Actuator-Systems

Edited by Prof. Dr.-Ing. Uwe D. Hanebeck // ISSN 1867-3813

Band 1 **Oliver Schrempf**
Stochastische Behandlung von Unsicherheiten in kaskadierten dynamischen Systemen. 2008
ISBN 978-3-86644-287-0

Band 2 **Florian Weißel**
Stochastische modell-prädiktive Regelung nichtlinearer Systeme. 2009
ISBN 978-3-86644-348-8

Band 3 **Patrick Rößler**
Telepräsente Bewegung und haptische Interaktion in ausgedehnten entfernten Umgebungen. 2009
ISBN 978-3-86644-346-4

Band 4 **Kathrin Roberts**
Modellbasierte Herzbewegungsschätzung für robotergestützte Interventionen. 2009
ISBN 978-3-86644-353-2

Band 5 **Felix Sawo**
Nonlinear state and parameter estimation of spatially distributed systems. 2009
ISBN 978-3-86644-370-9

Band 6 **Gregor F. Schwarzenberg**
Untersuchung der Abbildungseigenschaften eines 3D-Ultraschall-Computertomographen zur Berechnung der 3D-Abbildungsfunktion und Herleitung einer optimierten Sensorgeometrie. 2009
ISBN 978-3-86644-393-8

Die Bände sind unter www.ksp.kit.edu als PDF frei verfügbar oder als Druckausgabe bestellbar.

Band 7 **Marco Huber**
Probabilistic Framework for Sensor Management. 2009
ISBN 978-3-86644-405-8

Band 8 **Frederik Beutler**
Probabilistische modellbasierte Signalverarbeitung zur instantanen Lageschätzung. 2010
ISBN 978-3-86644-442-3

Band 9 **Marc Peter Deisenroth**
Efficient Reinforcement Learning using Gaussian Processes. 2010
ISBN 978-3-86644-569-7

Band 10 **Evgeniya Ballmann**
Physics-Based Probabilistic Motion Compensation of Elastically Deformable Objects. 2012
ISBN 978-3-86644-862-9

Band 11 **Peter Krauthausen**
Learning Dynamic Systems for Intention Recognition in Human-Robot-Cooperation. 2013
ISBN 978-3-86644-952-7

Band 12 **Antonia Pérez Arias**
Haptic Guidance for Extended Range Telepresence. 2013
ISBN 978-3-7315-0035-3

Band 13 **Marcus Baum**
Simultaneous Tracking and Shape Estimation of Extended Objects. 2013
ISBN 978-3-7315-0078-0

Band 14 **Benjamin Noack**
State Estimation for Distributed Systems with Stochastic and Set-membership Uncertainties. 2014
ISBN 978-3-7315-0124-4

Band 15 **Jörg Fischer**
Optimal Sequence-Based Control of Networked Linear Systems. 2014
ISBN 978-3-7315-0305-7

Band 16 **Marc Reinhardt**
Linear Estimation in Interconnected Sensor Systems with Information Constraints. 2015
ISBN 978-3-7315-0342-2

Band 17 **Gerhard Kurz**
Directional Estimation for Robotic Beating Heart Surgery. 2015
ISBN 978-3-7315-0382-8

Band 18 **Igor Gilitschenski**
Deterministic Sampling for Nonlinear Dynamic State Estimation. 2016
ISBN 978-3-7315-0473-3

Band 19 **Florian Faion**
Tracking Extended Objects in Noisy Point Clouds with Application in Telepresence Systems. 2016
ISBN 978-3-7315-0517-4

Band 20 **Martin Klemm**
Intraoperative Planning and Execution of Arbitrary Orthopedic Interventions Using Handheld Robotics and Augmented Reality. 2018
ISBN 978-3-7315-0800-7

Band 21 **Antonio Kleber Zea Cobo**
Tracking Extended Objects with Active Models and Negative Measurements. 2019
ISBN 978-3-7315-0877-9

Band 22 **Florian Pfaff**
Multitarget Tracking Using Orientation Estimation for Optical Belt Sorting. 2019
ISBN 978-3-7315-0932-5

Die Bände sind unter www.ksp.kit.edu als PDF frei verfügbar oder als Druckausgabe bestellbar.